Is America really heading to [...] answer is yes—unless we m[...] [...] change of course. Writing with the passion of a man who really believes what the Bible says, Mike brings a sobering, hope-filled challenge, calling every one of us to live as overcoming, uncompromising disciples of Jesus. The time to respond is now.

—MICHAEL L. BROWN, PHD
AUTHOR OF *HYPER-GRACE*, HOST OF THE LINE OF FIRE RADIO
BROADCAST, AND PRESIDENT OF FIRE SCHOOL OF MINISTRY

Mike Bickle is the greatest! His new book, *God's Answer to the Growing Crisis*, pinpoints the source of the catastrophe: abandoning God. All too often Christian seminaries and universities run from politics, believing the canard about "the separation of church and state" and self-applying a piece of duct tape over their mouths. The tragedy is that the last two to three generations of Christian pastors and leaders have surrendered the public square to a nonbiblical piety that separates the secular from the holy. Is it any wonder that "our inheritance has been turned over to strangers, our homes to foreigners" (Lam. 5:2)?

—DAVID LANE
AMERICAN RENEWAL PROJECT

GOD'S ANSWER TO THE GROWING CRISIS

MIKE BICKLE

CHARISMA
HOUSE

GOD'S ANSWER TO THE GROWING CRISIS by Mike Bickle
Published by Charisma House
Charisma Media/Charisma House Book Group
600 Rinehart Road
Lake Mary, Florida 32746
www.charismahouse.com

Cover design by Justin Evans

Visit the author's website at www.ihopkc.org.

Library of Congress Cataloging-in-Publication Data:
Names: Bickle, Mike, author.
Title: God's answer to the growing crisis / Mike Bickle.
Description: First edition. | Lake Mary : Charisma House, 2016. |
    Includes bibliographical references.
Identifiers: LCCN 2016045414| ISBN 9781629987354 (trade paper) |
ISBN 9781629987361 (ebook)
Subjects: LCSH: Bible. Psalms, II--Criticism, interpretation, etc. |
United States--Church history--21st century. | United States--Social
    conditions--21st century.
Classification: LCC BS1450 2d .B53 2016 | DDC 277.3/083--dc23
LC record available at https://lccn.loc.gov/2016045414

While the author has made every effort to provide accurate Internet addresses at the time of publication, neither the publisher nor the author assumes any responsibility for errors or for changes that occur after publication.

First edition

16 17 18 19 20 — 9 8 7 6 5 4 3 2 1
Printed in the United States of America

*To the sixteen thousand faithful believers who
have served full-time as IHOPKC staff, students,
or interns since our beginning days in 1999*

I want to express my gratitude to Marcus Yoars, who helped me greatly in writing this book. His skill, diligence, and humility made it a joy for me to work closely with him in writing it.

CONTENTS

FOREWORD

I N THIS BOOK my dear friend Mike Bickle presents a glorious eschatology to help prepare the church for challenges and persecutions and also kingdom advancement. I believe Mike's insights can stir faith for a victorious church that will impact history through the supremacy of prayer, even in the darkest of days.

I must admit, writing the foreword for a book containing elements of eschatology (the study of the end times) is a bit of a challenge for me, as I do not consider myself a master of the subject. More to the point, I have been troubled to witness how divisive making any reference to the end times has come to be among some sincere believers and leaders who deeply love God and one another. Oh, how I long to see the body of Christ come together in unity, to see them fast and pray for an awakening in the midst of the present crisis that is growing in the nations! Our passion and our unifying factor are the Lord Jesus crucified, raised on the third day, and ascended into heaven, who one day will return.

I am saddened to report that I have been in mass gatherings of prayer and evangelism where mighty ministries in Christ refused to participate because of varying views on how to interpret the present crisis in the nations from a biblical end-time perspective.

Are things getting better, or are they getting worse? What does the Bible say? According to Mike Bickle, the Bible is clear that things will *both* get better and get worse as we approach the return of the Lord. Isaiah said that God's glory will be manifest on God's people when deep darkness covers the earth (Isa. 60:1–2), and Jesus taught that the wheat and the tares will mature together at the end of the age (Matt. 13:30).

I still have many questions about the last days, as we all do, yet I remain open and challenged by Mike's insights; even more, I know from experience Mike's relentless devotion to the deepest truths of Christ. This man is a consecrated vessel raised by God for such a time as this. His understanding of the victory of Christ over history, the perseverance of the saints, and the great surge of the kingdom is worth your careful attention under the guidance of the Holy Spirit. I encourage you to read this book with an open heart, regardless of your present paradigm. In fact, I am hesitant to accept any articulation of the end times that has not been born in part from groanings over the Word combined with fasting and prayer. The Book of Revelation is not casually comprehended through mental apprehensions. Its secrets can be unlocked only from above and in the context of a consistent life of prayer. Mike is a man of both Word and Spirit.

And now I will be truly transparent. Before I moved to Kansas City, I didn't like Mike Bickle's eschatology! Part of the reason is that I had never heard him teach it. In other words, I was unwilling to receive it. Why? Because I assumed it was a purely defeatist, fatalistic eschatology; i.e., "It's only going to get worse, and there is no faith for victory or measures of dominion in the last days." That was my thinking until I moved to Kansas City and heard the message firsthand. Yes, there will be challenges, hardships, and persecutions. Yes, darkness will increase and the crisis will get more serious. But parallel to this, the Psalm 2 Christ will rise among His people to challenge powers and systems and demonstrate kingdom authority in the midst of worldwide rebellion.

I am ablaze with the hope of a victorious church in the last days, and if you will let him, Mike can lead you to this same hope. Along the way he will also confront you with other important truths that balance the picture. We must be careful not to read the Scriptures through our own theological lenses and refuse to acknowledge global upheaval that is present at this time and escalating rapidly. It's happening right before our eyes! To ignore the full complement of prophecy may produce a form of hope in the church, but I fear the blind hope that leaves us unprepared, perhaps even offended, when troubles come.

Mike boldly refuses easy, politically correct whitewashing of the last days. He would rather be spoken against than leave us unprepared. I see many people leaving their first love and becoming jaded; some even completely fall away because things haven't worked out in their lives as they had hoped. A true biblical eschatology prepares overcomers for the difficulties they must endure and helps them to stand with confidence that the greatest outpouring of the Holy Spirit is surely coming. Brothers and sisters, if we can't stand in our present trials, how will we then stand in the trauma of the times prophesied in Psalm 2, Isaiah 60–66, Daniel, and the Book of Revelation? Thank you, Mike Bickle, for your friendship and faithfulness to the whole counsel of God, and for your great courage to speak candidly and truthfully the word of God with full devotion. Thank you for delivering us from an escapist worldview and giving us one that prepares us to overcome and rule.

—Lou Engle
Cofounder and Visionary of TheCall

INTRODUCTION

WHEN VESTER FLANAGAN gunned down a television crew during a live broadcast in August 2015, killing his unsuspecting victims apparently was not enough. Within minutes of the shooting, Flanagan posted chilling videos on Twitter and Facebook of his approaching the scene with a gun and, as if in a first-person shooter video game, raising his weapon and firing upon those in his sights. He didn't want the world just to know his agenda; he wanted everyone to watch him follow through with it.[1]

The story stunned America and was sandwiched between two equally shocking shootings in which killers specifically targeted Christians. Only weeks prior to Flanagan's attack nine believers had been gunned down in Emanuel African Methodist Episcopal Church during a prayer meeting at the historic Charleston, South Carolina, site.[2] And within a few months another young gunman would walk into an Oregon community college and terrorize classrooms full of students. Only this time the killer would ask people directly, "Are you a Christian?" Those who professed their faith were immediately shot in the head, while non-Christians were shot in the leg.[3]

Welcome to modern-day America, where the seeds of hatred toward Christians, planted decades ago in a cultural revolution, are beginning to sprout in the open.

Within two generations our country has gone from honoring biblical values to despising them. Obviously persecution against Christians in the United States is nowhere near the level it is in countries that kill, torture, or imprison people just for confessing Jesus as Lord. But the animosity toward believers in America is

1

nonetheless real and growing. And as with Flanagan's case, the agenda to further that hatred within the public square is surprisingly overt.

This shouldn't come as a surprise. After all, the Bible is full of scriptures warning us of this animosity. Jesus stated more than once that those who follow Him "will be hated by all men for My name's sake" (Matt. 10:22). He also spoke of such hatred being part of a global time of crisis like no other. In Luke 21:25 Jesus described "distress" in the nations that would increase over the course of one specific generation. He mentioned believers who would see distressful things "begin to happen" (v. 28) and then assured them that their "generation will not pass away until all these things are fulfilled" (v. 32). Thus, within the time span of one generation an end-times global crisis would both begin and come to completion.

The heart cry of this book is to awaken people with urgency to the reality and implications of the real—and ever-growing—crisis that exists in this hour. We know from Scripture that the "distress of nations" Jesus mentioned in Luke 21:25 will be multifaceted and affect many spheres of society—financial, social, political, military, racial, cultural, meteorological, medical, and more. We also know it will continually escalate and eventually culminate in the battle of Armageddon and Jesus's triumphant return. But before then a crisis of unprecedented proportions will engulf the earth. Jesus's reference to this global distress harkens back to a prophetic psalm upon which this book centers: Psalm 2.

This key passage, written by King David, is one of Scripture's most relevant passages for us today and is also what I believe the Holy Spirit is speaking to the church around the world. In the first few verses of Psalm 2 David honed in on a spiritual crisis that will affect both the church and society in general. A rage against Jesus and His Word will begin with the public ridicule of people who value God's Word. It will grow to include hate-crime legislation that results in economic penalties for these believers (e.g., loss of job opportunities) and finally will culminate with violent persecution against them that includes prison and martyrdom.

David's vivid prophetic warning references the most intense, dangerous spiritual crisis in history—one that I believe has begun and will steadily increase until Jesus returns. It will result in a surge of lawlessness in society, global persecution against the church and Israel, and the abandoning of their faith by many believers. Paul prophesied of such a "falling away" in the end times (2 Thess. 2:3), saying that "the Spirit expressly says that in latter times some will depart from the faith, giving heed to deceiving spirits and doctrines of demons" (1 Tim. 4:1, NKJV).

Today many believers are intimidated and drawing back to the safety of silence because they fear being ridiculed and rejected in social circles. This is part of a dangerous spiritual crisis that has begun and that must be addressed today with clarity and urgency—thus the reason I am writing this book. It is crucial that we understand the times we live in and know what God is saying to us. As we will discover in these pages, being prepared for the growing crisis is vital for every believer.

CRISIS? WHAT CRISIS?

When a person who has contracted a serious disease first gets a doctor's diagnosis, it is often difficult to accept because there are few symptoms that indicate the disease's severity. The patient may even feel completely fine and healthy, yet the doctor knows that as time passes, the life-threatening disease will soon become more apparent.

So it is with the crisis we are in today. Many people—indeed, many in the church—do not believe there is a crisis. They think things are actually getting better as science, technology, and our understanding of life lead the way to a brighter future. How, then, do I know a crisis is here? A quick but discerning look at some of the key events in America in 2015 proves it does not take much to answer that question. Indeed, the year brought about seismic changes in our nation.

We will discuss the Supreme Court's legalization of gay marriage later in this book, but suffice it to say for now that this one law will have not only massive ripple effects on our culture but also a catalytic impact on the rest of the world. By legalizing, institutionalizing, and normalizing the gay lifestyle, America altered the course of its future and accelerated global sin.

For now, the Supreme Court's decision seems relatively harmless to many people, especially those who applaud the cause of tolerance and acceptance. Nowhere was this more evident than at ESPN's 2015 ESPY Awards, in which thousands of the world's top athletes and celebrities gave former Olympian Bruce Jenner—now known as Caitlyn Jenner—a standing ovation after he received the Arthur Ashe Courage Award for the "most courageous feat" of publicly transitioning from a man to a woman. I have great compassion for the pain, loneliness, and sexual confusion Jenner has experienced. But this one act of "courage"—and the glowing endorsement from many of the world's most famous and influential public icons—was hugely significant in normalizing and promoting sexual confusion around the world. The signals this sends to children and teenagers cannot be stressed enough.

Another example of the recent seismic changes took place during the writing of this book. The United States Department of Justice created a new position called the Domestic Terrorism Counsel. On the surface it was started to help prosecute terrorists in America, who the department says should be a greater concern for Americans than foreign terrorists. Yet at the center of this initiative we find the first stages of hate-crime prosecution that could—and I believe will—one day discriminate against those who publicly stand up for biblical values. The government will soon have the right to investigate, prosecute, and convict anyone it suspects is operating out of "anti-government views, racism, bigotry and anarchy, and other despicable beliefs," according to a department official.[4] Given that our nation's judicial system already criminalizes those who oppose gay marriage, it is just a matter of time until believers' views on the sanctity of life, marriage, and sex are deemed as "despicable beliefs" that warrant prosecution.

Views expressed in recent years clearly prove that those shaping our culture today—leaders not only in government but also in every sphere—do not want just to secularize America; they want to *de-Christianize* it. Many of our nation's most prominent voices adamantly declare that it is not enough to water down public faith in the name of religious equality; all this "Jesus stuff" must be completely washed away from our national ethos. After all, they say, it is merely superstitious belief anyway. We are smarter and more advanced now. We do not need to be held back by primitive mind-sets and religious, judgmental views. We certainly do not need any divine power to determine our value, ethics, or sense of justice; we can define those ourselves. In fact, the height of our humanness is to shrug off the foolish notion of supernatural entities—namely God—altogether and recognize that the best life is found through creating our own meaning and purpose.

This, in a nutshell, is what is now called secular humanism, and it is driving what might be the greatest shift in American history. Three hundred years ago men such as Immanuel Kant and Georg Wilhelm Friedrich Hegel paved the way for humanism, which elevates humans above God by saying that reason and rationality trump the divine or supernatural. Yet during the Age of Enlightenment these and other thought leaders still wrote with the backdrop of a Christian society.

That is no longer the case today, as Western postmodernism segued first into a post-Christian era and more recently into full-fledged secular humanism. If you look around, you can see evidence of secular humanism in virtually every facet of our modern culture.

In God We No Longer Trust
(Much Less Believe)

It starts, as is often the case in countries, with our judicial system. After all, that is where we officially define justice and distinguish right from wrong. So how does America's judicial system reflect this shift toward humanism?

Since removing public prayer and Bible reading from school classrooms in the early 1960s, the United States Supreme Court has continued to chip away at the biblical foundation of our nation. In 1968 the court opened the door for evolution to eventually become a mandated part of public schools' curriculum, while creationism and intelligent design became fringe or even extremist "theories."[5] In 1973 the Supreme Court legalized abortion, resulting in an estimated *fifty-eight million* babies murdered since then while culture celebrated a woman's right to choose to murder them.[6] And throughout the 1980s and following decades the nation's highest court and state supreme courts often ruled to remove any displays of the Ten Commandments from public courthouses and similar places.[7] Given this history, it was hardly a surprise when a federal district court declared secular humanism an official religion in America in 2014.[8]

But the bigger issue that must be considered is this: Are judges—federal, state, and in between—defining America's culture as moral "pioneers," or are they simply echoing what the masses have already declared in society?

The same question could be asked of those leading America's educational system. Most of us have heard the all-too-real stories of university professors lambasting Christian students in class for believing in the biblical account of creation rather than the big bang theory or of elementary teachers forcing homosexual values on first-graders. Not long ago in Fort Lauderdale, Florida, a teacher refused to allow a twelve-year-old student to read his Bible during a "free reading" session.[9]

Sadly these are no longer fringe cases. What used to be occasional outbursts from a tiny, God-hating minority has become everyday news. Today no one blinks when a spiritual leader such as Deepak Chopra says, "God is irrelevant, providing few if any practical benefits in daily life.... God only has a future if he (or she) becomes useful once more."[10]

Equally frightening are the studies proving that godlessness is more than on the rise; it is becoming the norm.

On the surface it is easy to see the spiritual shifts. In 2007, 78.4 percent of Americans claimed to be Christian. By 2014—only seven years later—that number had already dipped to 70.6 percent. Let's put these statistics in perspective: the overall population of Christians has dipped more than a full percent every year since 2007, which means almost *2.3 million* believers left the faith during those seven years.[11]

Still the United States has more Christians than any other country. Yes, the percentage may be on the decline, but we are still talking about seven out of every ten people calling themselves Christian, right?

Unfortunately a clearer picture of reality emerges when we dig into the actual beliefs of those who call themselves Christians. Only 35 percent of American believers—not all of the adult population, mind you, but only those who claim to be born-again Christians—believe Satan is real. A staggering 58 percent think the Holy Spirit is just a symbol rather than a real person. And perhaps most surprising of all, 39 percent of all those who claim to be born again believe that Jesus sinned while He was on the earth, while another 6 percent claim they do not have an opinion.[12]

Are you beginning to see the crisis we are in? Secular humanism not only has affected our country's secular culture; it has also shaped the emerging generations of those who claim to follow Jesus. In fact, an abysmal one-half of 1 percent of eighteen- to twenty-three-year-olds actually have a biblical worldview, according to a Barna Group study, while one out of nine older adults' beliefs line up with the Bible.[13]

"Although most Americans consider themselves to be Christian and say they know the content of the Bible, less than one out of ten Americans demonstrate such knowledge through their actions," says George Barna, whose research company has tracked such trends since the 1990s.[14]

LOSING FAITH ELSEWHERE TOO

The growing crisis goes beyond just our spiritual and moral decay, however. We can find a "Danger Ahead!" sign in every sphere of society.

Although the government and media trumpet every new high in the stock market or tiny dip in the unemployment rate, financial experts continue to warn us of how fragile the nation's economy actually is. One prominent expert called the crash of 2008 a "half-meltdown" in comparison with what is to come, and he predicts a massive collapse—in which "all the dominoes are going to fall"—within three years.[15] Is it any wonder, when 45 percent of all Americans do not pay a dime of federal income tax?[16]

At least half the states in America are on the verge of bankruptcy, with some reports claiming as many as forty-four out of fifty; federal law is the only thing prohibiting them from officially going broke.[17] And a staggering 49.2 percent of Americans—close to 160 million people—receive government entitlements. The math does not work on this. The "economic rubber band" is pulled so tight that when it breaks, these entitlements will be withheld, causing chaos and social unrest in the nation's cities, along with countless other implications.[18]

Meanwhile, faith in the political system is at an all-time low. With scandals, federal shutdowns, and political gridlocks now almost a weekly item, Americans' level of confidence in every facet of our government has reached record lows: a mere 7 percent of Americans trust Congress to accomplish *anything*. "[There's] no question," wrote political analyst Charlie Cook. "Politics has become more bitterly partisan and mean spirited as I have seen in thirty years."[19]

Indeed, when virtually all the nation's major media outlets consistently herald the sentiment captured by the *U.S. News and World Report* headline that "Americans Have Lost Confidence…in Everything," it is not simply a ploy to gain new readership; it is an accurate gauge of society's sense that a great crisis looms.[20]

And when recent Gallup polls showed that Americans' trust in virtually every major facet of society—from big business to the Supreme Court to organized religion—was either at historic lows or below historic averages, *U.S. News and World Report* columnist Ken Walsh wrote what most have already concluded: "All in all, it's a picture of a nation discouraged about its present and worried about its future, and highly doubtful that its institutions can pull America out of its trough."[21]

The problem is, our country faces more than a ditch. Clearly America is heading toward a cliff. And if we do not change our course soon, things will get much worse.

As someone who loves this country as much as the next patriotic American, why would I make such a statement? Because even if America's businesses start to take off, the US dollar strengthens once again, and the economy turns around, and even if every sector of our government suddenly regained public confidence, we still face the deeper, more critical crisis of our nation's clear choice to defy God.

French mathematician and philosopher Blaise Pascal once wrote, "We run carelessly to the precipice after having veiled our eyes to hinder us from seeing it."[22] The precipice before us today is the false god of humanism. In the process of running off the cliff of a spiritual crisis like never before, we have comforted ourselves by claiming that we are god. And that belief now permeates every aspect of our society.

We believe we no longer need God because we think our own strength is sufficient. In fact, the concept of American pride today has taken on an entirely new meaning. Accompanied by an "I'll show you" attitude, it is all about our individualistic resolve to fight through and persevere no matter what. Just believe in yourself, the saying goes, and you can do anything. And since you cannot expect anyone to hand you anything for free, you must "pull yourself up by the bootstraps," "take the bull by the horns," and "turn your dreams into reality." After all, if you can dream it, you can achieve it.

While such clichéd conviction is admirable, when God is not

at the core of against-all-odds perseverance, that spirit is often motivated by pride with defiance that refuses to acknowledge the Lord as our source of life, direction, and strength. Yet sadly that is where America stands today.

GLOBAL RED ALERT

It would be easy to stop there and address merely the crisis we face in America. Already we have established that the dramatic shifts seen over the last few years—from economic to political to moral and beyond—have set the stage for a crisis that will affect every sphere of society in our country.

But limiting our scope to America would be not only an inaccurate portrait of this crisis but also an unfaithful representation of what the Holy Spirit is saying today to the global church. This great crisis is not looming just in the United States; all of humanity is at a crossroads.

A simple snapshot of the world's biggest and most influential economies proves that trouble lies just at our doorstep. With both the Chinese and American economies creating more fears and uncertainties than confidence, even former British Prime Minister David Cameron was bold enough to declare at a G20 Summit that "red warning lights are flashing on the dashboard of the global economy."[23] Greece's bankruptcy exposed the sad reality that even a consortium of nations cannot save a country from ruin, and many predict it is merely the first domino to fall in a worldwide economic crash.

We see injustice rising in historic proportions through today's human trafficking industry. There are more slaves today than at any point in human history.[24] Meanwhile immorality continues to parade itself throughout the nations, which now celebrate it like never before. The pornography industry takes in $97 billion each year around the world (with at least $13 billion coming from the United States and another $25 million from South Korea), and a major segment of those earnings involves teenagers and children.[25] In fact, each year the latest, hottest porn trends involve acts so violent and repulsive they have begun to shock even mainstream liberal media.[26]

Among Millennials—those currently between eighteen and thirty years old—a staggering eight out of ten men and one in three women regularly use porn.[27] The current generation of children is the first in history to grow up in a pornified global culture in which the ubiquitous presence of sex is producing eight-year-old porn addicts in Australia,[28] while in the United Kingdom *10 percent* of all twelve- and thirteen-year-olds are addicted.[29] Although things will continue to digress on this moral front, we have clearly already reached a critical mass of depravity.

On the military front the stage is being set for a third world war. The Iran nuclear deal of 2015 will create a nuclear arms race in the Middle East. Terrorist groups will end up with nuclear weapons. They are pressuring Israel into a preemptive attack mode to save their nation, and yet Israel will be presented on the global stage as the aggressor of a world war. Satan is once again fueling anti-Semitism in the nations. Though the Holocaust is only a single generation removed, already leaders are rewriting history. What not long ago was a preposterous thought—that the Holocaust never happened—is becoming more common, particularly as radical Islam grows.

Indeed, radical Islam seems to be the spark that will kindle a new type of world war. The coordinated terrorist attacks in Paris that killed 130 people on November 13, 2015, provoked France and other European nations to fight Islamic State of Iraq and Syria (ISIS) with more aggressive military action. This is actually what some ISIS leaders want, as they and other groups have tried to bait Western nations into an open conflict. In the context of our demonstrating violence toward them, these Islamic terrorist groups will be able to recruit more people and raise more money as radical Islam proclaims the nobility of martyrdom and dominates the global conversation.

Because the Islamic State has no borders and is fueled by its ideology of hate and violence, the next world war will not look like the previous two. Rather than being fought within specific continental boundaries (such as Europe and Asia in World War II), it will likely be staged in many Western nations as part of a guerrilla-warfare-type attack in which small, seemingly independent terrorist cells engage in violence via shopping mall takeovers, school shootings, train station bombings, and even technological warfare (e.g., major website hacks, security breaches, and power grid shutdowns). Jihadist Islam is already at war with Western culture and its values—meaning the new world war will primarily be over ideology and secondarily over territory. Islamic extremists want their values, law, and religious practice to be enforced with violence across the whole earth.

Joel Rosenberg, the best-selling author whose books link the rise of radical Islam with the end times, has dubbed this movement "Apocalyptic Islam." "They want to establish their global Islamic kingdom where everybody has to follow Islam," he said. "And that is a...much more dangerous form of radical Islam than even Al Qaeda and Hamas and the Taliban....And these people are not just crazy—they're demonic."[30]

Radical Islam's primary enemy is America, which it sees as the "big Satan," while its secondary one is the "little Satan" of Israel. One ultimate goal is to take over Jerusalem and dominate the land of Israel to bring it under Allah, under the influence of the prophet Muhammad's teachings according to radical Islamists' dogma and interpretation. Since they cannot be victorious in Israel as long as America remains a global power, their focus is to weaken America in order to take Israel.

This complex military scenario is also intricately woven into the refugee crisis that has affected much of the world. Syria's ongoing civil war has displaced more than eleven million people— more than six million within the country and nearly five million leaving as refugees, mostly throughout Europe.[31] Islamic extremists have caused millions more to flee throughout the Middle East and Africa in countries such as Afghanistan, Somalia, Iraq,

Eritrea, and Sudan. In all, there are now more than sixty million refugees in the world.[32]

Radical Islamist terrorists want to piggyback on this crisis to come undetected into America and other Western nations in order to infiltrate in a far greater way. I have met with several groups of people who interact regularly with the White House or top US military leaders, and they are convinced of plans for a massive, orchestrated invasion of the United States by radical Islamists. The fear of such an invasion among Americans is causing a heated, sometimes xenophobic public conversation that began years ago with our own Mexican border crisis. Meanwhile Europe faces a similar problem as a massive influx of refugees forced to seek safety alongside terrorists in hiding has sparked racial tension in places such as Germany, Sweden, Greece, France, and Italy.

RACIAL CRISIS IN AMERICA

On July 5, 2016, a young black man named Alton Sterling was confronted by police in Baton Rouge, Louisiana. A video posted to social media that received scores of views shows Sterling being held on the ground by two white police officers. Moments after being restrained, Sterling was shot and killed by the police. The very next day a similar tragedy occurred near St. Paul, Minnesota. It was also captured on a video that went viral after it was posted on Facebook. It showed another young black man, Philando Castile, lying in his car with a blood-soaked shirt as a result of being shot by a white police officer. The videos of the deaths of these two young black men were seen by millions on social media. Within twenty-four hours the nation was filled with rage, grief, confusion, and frustration. The next day in various cities across America groups protested peacefully against police violence. However, in Dallas, Micah Johnson, a young black man filled with rage and pain, shot and killed five police officers. Johnson told police nego-tiators "that he was upset about recent police shootings, that he wanted to kill white people—especially white officers."[33]

Johnson's electronic devices gave evidence that he had been

influenced by a Facebook community titled "Black Power Political Organization" that claimed responsibility for the shooting of the five Dallas policemen. They promised more attacks. The next day they claimed their "sniper assassins [took] down five police officers." The same post also vowed more would be killed "in the coming days." This organization wants "to end the oppression" of black people in America. They seek to create the "United States of Africa." One of its rallying cries is: "Free yourself from the white men."[34] Obviously the vast majority of blacks in America have nothing to do with terrorist groups like this. However, we should not dismiss such small groups because, in my opinion, it takes less than 1 percent of a group of people to cause much trouble for others.

Today there are many heated debates about the root causes of the growing racial tension in America—it is common to see anger-filled arguments on popular news programs. Undeniably significant injustice has been shown to black people in our court systems, law enforcement, education, economics, and much more. The whole situation is very complicated, and I do not begin to understand all the dynamics involved in the pain, anger, fear, and offense that fuel the growing conflict in our culture.

But what is clear is that the intensity of the tension and conflict continues to increase at this time. No one knows where all this is going. *The social bonds in our culture are growing more and more strained.* This growing crisis is causing anyone who is paying attention to have deep concerns. It could move America to respond to God in either humility, repentance, and prayer or in more anger, bitterness, and violence. It will probably lead to both responses.

TARGETING CHRISTIANS

All these economic, justice, moral, military, and social factors alone indicate the crossroads we face in humanity. But if we return our focus to one important indicator of today's crisis—Christian persecution—the situation is direr than most realize. It is incorrect and truly insensitive to cite Muslims, white policemen, or militant blacks as the root causes of many of the issues mentioned above. And indeed we must remember that moderate Islam and jihadist Islam are anything but the same; it is a horrible mistake to see them as one. Just as most Christians disdain violence, so most Muslims do not condone it, and those involved with radical Islamic terrorist groups make up only a tiny percentage of the overall Muslim population.

Nevertheless, the numbers of radical Islamists are growing, as evidenced by the sudden rise of ISIS, and these extremists have ushered in a new era of public, glorified persecution against Christians worldwide. While hundreds of thousands of believers are killed, tortured, raped, and displaced throughout the Middle East by those who would like to terminate Christianity altogether, much of the world essentially sits on the sidelines unresponsive to the Christian plight and responding only when it makes political sense. Asia and Africa continue to give rise to a radical Islam that, like ISIS, is committed to the demise of all Christians. With such advancement of anti-Christian extremism, it is no wonder there are more Christians martyred today than ever before in history.

Around the world hatred for true Christianity and the Bible is becoming increasingly overt, even in nations with a rich heritage in the faith. The post-Christian landscape of Europe, Australia, and the rest of the Western world is already dominated by secular humanism, and what once was the hub for Christian influence around the world now sees God's Word as a book of fairy tales and archaic morals.

WHEN THE CRISIS GROWS

This all begs the question: Is it possible for us to turn back and avoid disaster? In the United States and around the world, can we somehow evade what seems like a crash course on nearly every front? Or is a global crisis of apocalyptic proportions imminent? Have we run so close to the cliff's edge that nothing can stop us from a catastrophic plummet?

I imagine in Europe in 1936 many people were asking similar questions. The relative world peace enjoyed after World War I had quickly faded. Under Adolf Hitler's Nazi party, Germany flexed its ever-growing military muscles by blatantly breaking a World War I pact and reoccupying the Rhineland. Italy had invaded Ethiopia and, led by its heavy-handed Fascist dictator Benito Mussolini, committed horrific war crimes. Civil war erupted in Spain. Russia's three-year "reign of terror" began with a bloody purging of Communist party dissidents that bolstered Josef Stalin's iron-fisted rule. Everywhere Europeans turned, it seemed they were surrounded by ruthless dictators and threats of war.

A godly Welshman named Rees Howells realized that Satan was using this scenario to hinder the gospel's spread. He was particularly concerned about Hitler, whom he rightly described as "Satan's agent."[35] So in March of that year, before World War II began and the United Kingdom entered the fight, Howells called the students of his Bible College of Wales to join him in prayer—morning, noon, and night—for God to intervene and remove Hitler so that the gospel could be preached to all. Until the war began, Howells often prayed that God would intervene to prevent war altogether.

He did not. On January 8, 1940, after four years of faithfully praying, Howells released a statement calling his nation to join him in prayer: "If all the righteous in the country will send up effectual prayer, we feel sure that we shall prevail."[36] Instead, on May 10, Hitler's troops invaded Belgium and the Netherlands, conquering them in less than a week. From there the English and French troops were driven down the coast of France until it became clear they would be trapped at Dunkirk.

Howells could have pulled back when it appeared his prayers were failing, but instead he continued to press in, and he encouraged his students to do likewise. Even as Hitler's troops were taking Belgium, Howells said to his students, "I think what a glory it is that we don't need to change our prayers one bit, in spite of the present developments.... The Lord has said, 'I am going to deal with the Nazis.'"[37]

In addition to praying throughout the day as they had for the previous four years, Howells and his students began interceding from 7:00 p.m. until midnight every night. Again they asked for God to intervene and cause the plans of Hitler to fail. Several days into their mighty prayer strategy Howells encouraged them, "We are going up to the battle, and I am as sure of victory as of the dawn. If you know you have faith for something, would you not go on until you got it?"[38]

Despite Howells's unwavering faith, victory seemed anything but sure—especially when hundreds of thousands of British and French troops found themselves pinned along the French coast by German forces. On the evening of May 19, 1940, Winston Churchill gave his first radio address as prime minister to the British people, speaking of the grave situation developing in France. The following morning Howells declared to his students, "The next twenty-four hours will be the crisis in this great battle. They are ready to take our country at any moment. Even before lunchtime the history of the world may be changed.... You do not know how much faith is needed.... Unless [the Lord] intervenes, we are lost.... I must be very careful [to continue to pray].... The only thing I want is not to doubt in the time of crisis."[39]

From May 22 to May 25 Howells shut himself in his prayer closet to cry out to the Lord day and night, leaving his staff to lead the students in the prayer meetings. He emerged on May 26 for the national day of prayer called by King George VI, who had asked the British people to turn back to God in a spirit of repentance and to plead for divine help.

The next morning, as British and French troops attempted to evacuate during the battle at Dunkirk, Howells was assured that "the Lord can do a mighty deed. Our people will see God answering their prayers, and they will have all the joy of it."[40] He admitted that faith was all he had left, given the increasingly bleak news of the situation he described as "hell upon earth."[41] And yet he and his students continued to turn to God.

On May 28 the group felt the Spirit come upon them during prayer, and they sensed they had been given an assurance that "something has happened." In the natural, things had not changed for the better but in fact looked worse. Britain and France were perilously close to losing the battle, which could result in both nations' conceding the war and Hitler's taking over.

"From a worldly standpoint there is no hope of victory," Howells said, "but God has said it.... If He is on the field of battle, He can change [bad news] and make it very good news. We are not to run into any panic thinking the Nazis are going to win.... We may have to go through far greater sufferings yet, but I am not going to doubt the final issue."[42]

The final issue came in miraculous fashion when, for reasons still unclear to historians today, Hitler issued a "halt order" on German attacks that gave a three-day gap for more than 338,000 British and French troops to evacuate. Howells and the students continued to pray fervently, as did many across Britain, and by June 4, all the troops had been evacuated—save a small battalion that remained as a rear guard—in what has been referred to as "a miracle of war."[43]

A small remnant of prayer warriors did not give up in crying out to God, despite the growing crisis that surrounded them. So it is today as we face what seems like a surging tsunami of "distress" in the nations. The crisis is here—we find evidence of that everywhere we look—yet it is nothing compared to what lies ahead. Those who believe in and study God's Word know there is much more to come.

Still, Psalm 2 assures us that God will intervene. Despite a global crisis few can imagine and even fewer can endure, His will shall be done on the earth as it is in heaven, Satan will be overcome, and Jesus will reign in victory. As Howells said, "We may have to go through far greater sufferings yet, but we are not going to doubt the final issue."[44]

PART I
THE CRISIS

Chapter 1

THE BIBLE TELLS US SO

L *OVE WINS!"*
The phrase appeared in everything from newspaper headlines to Twitter hashtags to marketing campaigns, all in celebration of the US Supreme Court's monumental decision to legalize same-sex marriage nationwide. Facebook quickly gave users an option to filter their profile pictures with a rainbow to show support to the gay community—and these pictures received more than half a *billion* likes within the first few hours following the ruling. Twitter offered a specially designed rainbow emoji. Ice cream company Ben and Jerry's renamed one of its top-selling flavors to mark the occasion. And most of the nation's biggest companies—from Target to Visa to American Airlines—ran congratulatory ads or social media campaigns with such phrases as "Love reigns from coast to coast" and "Love. Accepted Everywhere."[1] In sweeping fashion, America celebrated a cultural truth that love, indeed, had won the day.

For those committed to God's Word, though, there was a profound problem: love *didn't* win.

It is not that God does not love those who call themselves gay, lesbian, bisexual, transgender, queer, intersexual, or asexual. His love is as strong as ever for all people, regardless of their sexual practices and ideology. But God's definition of love is vastly different from the one America offers today.

Our culture believes we should each have the right to express this "love" however we want, with whomever we want. This definition of love is rooted in accommodating whatever people want—and accommodation and tolerance are the twin values upon which secular humanism thrives.

So if a man says he loves another man and wants to marry him, who are we to say they should not be allowed to marry? This argument is used everywhere as the fundamental rationale for same-sex marriage. And as long as you define love by purely human terms, it makes sense (which is one of the main reasons why the Supreme Court was willing to overturn a standard that has stood for centuries).

Love, however, is not a human idea. It is not a human creation. First John 4:7 says that "love is from God" (ESV). Love, in fact, is a divine person, and His name is Jesus. In Jesus we find the perfect definition of love and the perfect depiction of love incarnate. God sent His only Son, Jesus, to the earth so that we could know and be in relationship with this perfect love.

Yet what happened two thousand years ago when Love walked the earth still happens today: We reject His "version" of love and opt for our own. In the spirit of humanism we declare ourselves our own god, with our own right to define what love is and is not. And in so doing, we assert that our definition stands as absolute truth.

This is why those in the humanistic and gay movements are so fervently bent on tearing down the "old-fashioned" morals of Christianity. The leading voices behind these movements do not just attack biblical faith; they present their values and doctrines as far superior to those espoused by Christians, honestly believing that they express the moral high ground. They see God's Word and His ways as antiquated, intolerant, and irrelevant to today's more advanced, intelligent, and accepting moral code. After all, what kind of God calls Himself loving and kind yet will not allow two people who love each other—and who just happen to be of the same sex—to be joined in marriage?

I love gay and lesbian people. I truly do. I have great compassion for those in same-sex relationships, and, just as Jesus would, I embrace those struggling with their sexual identity or same-sex attractions as well as the many heterosexuals who feel trapped in immorality in either a physical or virtual expression (pornography). Homosexuals are not a mass of unidentified faces that we can easily distance ourselves from by labeling them "them"; a homosexual is a precious and valuable person, just like anyone else dealing with an issue. So when I meet a man who says he is gay, I want to know him, understand him, and love him. I want to show him God's love and tell him about how the Lord can lead him out of whatever pain, disorientation, identity crisis, or confusion he is experiencing.

At its core, however, the crisis of the Supreme Court's decision is not actually about an individual. This is about a single law opening the legal door for something far greater than a person's right to marry someone of the same sex. Indeed, the Supreme Court's ruling on same-sex marriage is just the tip of the moral and spiritual iceberg.

What is seen as love triumphing is actually the opening of a door to enforce the systematic presentation of a demonically driven, immoral agenda upon future generations. The ramifications of opening this door are serious and significant.

Within a few years people will use the same "love wins" mentality to argue for the legal rights of an adult who "loves" a twelve-year-old and thinks they should be allowed to marry. We will see court cases pushing for bigamy, polygamy, and eventually even incestuous marriages. Indeed, the ruling on June 26, 2015, by our nation's highest court that legalized gay marriage and, in fact, institutionalized immorality goes far beyond what people do in the privacy of their bedroom. As a result of that one judicial decision our nation's government will demand by law that the gay agenda is methodically presented in every public elementary school. Seven- and eight-year-olds will eventually be forced— again, by law—to learn not just about a woman's right to have sex with another woman but also about the details involved in her actions. By mandate of law eight-year-olds will have to study why a man should be commended for dressing like a woman.

We have only to look across the pond to see where we are

headed. In France four- and five-year-olds in some schools now engage in exercises that help them avoid stereotyping sexes. They are taught to think gender-neutrally. Meanwhile twelve- to fourteen-year-old students continue this "education" by watching films that celebrate boys who act like girls and girls who act like boys (and who then fall in love with members of their own sex). In some German elementary and middle schools teachers and students celebrate "gender equality day" by dressing as the opposite sex. Seventh-graders there must complete a written exercise that asks loaded questions such as: "When and why did you decide to be heterosexual?" "Is heterosexuality only a phase which you'll overcome?" "Is it possible that your heterosexuality is the result of the neurotic fear of the people the same gender as you?"[2]

In Switzerland some kindergartners receive "sex boxes" complete with plush toy genitalia to mix and match, queer dolls they can cross-dress, and illustrated books with an assortment of gender identities explained.[3] One state-funded Swedish kindergarten treats children as if they have no gender and strictly forbids calling a child "he" or "she" (instead referring to a child of either gender as an "it").[4] And in Norway the government has proposed legislation that will allow seven-year-olds to decide (with their parents' support) their own legal gender.[5] In fact, across Europe many government ministries of education now push the belief that children are born gender-neutral and should be exposed to every sexual preference possible at an early age so they can choose for themselves.

Because of the Supreme Court's decision, America is not far from taking such radical steps toward gender neutralization. We are only a decade or two away from a great increase of the current emotional and sexual chaos running rampant among our children. That may sound preposterous and even laughable today—after all, we pride ourselves in knowing right from wrong. But even the most logical secular humanists should be able to see the slippery slope we are on once we define love, sex, and gender by our own standards rather than God's.

Yet that is exactly the problem: they cannot see because, as Scripture says, "The god of this age has blinded the minds of unbelievers" (2 Cor. 4:4, NIV). Because so many worship the false god of humanism, they are unable to see their own double-mindedness or intolerance. Their blindness allows them to lobby for tolerance for everyone in one breath yet lambaste Christians in the next, and ironically their hatred for believers stems from their claim that we are so "intolerant."

Is it any wonder that Satan—the ultimate "god of this age" that Paul referred to in the verse above—needs little help in getting humans to defy God and define their own truth? Since the Garden of Eden he has baited us with the same hook: *Did God really say…?* History proves humans will repeatedly fall for this line and, in our fallen nature, do whatever it takes to stand in direct opposition to God's Word.

Don't Say I Didn't Warn You

What if I told you that someone had forecast the Supreme Court's ruling and its ensuing ramifications? That would not be a big deal, given the many voices that have warned America of this slippery slope. But what if that prediction was not made just a few years ago or even a few generations ago, but in fact more than *three thousand years ago*? That would add significantly more weight to this person's words, wouldn't it?

But what if I said this same person accurately described how leaders around the world today would collectively shake their fists at God, believe that His Word no longer had relevance, and actually call His ways antiquated? And what if this person also alluded to governments passing laws that directly opposed God's ways, specifically in the areas of love and marriage?

Do I have your attention yet?

The truth is that the Bible, in a single chapter, paints an astoundingly vivid and precise picture of what we are beginning to experience today. Even more concerning, it gives an account of what is to come—and (spoiler alert!) the picture is not pretty for those who oppose God.

More than three thousand years ago David, the great king of Israel who penned much of the Book of Psalms, foresaw what is happening today. Under the guidance of the Holy Spirit he wrote a prophetic warning that we now know as Psalm 2. His words not only depict the global scene for generations today but also provide key insight for the generation of the Lord's return—a generation that could be living now.

We do not know exactly what year this psalm was written or what David was experiencing at the time he wrote it. In the next chapter we will explore more about the context and importance of this pivotal passage of Scripture, which is actually the most quoted psalm in the entire Bible. What I want us to consider for now, though, is just how remarkable it is that God would give David such clear and specific direction for this generation.

I remember how amazed I was years ago when the Lord gave me information of something that would happen in the future of our church family. It stirred my faith and moved me to love Him even more. Let me explain.

In 1985 our church plant in Kansas City was two years old and continuing to grow. We were renting an auditorium in a nearby high school and had been asking the Lord to provide a building for us so we could house our one-thousand-member young-adult congregation.

During the Sunday service on February 3 a visiting friend went up to the platform to bless our church and surprised us all by prophesying that we would have our new building specifically by June 1. The people applauded, but I was not happy with him (and later spoke privately with him) for giving such a specifically dated prophetic word in public without first submitting it to our elders. At the time we had no potential buildings in sight to purchase for our new church home. Three months went by, and nothing promising happened related to getting a building for our local church.

We had no money saved up for a down payment for it, so I was doubtful that anything would happen by June 1.

By the beginning of May that year the situation had not changed. We still had no good prospects for a new building. But on May 15, to our total surprise, two men took the initiative to contact me and offered to sell us a building without any down payment, and they offered to give us an interest-free loan to buy the building from them. Equally as significant, they said we could move into the building two weeks later. In fact, we could move in *exactly* on—you guessed it—June 1. We were amazed that the Lord had given us such a specific prophetic word and promise just four months earlier.

Indeed, it is amazing when God gives us a prophetic word or vision for something that happens a few weeks, months, or even years in the future. But think of how that pales compared to a vision that isn't fully fleshed out for more than three thousand years!

This fact alone certainly adds gravity to Psalm 2. I believe God intended it to be a word of encouragement for those who, like the sons of Issachar mentioned in 1 Chronicles, would have "understanding of the times" (1 Chron. 12:32, NKJV). God wants us to discern some of the key events of our day so that we can respond with His wisdom and love. The fact that He would begin to reveal the full application of Psalm 2 in our generation today confirms just how much He desires for His people to walk in intimacy and partnership with Him, even amid the coming troubles. But sadly, for those who refuse His love and continue to reject Jesus's leadership despite warnings that, like this one, go as far back as three millennia, the consequences are grave.

> Why do the nations rage,
> and the peoples plot in vain?
> The kings of the earth set themselves,
> and the rulers take counsel together,
> against the LORD
> and against His anointed, saying,

"Let us tear off their bonds
   and cast away their ropes from us."
—Psalm 2:1–3

In the first three verses of Psalm 2 David speaks of the nations raging against God and His anointed, who is Jesus. He describes leaders from around the world who will be working together *to remove the influence of God's Word from society.* Despite the fact that many of these leaders will possibly come from Christian heritages, they will believe that God's Word is outdated, irrelevant, and restrictive in light of their more advanced way of the thinking. David even mentions that this coalition of leaders will enforce laws in direct opposition to God's ways.

Does this not sound eerily similar to what we see today?

Across the world there has been a rapid acceleration of the hostility toward God's ways and those who follow them. I was born in 1955 and can remember well the upheaval in the 1960s—the countercultural sexual and social revolutions.

When *Time* magazine famously asked "Is God Dead?" on its cover in 1966, the general public was shocked and critical of the magazine for insinuating God's demise in a nation rooted in Christianity. Yet the changes that era brought seem small compared to what has happened in recent years, where popular culture—particularly in America—has gone from being opposed to God's Word to outright loathing it. I have never seen the cultural climate shift as quickly as it has in the last five to ten years.

Christians in the Crossfire

As a result of this remarkable shift Christians are getting caught more in the cultural crossfire. What used to be the exception— believers being maligned for standing on God's Word—is in its early stages of becoming the norm. Consider some of these well-known US cases in the long and growing list of believers ridiculed in recent months for their public stances on biblical values:

- Kentucky clerk Kim Davis spent five days in jail after defying a federal court order to issue same-sex marriage licenses in Rowan County. Amid an intense national debate, major media outlets and everyday bloggers alike lambasted Davis for her Christian faith, particularly when her e-mails went public and revealed that she called herself a "soldier for Christ" and, amid the increasing backlash from her stance, said "God is still alive and on the throne."[6]

- Christian bakers Melissa and Aaron Klein closed their Oregon business following ongoing threats, protests, and harassment from the LGBT community. After refusing to bake a wedding cake for a lesbian couple in 2013, the Kleins were ordered by the state to pay $135,000 in damages and slapped with a gag order that prevents them from speaking about their decision.[7]

- The Kentucky Department of Juvenile Justice revoked chaplain David Wells's credentials as an ordained minister along with those of several other volunteer chaplains from churches in Warren County who also refused to sign a state-mandated document ensuring that they would never call homosexuality a sin in their work with young inmates.[8]

- Toledo, Ohio, Municipal Judge C. Allen McConnell was threatened with disbarment after he refused to perform a same-sex wedding due to his Christian beliefs. In response to the seventy-one-year-old's biblical stance, an Ohio Supreme Court advisory board quickly deemed that any judge in the state who refused to grant such marriages while continuing to perform traditional marriages would be acting contrary to the judicial oath of office and showing prejudice.[9]

- Former Alabama state representative Jay Love (R) was hired by Apple for lobbying work in Alabama but fired just a few days later when the company, the CEO of which is openly gay, discovered Love was a staunch defender of traditional marriage.[10]

These cases are only in America. Throughout Europe, where Christianity has long been on the decline, the situation is decidedly more severe because of laws passed in the name of securing human rights (including religious freedom) that in fact stigmatize Christians. For example:

- A hospital in Eksjö, Sweden, fired nurse Ellinor Grimmark after she said she would not perform abortions due to her Christian beliefs.[11]

- Christian pediatrician David Drew, who had an unblemished thirty-seven-year record as a clinical director at Walsall Manor Hospital in England, was fired according to a review panel for trying to motivate his coworkers by sending out a sixteenth-century prayer of Saint Ignatius Loyola.[12]

- In Cornwall, England, Christians Peter and Hazelmary Bull opened their home as a bed and breakfast but were fined, harassed, and eventually forced to sell the property after refusing to let a gay couple share a double room there because they believed "in the importance of marriage as the union of one man and one woman."[13]

- German government officials jailed and heavily fined at least eight German fathers for keeping their children out of a mandatory sex-education class that taught nine-year-olds how to engage in sexual intercourse using rubber penises and plush vaginas.[14] When the case went to court, Germany's Federal Court of Justice ruled that forcing Christian parents to send their children to such programs did not breach the parents' religious freedom. Though many objecting parents have taken similar cases to the European Court of Human Rights, all have been dismissed.[15]

- Polish gynecologist Bogdan Chazan was fired as director of Holy Family Hospital in Warsaw after defying Polish law that said he must perform an abortion on a patient or refer the patient to another doctor or medical establishment that would do so. Chazan refused to do either and was subsequently dismissed, fined, and maligned by Polish media.[16]

- In France attacks against Christians have become so common and increasingly violent—while authorities have responded with indifference—that 115,000 French believers sent Pope Francis a petition requesting he address the issue with the country's president. In 2012 eight out of ten vandalism cases involved Christian homes, businesses, or sites, and many of those cases lacked any follow-up from public authorities.[17]

- Russian President Vladimir Putin signed an antiterrorism law in July 2016. It has strong negative implications for Christians in Russia. As *Charisma News* reported, "Foreign guests are not permitted to speak in churches unless they have a 'work permit' from Russian authorities. If a friend...from outside Russia wishes to share his/her faith in your home the guest will be fined and expelled from Russia. Any discussion of God with non-believers is considered missionary activity and

will be punishable....Example: If one traveling on
a train shares his faith without written permis-
sion the offender will be taken into police cus-
tody....Religious activity is no longer permitted
in private homes. Most churches in Russia meet in
homes. Every citizen is obligated to report religious
activity of neighbors to the authorities. Failure to
be an informant is punishable by law....In church
buildings, it is not permitted to invite people
to turn to God. Worship services are permitted
but making a non-believer a follower of Christ is
against the law."[18] The church leaders in Russia are
appalled at the news of the new law.

FRIENDLY FIRE IN THE CHURCH

These situations—and hundreds of others like them—prove that
we are experiencing a dramatic change in the cultural climate,
both in the United States and around the world. The temperature
is rising, as is the heat against Christians in particular.

As believers we would be foolish to expect sympathy from the
secular world. Jesus promised us, "You will be hated by all nations
for My name's sake" (Matt. 24:9).

Is it any wonder, then, that there has been such little media cov-
erage and response from world leaders (other than the obligatory
condolences and empty promises to bring about justice) to ISIS's
beheading of Christians in droves, or to churches being blown up
throughout the Middle East, or to entire towns of Christians in
India being slaughtered? Truth be told, such murdering and tor-
turing of believers was on the rise years before ISIS emerged. So
the global apathy is not surprising.

What is alarming, however, is the growing trend of considering
Christian persecution a mere myth. And what should concern us
even more is who is helping to promote this idea.

The argument is simple: Christianity is the majority religion in
the world, with more than 2.2 billion people—about one-third of

the world population—claiming an association with the Christian faith; therefore any reports of persecution toward Christians are part of a deceptive scheme from them to keep the masses sympathetic toward their cause. As one cynical columnist wrote, "Who can resist the deliciousness of having both the upper hand of power and the righteousness of the oppressed?"[19]

In America this argument is frequently voiced with both reason and subtlety. The logical objection is that, unlike most nations in the world, the United States still upholds the ideal of religious freedom. Therefore to say Christians are persecuted in America is nothing more than a myth—after all, none of the believers listed in the previous section lost their lives, nor were they tortured for their faith.

Indeed, the United States and many "post-Christian" nations have a long way to go before their level of Christian persecution can compare to places such as North Korea, Somalia, Iraq, or Syria. Though I pray that level never increases, the point remains for those of us in America: the cases listed above—and countless others—are still reminders that our country is rapidly shifting even farther away from its Christian roots. And within the last decade the acceleration of decidedly anti-Christian activity is startling.

If Christians do not wake up to see what is happening—both overtly and behind the scenes—we will end up accelerating our own persecution. How do I know this? Because we can already see that one of the enemy's methods to increase the persecution of Christians is to use Christians themselves to say such persecution does not even exist!

You would think that when believers publicly stand their ground for biblical values, they could expect support from fellow believers. At the very least the Christian community should be a safe haven for those who have been ridiculed, mocked, or penalized in the public square for their faith. Yet often the leading voices in America's secular media touting the "myth" of Christian persecution are believers—many from a more liberal viewpoint—who claim to represent the church as a whole.

Even among smaller Christian media outlets instances of Christian persecution—particularly the high-profile ones stirring national debate—draw out the worst in believers and often lead to friendly fire within the church. One of the most common shots fired is that believers exaggerate by calling it "persecution" in the first place. Benjamin Dixon, a former pastor and author of *God Is Not a Republican*, says Christians in America claiming to be persecuted "are embarrassing the faith because it would appear that [they] can't even endure what essentially amounts to someone no longer being the popular girl in school."[20]

These fellow believers' main argument is that American Christians cannot claim to face real persecution as long as we are the majority of the population. Granted, I understand the dilemma of comparing the current persecution of Christians in America to that of Christians in countries where believers are beheaded for their faith. Clearly these are completely different levels of persecution. But at what point does persecution become "real" persecution? How badly must we be attacked before our cries for the church to wake up are heeded? How much hatred do we have to endure for us to realize that our culture has shifted and that we have entered into a new era in which persecution for standing up for God's Word will continually increase?

History repeatedly proves that even a majority can be the weaker victim of discrimination to an aggressive, powerful minority. From Adolf Hitler's Nazi regime to South Africa's apartheid, outspoken minority parties have shaped countries and even the world by following through with an uncompromising agenda. So just because Christians are statistically the majority in the United States does not mean the fiercer minority that hates their God cannot discriminate against them.

As mentioned in this book's introduction, unfortunately only a portion of those who claim to be Christian actually walk in accordance with or even believe in God's ways as defined in His Word. Though none of us have the right to judge who the "real" Christians are—only God sees the heart—we do know that when we truly follow Jesus, we will face opposition and persecution. Jesus exhorted us to rejoice when this happens, knowing that our reward in heaven is great (Matt. 5:12). Nominal and lukewarm Christians—those who make up the majority of America's "Christians" according to the Barna study on those with a biblical worldview[21]—do little to draw persecution upon themselves because their beliefs are shaped more by popular culture's opinions than by what God's Word actually says. This type of "Christian" will do whatever it takes—in beliefs and actions—to fit in with what culture says is true and right. Yet those willing to take a countercultural stand, those who will declare God's truths even when they are unpopular, will face resistance in an ever-increasing way.

Again, Jesus promised that we would be hated for following Him (Mark 13:13; Luke 21:17). For some that hatred leads to death; for others it involves being ridiculed. But whatever the degree, we cannot ignore or even downplay the attacks simply because they are not as severe in the United States as in other countries. The growing trend of ridiculing Christians signals where our nation is going. Thus the body of Christ in America must brace itself to stand strong in the face of increasing ridicule and resistance along with more intense expressions of persecution. While we still have the freedom in this country, believers must boldly speak God's truth in love—both to affect our attackers and to wake up the conscience of a church that, for the most part, has slept through the radical cultural changes thus far and done little to respond. Many Christians have been like the frog in the classic story of a frog placed in a kettle of boiling water—content to enjoy the rising heat and doing nothing until his own demise.

That is not God's desire for those who follow Him. He has given us His Holy Spirit, who lives within us and can help us to understand these times. I believe that same Holy Spirit is calling the American church—and believers all around the world—to recognize the growing crisis and respond according to His will, as shown in Psalm 2.

A Unique Generation

Those who stand strong against the cultural tides, even in the face of increasing persecution, can actually be encouraged by this astounding truth: only one generation in history will witness the complete fulfillment of the prophecy of Psalm 2. Let me explain what I mean by that.

As we will explore more in the following chapters, Psalm 2 has significant end-times implications. Biblical prophecy often works in such a way that prophecies take on a dualistic nature of being partially fulfilled during a set point in history as a foreshadowing of the complete fulfillment in the end times.

For example, when Jesus prophesied that Jerusalem would be surrounded by hostile Gentile armies (Luke 21:24), He was not *only* referring to the Roman Empire's attack against Jerusalem in AD 70, but He was also giving a prophetic picture of Jerusalem in the end times.

Psalm 2 is somewhat similar in that it may have a past historical application. Bible scholars debate about exactly when the psalm was written and in what context. It is possible David wrote it after gaining victory over surrounding enemy nations, as is indicated in 2 Samuel 5:17–25; 8:1–14; and 10:1–19. Or he could have written it after ascending the throne as Israel's king. Some even go so far as to debate about whether the author was David at all, though we know this is the case because the Bible tells us so. While quoting from Psalm 2, Acts 4:24–25 says, "Lord, You are God…who by the mouth of Your servant David said…"

Regardless of scholars' varying opinions, any of which are pure conjecture, they must all agree that this psalm has not yet been completely fulfilled. Even those who do not believe Jesus is the centerpiece of this psalm must recognize that no one person has ever been given "the nations for [his] inheritance, and the ends of the earth for [his] possession" (Ps. 2:8). As vast as the empires of Napoleon, Alexander the Great, and Genghis Khan were, none of those men ruled the entire world. That promise is made exclusively for one person: Jesus Christ. Upon His return to the earth, He will reign as King and Ruler of all.

Because of this truth we know that only one generation in history will see Psalm 2 come to complete fruition. In my opinion, that generation may arrive sooner than some think, particularly when we consider the psalm's first three verses. We are beginning to see the nations rage against Jesus today. There is an unprecedented acceleration of hostility toward His Word and hatred toward His followers. Society's rulers are starting to join together, seeking to remove any influence of God's Word from the culture (v. 3). Although there are elements of Psalm 2 that have yet to be fulfilled, much in the psalm has begun to take shape. The stage is being set, the players are moving into position, and the tension is rising.

My Personal Opinion

I can already imagine your response: "Mike, are you saying you think Jesus might return within our lifetime? Wait a second—even Jesus said nobody but the Father knows when that day will come." You are exactly right—Jesus did say that. In Matthew 24:36 the Lord spoke to His disciples about His return: "Concerning that day and hour no one knows, not even the angels of heaven, but My Father only."

There is a difference, however, between knowing the exact day and hour and knowing the season or "times," as the Bible often refers to it. Many believers argue that it is not important for believers to know if they are in the generation of Jesus's return; what matters is simply that we are spiritually prepared for it. Though the latter is incredibly important, we cannot ignore the fact that the Lord also commanded His people to know the conditions of the generation leading up to His second coming (Matt. 24:33, 42, 44). The Scriptures have an abundance of information on this topic because God wants His people to know if they are in or approaching that generation by the biblical signs of the times given by Jesus. Jesus made it clear that it is actually the responsibility of the generation of believers living when He returns to *know* the signs of the times (Matt. 24:32–34; Luke 21:25, 28–36).

In my opinion, there are people alive today who might see Jesus return. Those within that generation might be only young children right now—I don't know. Nobody can know for sure at this time. Scripture clearly lays out a seven-year period immediately prior to Jesus's second coming, and that prophetic time could begin in the near future or may still be several decades from now. I want to stress from the beginning of this book that this is just my personal opinion based on my observations of the biblical signs of the times—it is not a based on a personal prophetic revelation.

I am often asked, "Can we know if we are living in the generation of the Lord's return?" The biblical answer is that the one generation will certainly know. How can they know this? By the signs that Jesus told them about. Jesus did not speak in code regarding the end times. He was not mysterious or vague beyond understanding. In Matthew 24 alone we have an entire chapter in which He spoke specifically about these signs—and how we are to respond. Mark 13 and Luke 21 give other renditions of what is commonly called the Olivet Discourse (because Jesus said these things on the Mount of Olives).

We will go into this topic more toward the end of the book as we discuss how believers are to respond in the season of growing crisis. But for now it is important to recognize this: understanding these biblical signs and recognizing when they appear is crucial for the church; it is part of the spiritual preparation of God's people for the Lord's return.

TODAY'S REALITY, TOMORROW'S HOPE

As we prepare, we can be encouraged by what God has promised in His Word regarding what is coming in the days ahead. I realize this chapter may have seemed somewhat bleak in its portrayal of what is happening and what will continue to increase in the world today. Indeed, we cannot sugarcoat the crisis at hand, nor can we as Christians continue to overlook the increasing ridicule of, resistance against, and persecution of God's people. What David prophesied more than three thousand years ago in Psalm 2 is now beginning to come to pass.

It is important to remember, however, that Scripture teaches that both darkness and light will simultaneously increase in the days to come (Isa. 60:1–2).

What does that mean? On one hand, we will see things getting worse. In fact, we will witness the deepest level of sin this earth has ever seen. Man's depravity and the expressions of his wickedness will increase in ways we cannot imagine. Satan's works of darkness will increase both in the hearts of people and in their visible expressions. Demonic activity and strongholds will increase as society embraces and even celebrates evil in unparalleled ways. And tragically perversion and deception will run rampant through the nations, causing many to fall away from the faith.

Yet on the other hand is the promise of the victorious church walking in the glory of God, which is clearly set forth in the Scriptures. Amid the growing darkness the light of Jesus will also continue to expand. We will witness the greatest revival this planet has ever known. Even as sin increases in societies, this revival will usher in the greatest harvest of souls ever. Millions upon millions will stand up against the cultural tidal wave of darkness and commit to follow and love Jesus with all their hearts. The end-time church will walk in unprecedented power and fulfill what Jesus promised when He said, "He who believes in Me will do the works that I do also. And he will do greater works than these" (John 14:12). These greater works of signs, wonders, and miracles will astound the world and declare Jesus's true authority over all. Indeed, I believe that the church's finest hour is sure to come.

Why do I believe this, especially since the mainstream media regularly remind us of all the studies proving the church's so-called demise? First, I know it because God's Word says so.

Arise, shine; for your light has come, and the glory of the
LORD has risen upon you. For the darkness shall cover the
earth, and deep darkness the peoples; but the LORD shall
rise upon you, and His glory shall be seen upon you.

—ISAIAH 60:1–2

Both light and darkness will increase in the end times. The light
is God's glory—this speaks of His glory resting upon believers.
The darkness is sin, demonic activity, and the celebration of wickedness that will pervade the earth. Both will expand during the
coming crisis until the return of Jesus. A great ingathering of
souls and a great falling away from the faith will happen simultaneously. Amid extreme darkness God's glory will arise on His
people and will be openly manifest. Paul emphasized this glory
among believers in Ephesians 5:27 when he said that Jesus would
"present to Himself a glorious church, not having spot, or wrinkle,
or any such thing, but that it should be holy and without blemish."
Indeed, the church will manifest glory in a measure beyond any
time in history.

I believe the church's finest hour is yet to come. The signs of
it have already begun. It is true that the number of professing
Christians who attend church in the Western world is declining.
But it is simultaneously true that for more than fifty years the
number of professing Christians in Africa, Asia, and South
America has grown exponentially. China's underground revival
alone is the greatest numerically in history, yet how often—
outside of a few Christian channels—is this told? Africa and Asia
now seem to be the hub of Christendom, and Christian influence
around the world continues to grow. God is truly cleansing His
church, the bride of Christ, with believers who will not yield to
culture's standards—including its definition of love.

In addition, the Holy Spirit's miraculous work is on the rise.
Ten or fifteen years ago news sources such as *Charisma* magazine
would highlight someone's being raised from the dead or healed
in a dramatic way because it was so rare; today many of the international healing ministries I know have experienced these kinds

of miracles firsthand. An army of nameless, faceless believers is emerging in various places on the earth and bringing about God's kingdom with supernatural power.

This is good news, and it is the reality of both today and the days to come. Too often Christians speak of the end times with a sense of gloom and doom. Even mentioning the phrase *end times* evokes for many the image of a sign-toting street preacher agitatedly proclaiming, "The end is near!" For generations the church's dealing with this topic has been either to skirt it or, for those bold enough, to address it in the wrong spirit and with wrong ideas. We have often promoted fear over God's love and doom over the hope God offers.

It is true that the end times will usher in terrible things. Scripture makes this clear. We must not take this lightly.

But we also must not forget God's loving, redemptive nature, which will remain just as constant through the end times. God will do whatever it takes—including removing any obstacles to His love's prevailing—to redeem this planet.

Remember, His definition of love is not the same as the definitions in our culture. And in His love God will cleanse the planet of evil and darkness. Though He has allowed Satan to sift humanity for a time and has appointed men and women to be given over to their own evil ways (Rom. 1:24–32), Jesus will reign as the only rightful Ruler. Amid the chaos, amid the surging crisis, Jesus is preparing His bride, the church, to rule and reign with Him for eternity (Rev. 19:7; see also Rev. 5:10).

Beloved, this is good news! It not only gives us hope as we look at what is happening around the world today but also encourages us to delve deeper into what the Holy Spirit is currently saying to us as He prepares His people for the coming times. That includes receiving greater insight regarding Psalm 2, which I believe He is highlighting for the church to understand more.

So let's continue to look at the powerful prophecies found in this key passage of Scripture.

Chapter 2

THE DIVINE DRAMA OF PSALM 2

THE HOUSE LIGHTS in the large auditorium finally dimmed. Silence blanketed the room and every eye in the room looked to the stage. As the massive velvet curtain lifted, I leaned forward in my seat, eager to see what waited behind the drape.

It was my first time seeing *Les Misérables* at Queen's Theatre in the West End of London, and I will never forget how attentive I was when the first act began. From that moment on, each time the curtain closed and reopened for the play's different acts, I took in with great attentiveness the changing scenes—the vibrant colors of the stage set, the detailed decorations and props, the actors in new places with new costumes. Then there were the intense emotional swings that the audience went through as the story line unfolded—watching Jean Valjean experience God's mercy and then responding by showing kindness to Cosette and Fantine, all while being relentlessly hunted by Javert...and so much more. It was an evening I will always remember.

In the same unforgettable way Psalm 2 unfolds like a great play set on an even grander stage. The verses of this prophetic end-times scripture comprise a drama the entire world will one day watch to its fulfillment. In fact, the greatest stage productions in history will pale in comparison to this divine masterpiece, complete with a star-studded cast and a story for the ages.

Nineteenth-century preacher Charles Spurgeon knew just how spectacular and dramatic Psalm 2's story is. He described the psalm as "a four-fold picture" in the same vein as a theatrical drama.[1] Anyone familiar with the London theater scene in his day would have followed Spurgeon's analogy. Theaters of all sizes surrounded him in that city, where he served as pastor of the historic New Park Street Chapel (later the Metropolitan Tabernacle) from 1854 to 1892.

Spurgeon certainly understood the power of a dramatic story and its effect on people. As one of England's greatest orators ever, he would often draw crowds of five to ten thousand with his preaching, and it was said that people hung on his every word. His voice was powerful enough that he once spoke to a crowd of more than twenty-three thousand people without using a microphone or any amplification system (such a system wouldn't be invented until the twentieth century).[2]

I imagine the London theaters were on his mind as he wrote his Psalm 2 commentary and used the analogy of a great drama. So as we go through this psalm, picture a spectacular drama unfolding in a grand theater and fascinating you with each act, just as I was fascinated at *Les Misérables* in London.

The Script

Psalm 2 has four distinct parts, as evidenced not only by what is being addressed in each part but also by who is delivering the messages. Spurgeon described Psalm 2 as a drama with four acts in which each presented a different key figure who was taking center stage.

Each of these four acts contains profound implications for today—in fact, each phrase of each verse does. I believe our understanding of both the overarching message *and* the many nuances of Psalm 2 is crucial to our not only discerning the times but also discovering how the Lord desires for us to stand during these days. As I mentioned in the previous chapter, things will get progressively worse *and* better at the same time. Opposition to and hatred for Jesus will continually increase, which means those who claim to follow Him will be despised as well. As the darkness grows, so will the light; we as the church must know what the Holy Spirit is saying and how He is guiding us during these times.

Before we go any further, however, let's first look at Psalm 2 in

its entirety so we can establish an overview of this critical passage
of Scripture:

> Why do the nations rage,
>> and the peoples plot in vain?
> The kings of the earth set themselves,
>> and the rulers take counsel together,
> against the LORD
>> and against His anointed, saying,
> "Let us tear off their bonds
>> and cast away their ropes from us."
>
> He who sits in the heavens laughs;
>> the LORD ridicules them.
> Then He will speak to them in His wrath
>> and terrify them in His burning anger:
> "I have installed My king
>> on Zion, My holy hill."
>
> I will declare the decree of the LORD:
>
> He said to me, "You are My son;
>> this day have I begotten you.
> Ask of Me,
>> and I will give you the nations for your inheritance,
>> and the ends of the earth for your possession.
> You will break them with a scepter of iron;
>> you will dash them in pieces like a potter's vessel."
>
> Now then, you kings, be wise;
>> be admonished, you judges of the earth.
> Serve the LORD with fear;
>> tremble with trepidation!
> Kiss the son, lest He become angry,
>> and you perish in the way,
> for His wrath kindles in a flash.
>> Blessed are all who seek refuge in Him.

Now let's briefly summarize each of the four acts, as if they were part of a play, to gain a greater perspective of how this great drama unfolds in just twelve verses.

Act I: Earth's Kings and Rulers (vv. 1–3)

[Curtain rises]

In the drama's first act the kings and rulers of the earth take center stage. In these three verses the leaders of the nations present their case against God and His Christ, yet they reveal their hearts entirely with only one line of speech: "Let us tear off their bonds and cast away their ropes from us" (v. 3). The kings and rulers essentially shake their fists at the Lord in utter rage and contempt for Him. More specifically they oppose Jesus, God's anointed One, and they want to remove the influence of His Word from every part of their societies and dominions. They believe they will be free when the Word of God is no longer holding them back, and they unite to plot against God. They see God's Word as "bonds" and "ropes" that hold them in bondage and captivity.

[Curtain falls]

Act II: The Father (vv. 4–6)

[Curtain rises]

Act II places God the Father at center stage. David sums up the Lord's initial response to the kings' and rulers' opposition with one word: laughter. As the master of the universe God laughs at the notion that these earthly leaders think their plans to oppose Him will amount to anything. His mocking laughter eventually turns into terrible wrath, however, as He confronts the rebellion against Jesus by both unleashing His vengeance and exalting His Son, Jesus, as the true King of all.

[Curtain falls]

Act III: Jesus (vv. 7–9)

[Curtain rises]

After receiving such honor from His Father, the spotlight now shines brightly upon Jesus, God's anointed King. In three verses

Jesus responds both to the earthly hatred against Him and to His Father's response to the kings and rulers. In perfect humility Jesus does exactly what He did while walking on the earth: He speaks out only what He hears the Father saying (John 12:49). In verses 7–9 Christ repeats His Father's words, which are an edict declaring God's promises to Him. In essence, Jesus is interceding in agreement with the Father's decrees, confirming once again that even as King of the earth He is still the Great Intercessor of heaven. From this position of rightful authority and kingship Jesus inherits the earth and destroys all opposition.

[Curtain falls]

Act IV: David (vv. 10–12)

[Curtain rises]

Though God ultimately gets the last word, in the final act of Psalm 2 David actually gets to speak last. In the concluding three verses Israel's king encourages his fellow kings and rulers to humble themselves by serving the Lord. Essentially David says they should willingly throw themselves at Jesus's feet in godly fear and love, considering He is the mightiest King of all. Their resistance to Him will never succeed, David points out, so it would be wise to serve God on His terms rather than to resist His leadership. He exhorts them to "kiss the son" as a loyal servant would bow before a king in both humility and adoration (v. 12). Finally David encourages all who trust the Lord—those who understand that out of godly fear come true intimacy and friendship—by reminding them that trust leads to eternal blessing.

[Curtain falls]

Four acts. Three verses each. Only twelve short verses in all. And yet within this relatively small chapter is the culmination of the earth's history, as the majority of people on the planet rise up to oppose Jesus in a showdown of eternal significance and consequences. The kings and rulers of the earth draw together with one common denominator: their fervent hatred for Jesus and His Word (vv. 2–3). Out of this common loathing they unite in opposition.

But their plans and schemes amount to nothing because we know who wins: Jesus. It's not even a contest. There may be a showdown, but ultimately the battle is over before it begins.

The Bible makes it clear that all opposition to Jesus is for naught, that the rebellious leaders will be smashed "in pieces like a potter's vessel" (v. 9) and that He will reign over the nations. If this is the end result, then what is the point in studying Psalm 2? Why bother with understanding more about this passage? Aren't we reading too much into such a simple psalm in the first place? If at the end of the day we all know Jesus wins and Satan loses, then why concern ourselves with the increasing darkness and opposition?

The answer to that last question—which actually answers the previous ones as well—is simple: because many will succumb to the darkness. When the overwhelming majority of people on the earth rise up against Jesus, opposing Him with violent hatred, it will become difficult for believers to stand against such an onslaught and stay true to Christ without understanding what is happening on the earth from God's point of view. By understanding the depths of what Psalm 2 reveals to us, we can gain insight into the coming days so that we will not be offended or overwhelmed and, more importantly, so we will be spiritually prepared to face the surging darkness and opposition.

But let me expound on why understanding Psalm 2 is so important, even when we know that, yes, the light of Jesus ultimately overcomes this darkness.

When the Holy Spirit Highlights

In May 1983 many in the young-adult church that I was pastoring went on a twenty-one-day fast. We met many hours each day to pray together, and during this time the Lord spoke a word we did not understand then but that later proved to be one of the most significant words God has ever given me or our church body. Let me share what happened.

As we were together worshipping, praying, and seeking the Lord one day, I was gripped by Psalm 27:4, in which David prayed that he may "dwell in the house of the LORD all the days of [his] life, to see the beauty of the LORD, and to inquire in His temple." All day as I paced in that prayer meeting, I whispered David's prayer to God: "Oh, that I could dwell in Your house to gaze on Your beauty." I was not entirely sure what that sentence meant, but I felt compelled to keep saying it to the Lord throughout the day. I may have prayed it thousands of times that day.

The next day Bob Jones, a man with a proven prophetic ministry, came to me and said that he had heard the audible voice of the Lord in a dream the night before. The Lord told him that He "gave Mike Bickle a prayer the day before from Psalm 27:4." I was surprised to hear this because I had not shared with Bob or anyone else the fact that I had prayed that same verse, Psalm 27:4, throughout the previous day. Given this remarkable insight, I asked Bob if he knew what it meant, and he said it meant that one day the Lord would enable us "to do 24/7 prayer in the spirit of the tabernacle of David."

It was as if he was speaking Chinese to me. I had no idea what that phrase meant. Bob expounded by saying we would hold 24/7 prayer meetings led by worship teams as David did in the tabernacle in the Old Testament. I still did not understand what that meant. However, we put the phrase he said on a sign in our church's prayer room, and it remained there on the wall for almost fifteen years until we started the International House of Prayer of Kansas City in 1999. Now many years later, after the Holy Spirit highlighted a specific scripture to me and further explained it through a prophetic word, I understand much more.

The Holy Spirit is always at work. We know that in His omnipresence God has the ability and capacity to move an infinite number of different ways at once. That means His Spirit is always moving around the world, working on the hearts of men and women everywhere.

But there are also times and seasons when God seems to specifically pinpoint certain things so as to prepare His people for a wave of His Spirit. He does not desire for us to be unprepared and overwhelmed when the Holy Spirit sweeps over the earth with power; instead He wants us to be His vessels, working in tandem with Him to extend the Spirit's work.

That is one of the reasons certain passages of Scripture seem to be given more prominence in certain seasons of history—not because they are more important than any others but because they are a *kairos* word to the body of Christ. *Kairos* is the Greek word meaning "time" or "season." It refers to not just any time or season but an *opportune* time or a *fitting* season.[3] A *kairos* word is one that fits perfectly for the season—it is the exact right word delivered at the exact right time in history.

Often the Holy Spirit will take His divine highlighter and high-light a *kairos* word from Scripture for the global church. He will accentuate a certain passage of God's Word that not only pro-vides insight into the times but also contains power needed for that moment.

In church history, for example, we know that the Holy Spirit used Romans 1:16–17 to propel Martin Luther to study more intensely how "the just shall live by faith." That scripture, along with others such as Ephesians 2:8—that it is "by grace you have been saved through faith, and this is not of yourselves"—changed history because Luther's conclusion, boldly declared in his Ninety-Five Theses, was used to spark the Protestant Reformation.

I believe the Holy Spirit is highlighting Psalm 2 today not just in a few local churches and not just in the United States but throughout the entire world. Why? Because this scripture helps us to interpret the crisis that is unfolding globally right now. As we have already discussed, that crisis is escalating rapidly. It will not mellow out and fade away. We know from both Scripture and his-tory itself that it will continue to swell until it comes to the point of a full rage among the earth's kings and rulers against the Lord.

When we grasp the full meaning of Psalm 2, we will not be confused, fearful, or offended by the wickedness that occurs. Instead we will be prepared to face the times, fully aware of God's big-picture plan while discerning how the smaller developments of the growing crisis relate to it.

Ignoring and Rejecting the Holy Spirit

Sadly, however, much of what the Holy Spirit is saying and doing today regarding Psalm 2 is being either ignored or rejected. Even worse, it is being ignored or rejected by those who claim to follow Him—the church! Obviously I am not referring to *all* of the church, but many who call themselves Christians today deny the notion that there is such an increase of vitriolic opposition to Jesus. They think that fellow Christians stretch the truth regarding such things as the increasing darkness and Christian persecution.

Forgive me for my bluntness, but this viewpoint—that the whole professing church loves the ways and teachings of Jesus—is equivalent to burying your head in the sand on the battlefield during a war. (Not to mention that it distorts the full truth of who Jesus is.)

Other believers in the church are desperate to seek the favor and acceptance of the kings and rulers in society. These Christians want peace above all. They want things to go well. They want their ministries to grow, and they want to be accepted and liked by many. They are hoping the crisis will pass and that everything will work out in the end. They have decided to play it safe in the name of being peacemakers. They are content to remain silent on biblical issues because they do not want to offend anyone or burn any bridges—all in the name of becoming "all things to all men" (1 Cor. 9:22).

Jesus clearly said, "He who is not with Me is against Me" (Matt. 12:30). He also said, "Whoever will confess Me before men, him will I confess also before My Father who is in heaven. But whoever will deny Me before men, him will I also deny before My Father who is in heaven" (Matt. 10:32–33).

This is not the hour for silence. It is not time to side with the popular statements in culture and resist the stigma of taking a stand with the Lord. It is not the season for cowering at opportunities to speak the truth in love. Things will not get any easier than they are now. In fact, things will continue only to get more intense. This crisis will not come and go like a summer day's rain; it is the hurricane of all hurricanes. We are talking about the culmination of natural history here. That is why Jesus used such strong language in explaining both His purpose on the earth and the narrow way for those who would dare to follow Him.

In Matthew 10:34—a verse that has always given Christians problems—Jesus said, "Do not think that I have come to bring peace on earth. I did not come to bring peace, but a sword." Jesus's message is divisive and offensive to many. Because of Him, "a man's foes will be those of his own household" (v. 36). Family members will turn on each other over the issue of standing with Jesus or standing with popular culture.

Jesus has never been a fan of following popular culture. While on the earth He preached a gospel that was decidedly countercultural and offensive to most of His listeners. What religion built up, He tore down. What meaningless tradition upheld, He disassembled.

He described the way to His kingdom—the path required for those who want to follow Him—as decidedly narrow:

> Enter at the narrow gate, for wide is the gate and broad is the way that leads to destruction, and there are many who are going through it, because small is the gate and narrow is the way which leads to life, and there are few who find it.
> —MATTHEW 7:13–14

It is no wonder that one of the topics Jesus spoke about most in the context of the coming crisis was believers veering from the narrow path.

THE GREAT DECEPTION

The Bible contains at least 150 chapters in which the end times are the major subject. In fact, almost twice as many chapters of Scripture deal with Jesus's second coming as deal with His first coming.

So it is safe to say this is no small subject matter. God wants us to know about His plans for the end times, and He wants us to discern the times in which we live. But this is also why, when speaking about the end times, *Jesus gave more warnings about deception than about tribulation.* The church has often been fixated on the Great Tribulation—the three-and-a-half-year period just prior to Jesus's return to the earth. We speak, often with a sense of dread and fear, of the fact that God will release unprecedented judgments on the Antichrist's kingdom and that unparalleled darkness and opposition will surround those believers still alive during that time. Note that this judgment is on the Antichrist's kingdom and his followers, not on the church.

These facts are true. Yet if Jesus spoke far more often about the deception, then we need to be focused more on that than on how bad the coming pressures will be. As Jesus said, "Do not fear those who kill the body but are not able to kill the soul. But rather fear Him who is able to destroy both soul and body in hell" (Matt. 10:28). Jesus was referring to the Father when He said this, as He is obviously more powerful than anyone or anything. Only He— not Satan—has the power to throw someone into hell. And the Father has given the keys of death and Hades to Jesus, who now has absolute dominion over hell (Rev. 1:18). Yet we must be aware that the great deception will be one of Satan's last-ditch efforts to draw as many into hell as possible.

Make no mistake; the Great Tribulation will be difficult. As we have discussed, I believe that the end-time global attack against God's people has already begun. Such hatred toward us has been present throughout history and continues today. But the rage against Jesus's people will escalate to the point at which persecution will no longer be in isolated situations or nations. The day is coming when the kings and rulers *of the earth* in their rage will establish legislation to kill believers throughout the world (Ps. 2:1–3; Rev. 13:14–18). It will be open season, fair game, and sadistic sport—all in one—just as it was for the early believers in the Roman era.

Yet it is significant that Jesus, fully aware of the scope and depth of this tribulation, warned us more about being deceived and falling away from the truth. Why do you think that is?

I believe it is because this great deception will be the subtlest, most effective, and most efficient way Satan leads the eternal souls of millions upon millions into darkness forever. What the enemy did in ancient Rome and through the Holocaust in terms of physically murdering God's people, he will seek to do spiritually—multiplied exponentially—through the great deception of both believers and unbelievers.

JESUS'S WARNINGS

Jesus warned about this great deception in Matthew 24, which is the longest passage we have in the Gospels dealing with the end times. At the beginning of this key chapter Jesus's disciples are somewhat in shock after some of the statements He has just made about murdered prophets, a desolated Jerusalem, and the great temple destroyed (Matt. 23:37–24:2). Bewildered, they do what most of us would do in that situation: they ask their teacher to throw them a bone…of understanding.

> As He sat on the Mount of Olives, the disciples came to Him privately, saying, "Tell us, when will these things be, and what will be the sign of Your coming and of the end of the age?"
> —MATTHEW 24:3

As usual, Jesus's answer is probably not what they expected. They wanted to know exactly when He planned to return to Jerusalem to overthrow the Roman government. It is likely most of the disciples were still thinking in terms of the political uprising they believed Jesus would lead to finally restore the kingdom of Israel.

Yet it is both significant and extremely telling that Jesus's first words to answer them have nothing to do with political power and everything to do with losing one's soul through deception:

> Take heed that no one deceives you. For many will come in
> My name, saying, "I am the Christ," and will deceive many.
> —Matthew 24:4–5

Only a few verses later Jesus offers a similar warning specific to the great deception: "And many false prophets will rise and will deceive many" (v. 11).

And finally, in verse 24, He says, "For false christs and false prophets will arise and show great signs and wonders to deceive, if possible, even the elect."

In four different verses within the same chapter on the end times Jesus warns His followers about those who would deceive many through their words and miracles. False christs are simply those who pretend to be and overtly claim to be the Messiah. History shows that there have always been those who claimed this, yet in recent years it seems the number of such cases is dramatically increasing. I am sure our modern-day era of ubiquitous media has made them more prominent, both by providing opportunities for false christs to promote themselves and by seizing every opportunity to prove they are "crazy." Indeed, these days few people take such delusional cases seriously.

Yet Jesus's warning was no joke. I highly doubt He was alerting us to the existence of phonies and frauds you could spot from a mile away. Verse 24 indicates that there will be a day when even "the elect"—God's people—will be duped by those claiming to be an anointed leader sent by God, which means the false christs will become more and more convincing as the global crisis increases. We must take that warning to heart.

The same is to be said of false prophets—those who claim to speak the word of the Lord but do not. False prophets, as Jesus calls them, operate with a deceptive spirit. In Matthew 7:15 He further clarifies: "Beware of false prophets who come to you in sheep's clothing, but inwardly they are ravenous wolves." Whereas false christs may be more overt in their claim to be Jesus, false prophets are subtler deceivers (at least this is true today). They will often tickle people's ears with smooth teachings, inspirational messages, and feel-good "words" from the Lord—all for personal gain. They discredit the gift of prophecy by acting as God's mouthpiece even though their words are empty and anything but Spirit inspired.

Notice, however, that Jesus warns us specifically of the power both false christs and false prophets will have as the end times near. It will become more difficult for people without spiritual discernment to distinguish these deceivers from true believers because they will come in Jesus's name with miraculous powers following them. By all appearances they will seem to be doing the work of God. Yet remember, Satan seeks to do things that counterfeit Jesus. Therefore he will use these deceivers to first do incredible signs and wonders that will leave many—believers included—in awe. Many people will actually believe that God has sent these deceivers because, after all, their supernatural powers validate that it must be His doing. Yet once these deceivers are trusted, Satan will use them to pervert the truth and draw people away from God.

We would do well to remember Jesus's warning from Matthew 7:21–23:

> Not everyone who says to Me, "Lord, Lord," shall enter the kingdom of heaven, but he who does the will of My Father who is in heaven. Many will say to Me on that day, "Lord, Lord, have we not prophesied in Your name, cast out demons in Your name, and done many wonderful works in Your name?" But then I will declare to them, "I never knew you. Depart from Me, you who practice evil."

PAUL'S ADDITIONAL WARNINGS

The apostle Paul was all too familiar with dealing with deceivers in the church. Several of his messages to various church leaders include how to handle false prophets and those who willingly distort the truth of God. To the church leaders in Ephesus, for example, he said, "For I know that after my departure, dreadful wolves will enter among you, not sparing the flock. Even from among you men will arise speaking perverse things, to draw the disciples away after them" (Acts 20:29–30).

In his letter to Timothy he went so far as to name some of those men and say that he had "delivered [them] to Satan that they may learn not to blaspheme" (1 Tim. 1:20). Ouch!

Paul offered church leaders then—and now—a specific model for dealing with false prophecy in the local church context. But he also issued multiple warnings of a greater deception to come—the one Jesus referred to in the Olivet Discourse.

We recall Paul's warning from 2 Thessalonians 2:9–10:

> ...even him, whose coming is in accordance with the working of Satan with all power and signs and false wonders, and with all deception of unrighteousness among those who perish, because they did not receive the love for the truth that they might be saved.

In 2 Timothy 3:13 Paul affirmed Jesus's description of the last days by saying, "Evil men and seducers will grow worse and worse, deceiving and being deceived." Earlier, in his first letter to Timothy, the apostle prophesied in detail about the generation in which the Lord returns and specifically about the deception that would abound. In that letter he wrote:

> Now the Spirit expressly says that in latter times some will depart from the faith, giving heed to deceiving spirits and doctrines of demons, speaking lies in hypocrisy, having their own conscience seared with a hot iron, forbidding to marry, and commanding to abstain from foods which God created to be received with thanksgiving by those who believe and know the truth.
>
> —1 Timothy 4:1–3, nkjv

It is interesting that Paul began this chapter by saying, "The Spirit expressly says...," which added weight to what followed—namely that some will fall away because of the deception. This is the first time, however, that demonic influence is mentioned behind such deception. We know that Satan is the father of lies (John 8:44); therefore such deception is described as "doctrines of demons."

What are doctrines of demons? I believe these are doctrines that obscure the essential truths of salvation and therefore cause people not to follow the Lord or not to receive Him according to the spirit of truth. Doctrines of demons are ideas or beliefs that distort the truth of God and obscure the truths about Jesus, His commands, His claims, the nature of His salvation, who He is, and so on.

For example, there is only one way of salvation. Jesus made it clear that He is "the way, the truth, and the life. No one comes to the Father except through Me" (John 14:6). Peter confirmed this truth when he declared to the Sanhedrin in Jerusalem, "There is no salvation in any other, for there is no other name under heaven given among men by which we must be saved" (Acts 4:12). Yet today one of the most prominent beliefs in the world is that there are many paths to God. Even professing Christians claim that they can "find" God in a buffet-like selection of different faiths—with a dab of Hinduism, a spot of Buddhism, a little Islam on the side, and maybe even a bit of Scientology or Kabbalah sprinkled in for good measure. Although organized religion is out of style, being "spiritual" is once again in, which is why celebrities and cultural leaders around the world are promoting the false idea that God can be found in all faiths.

The concept that there are many paths to God is a lie from the pit of hell. There is only one path to God, and that is through His Son, Jesus Christ. He was the only Man in eternity who was completely innocent yet became the perfect sacrifice for sin and paid the price so that those who are guilty—you and I—could receive the free gift of eternal life and be united with God. Muhammad did not become sin for us and pay our debt. Buddha did not. L. Ron Hubbard didn't either. None of the religions of the world had a man who was innocent and who took upon himself the guilt of the nations so that the guilty could have free salvation. All paths do not lead to God. There is only one path, only one way.

This claim is not elitism. It is not unfair or unenlightened. There is only one Man who paid the debt—it is as simple as that. It is not about our religion being better than others; it is about a Man who lived in perfection and paid the debt of sin.

It is not by chance that scholars are debating this fact with new fervor in our nation right now. The crisis is escalating, and the very debate itself—the fact that many refuse to accept the truth of what Jesus did—shows how the doctrines of demons are at work. Demonic forces are obscuring the truth, and their activity will increase in the days ahead.

How Far Will the Deception Go?

Notice one of the tiny phrases Paul included in his depiction of the end-times deception that I quoted earlier. In 1 Timothy 4:3 he added three small words in his list of what will happen amid the great deception: "forbidding to marry." Paul wrote this letter to Timothy almost two thousand years ago, and yet he prophesied that the days were coming when marriage would be *forbidden*. In other words, rulers will outlaw marriage in parts of the earth. This means not only marriage between people of the same sex, not only incestuous marriage or polygamy, but marriage in its entirety.

To most of us that sounds absurd. Marriage is one of the foundational pillars of human society; how could it ever be outlawed? Was Paul just being extreme with this inclusion? Maybe he got carried away while writing his letter, possibly because he was so fed up with the deceivers he had to confront in the churches where he visited.

I do not believe it was by mistake that Paul starts this chapter with the emphatic, "The Spirit expressly says..." (NKJV). Neither do I believe it was by mistake that Paul included the banning of marriage as one of the indicators and fruits of the great deception. In recent years we have crossed one of the thresholds of biblical marriage: that it is between one man and one woman. We have perverted God's definition of it.

Ten years ago most cultures did not accept the notion of same-sex marriage; today not only do laws allow it, but also polls prove that most people approve of it.

Why, then, do we think society's views on the sacredness of marriage and its role in society will remain the same? Our definitions for what is moral and what is not are changing with incredible speed, and the institution of marriage is no exception. So what seemed difficult to even imagine ten years ago—that marriage would be outlawed—is, sadly enough, already in the works toward becoming reality. Whether that is five years or fifty years away, I do not know. But what was unthinkable only a handful of years ago is now part of a cultural dialogue.

Interestingly enough the public discourse about marriage's relevance has shifted too. More than ten years ago, amid the early stages of debating same-sex marriage's legality in America, scholars and sociologists questioned whether marriage was eroding or simply evolving.[4] Today key political voices that have long defended marriage—and were even part of the debate a decade ago—now describe it as officially "disappearing" and "dying." Some have said we are in a "new marriage revolution" that, like the sexual revolution of the 1960s, will not only redefine our views on the purpose and benefits of marriage but also could eventually make it obsolete.[5] Indeed, lawyers, professors, philosophers, bloggers, and talking heads alike are asking the same question: Should we abolish marriage entirely?[6] Much of this questioning revolves around the government's legal involvement in civil unions, yet almost universally those debating the issue agree that marriage is becoming more and more controversial. Now that federal law endorses gay marriage, at what point must we also allow other relationships—incestuous, polygamous, and so on—that may be seen as taboo today but in ten years may be looked upon with more acceptance?

There is, of course, a difference between marriage being

completely and globally abolished and its being outlawed in various parts of the world. We might still be some years from the latter's coming to pass, yet who would have thought that we would see such a rapid, dramatic shift in culture's views toward divorce, unmarried people living together in a sexually active way, and gay marriage, as we have in the last two generations—or even the last five to ten years?

WHEN EVIL IS ENDORSED

The first three verses of Psalm 2 remind us that as we get closer to a global rage against Jesus, things we thought impossible can become reality. We are in a time when people "call evil good, and good evil; [they] exchange darkness for light, and light for darkness; [they] exchange bitter for sweet, and sweet for bitter!" (Isa. 5:20).

But how have we so quickly come to a place where what was false is now considered "truth"? How will we now call what once was wrong "right"? In the famous tale of "The Emperor's New Clothes" a little child was able to point out the absurdity of what everyone else was too scared to say. Surely someone can simply stand up and point out how absurd, illogical, and harmful our culture's current progression is. Surely more people should lift their voices against this madness—yes, speak out, but in a loving, tender, and biblical way.

You would hope that would be the case. You would hope that more people would speak out for God's values. You would hope that the church would rise up in the face of opposition and speak the truth. Sadly, though, that has not been the case so far, nor has it been the case in recent history.

Corrie ten Boom's personal story of surviving the Nazi regime in Europe during World War II is well known around the world because of her inspiring book *The Hiding Place* and the subsequent movie based on it. But when she was freed from prison camp and began speaking to crowds around the world after the war, her broader story about the church's response to evil came as a shock to many. Throughout the early 1930s, as Adolf Hitler and his Nazi party quickly rose to power, the church in Germany assured people that all would be fine and that trouble was not coming. Church leaders regularly proclaimed that Hitler was seeking to bring peace and blessing to Germany and therefore should be supported.

Amid this "assurance," however, many German believers fell away from their faith under the mounting pressures of the Nazi regime—and indeed, historical numbers prove that was the case. From 1934 to 1935 about one hundred forty thousand people left the Protestant or Catholic churches; from 1937 through 1942, as Germany rose to power and began the global war, *two million* people left.[7] They were completely unprepared for what was happening. Many in Germany at that time thought God was raising up Hitler to restore their economy, bless their homes and families, and give them liberty. They figured God was redeeming what had been lost from World War I. This idea led many church leaders to support Hitler because of the great economic gains and national honor that was being restored. And for a season, while the Nazi party publicly claimed to be Christian-supporting, the church gave a thumbs-up, expecting that good times were on their way.

When the exact opposite happened and "blessing" quickly turned into mass murder, many believers crumbled in their faith. Rather than face persecution, hardship, or death, people gave in to Hitler. Others fell away from the Lord entirely because they felt that what they were experiencing did not line up with what they believed about the love of God and the good promises in His Word. They had heard preached nothing but a gospel of blessing, and yet only suffering surrounded them. Because of this dichotomy many concluded that they could not trust God because His Word was not true. Though they had been misinformed and duped into an easy gospel by church leaders, they blamed God nonetheless.

In addition, Germany's church leadership continued for the most part to remain silent in objecting to the Nazi evil. A few dissenters such as theologian Dietrich Bonhoeffer and pastor Martin Niemöller rose up in objection to the party's brutal tactics, racialized theology, and treatment of Jews. But for the most part Protestant and Catholic church leaders, as well as everyday believers, were complicit in Hitler's rise through their silence—something that haunted them for generations following the war.[8]

Not standing up to Hitler was arguably one of the greatest failures of the church in all history. His reign was certainly one of the darkest, most shameful periods in Christian history. The way the church responded was the complete opposite of the way a Christian should have responded. Because of the church's failure I fully understand the utter disdain many Jewish people still have today when they hear the word *Christian*, for when they most needed the church to be the extension of Jesus's love for them, we failed them miserably.

Whose Side Are You On?

When crisis comes, it reveals what is inside. Fire has a way of revealing the inner properties of whatever it consumes. The German church during the Nazi regime is a sobering reminder that as the coming crisis intensifies, things will not get easier. Instead we must be prepared because they will actually get more difficult. We cannot coast as believers. We fool ourselves if we think things will get easier or smoother. At some point each of us will be forced to make a difficult decision: Do we stand with Jesus and endure to the end through the growing pressures, tribulation, and possibly even death; or do we take the easier route—at least for now—and yield to today's cultural truths? As Jesus said, we are either for Him or we are against Him. There is no option in between.

My guess is you are reading this book because you intend to side with Him. If that is true, then His warning of the great deception in the times ahead must permeate your heart. We must not lose sight of the fact that Satan will do whatever he can to seduce us with lies—even through people who appear to be sent from God.

There are many voices in the church today clamoring to be heard. Many are prophesying of great trouble ahead. Others say,

"No, great revival is coming!" And still others believe that everything is going well as it is. So which is it?

It is true: we are entering an hour of great revival—of unprecedented numbers coming to Jesus and committing to stand with Him despite persecution. I am standing with many other leaders who are personally believing God for more than a billion new souls in His kingdom in the great end-time harvest. But we are also entering an hour of great deception, a time of great numbers of people falling away. Both will happen simultaneously.

Jesus promised that it would be this way, so we should not be surprised when it happens. When He shared the parable of the wheat and the tares in Matthew 13:24–30, He said both would *mature together at the end.* In fact, He specifically explained the meaning of this parable in detail to His disciples, saying that "as the tares are gathered and burned in the fire, so it will be at the end of this age" (v. 40, NKJV).

There will be a great revival and harvest of souls, and there will be a great falling away of them too. The level of deception in the world and in the church will be at an all-time high—so much that God's people will have to rely on the truth of His Word as if it were their next breath. That is why we must commit *now* to stand true. We must grow in our love for Jesus so that when the heat rises to temperatures we do not think we can endure, we will look to Him for salvation rather than siding with culture.

I want to stand with truth. I want to be a faithful witness. Amid the great end-times drama that Psalm 2 so vividly depicts, I do not want to be among those raging against Jesus, as many will do according to Psalm 2:1; I want to be among those He can count as faithful, the ones He can trust to the end.

How about you?

Chapter 3

ACT I: THE GLOBAL OPPOSITION

Why do the nations rage, and the peoples plot in vain? The kings of the earth set themselves, and the rulers take counsel together, against the LORD and against His anointed, saying, "Let us tear off their bonds and cast away their ropes from us."
—PSALM 2:1–3

IT WOULD BE a truly historic event for literally *all* the world's kings, queens, presidents, prime ministers, political leaders, top business executives, and top culture-shapers to come together around one plan and agenda. In fact, I would call that an absolute miracle.

Even if that could happen—as far-fetched as it might seem—it would be even more staggering if those world leaders got together and agreed not only on a single thing that needed to get done but also, more specifically, on how to get that one thing done. Yet that, in a nutshell, is the surprising phenomenon of Psalm 2's first act in this great end-times drama.

The fact that this psalm paints a picture of a unified world coalition of national leaders and people groups from its first verses shows us how entirely rare this moment will be in human history. Think about it: Other than the two world wars, can you think of any other event or situation that has literally drawn every nation and every people group together? I cannot. And yet there is one thing in history that will unite the nations of the earth like never before: a *raging hatred for Jesus*.

Even in the two world wars of human history, and even in the earth's greatest empires that covered much of the globe, nations remained divided. They were most certainly not united for one purpose. And yet in Psalm 2's prophetic picture of the end times, we find the kings and rulers of the nations standing unified in their rage against Jesus. The apostle John confirmed this in his prophetic vision in Revelation 19:

> And I saw the beast, the kings of the earth, and their armies, gathered together to make war against Him...
> —REVELATION 19:19, NKJV

Before we go any further with this story, however, we need to rewind a bit and understand how we got to this point. How could Jesus go from being a perfect, completely innocent baby in a manger—God's incarnate love expressed to all humanity—to the most hated Man in history? And how did the nations and people groups of the world go from quarreling with and warring against one another to warring together against a single Man?

David begins Psalm 2 with a similar question: "Why do the nations rage, and the peoples plot in vain?" (v. 1). In other words, what possible reason is there for such passionate anger from the kings and rulers of the earth? And what in the world—literally, what is there in this world—that could make everyone gather together for a singular plan?

THE BACKSTORY TO A GLOBAL HATRED

In verse 1 David mentions "the nations" and "the peoples." This means what it sounds like: many nations of the world will be united together to plot against Jesus.

In verse 2 David specifically mentions another piece of the puzzle: kings and rulers.

The kings are just that—kings of the nations. With that one word we can safely assume these are the top governmental leaders—the king, queen, president, prime minister, and so on—of many countries.

Defining the word *rulers*, however, gets a little trickier. I do not believe David is referring only to those who politically rule a nation, such as dictators. I think he means those who rule society, which would then include the top leaders who shape culture in a significant way. These culture-shapers are the top leaders of every sphere of society.

In 1975 God gave the same vision to Youth With A Mission founder Loren Cunningham, Campus Crusade for Christ (now known as Cru) founder Bill Bright, and theologian Francis Schaeffer while each was in a separate place. When the three compared notes, they found God had given them each the same message: that to impact any one nation, the church had to reach the major spheres found in every society. These seven spheres or mountains have been defined as business, government, media, religion, education, family, and arts/entertainment.[1]

When David uses the word *rulers*, I believe he is referring not only to literal rulers of countries but also to the rulers in each of these societal spheres or mountains. Business executives, scholars, movie stars, celebrity TV figures, doctors, pastors…these (and others) represent the leaders who shape our culture. Certainly in America these people actually do more to influence our culture and our daily lives in a practical way than some presidents or vice presidents do.

So Act I has its key players, its main actors, on stage now. But still, why is there such hatred for Jesus?

The truth is that the kings and rulers of this earth do not just one day wake up and suddenly decide to hate Jesus. Such extreme vitriol would have to develop over time, starting as a tiny seed and growing into a monstrous, violent rage.

My theory is that out of a group that large, some of these leaders would undoubtedly have had a background of faith. Some probably had deep experiences with God that made an impact on their lives, while others may have walked with the Lord when they were young. But whatever their background with God, verse 2 clearly indicates that those days of closeness will be long gone. Some of these kings and rulers may turn away from their past relationships with God out of disappointment or hurt. They may feel that God let them down when they needed Him most. Maybe sin entangled them to such a degree that they could not feel His presence, love, or forgiveness. Others possibly succumbed to the great deception Jesus warned of and fell for the lies of a false christ or false prophet. Whatever the issue or cause, I imagine some of these kings and rulers at one point in their lives will have felt a measure of love toward God. Yet as they take the stage for Psalm 2's drama, that sense is far, far removed.

In Matthew 24:12 Jesus warned us that in the last days, "the love of most will grow cold" (NIV). Coldness turns to apathy, and apathy leads to hard-heartedness. When your heart is hard for a long period of time, anger can grow very strong. And wherever there is anger or bitterness in your life, the enemy has an open door to gain control and quickly shift things into full-fledged rage. This demonic progression—a common theme among these kings and rulers—is how Jesus will become Enemy Number One for the world's leaders.

Declaring a Position

David asks, "Why do the nations rage?" The truth is, the nations are not yet raging today. Obviously hatred for Christians, Jesus, and for God's Word can be found around the world. And obviously some of that hatred has built to the point at which ordinary men can today walk into a school, ask for all the Christians to raise their hands, and selectively gun them down in the most brutal way possible. But these are mere flare-ups on a global perspective. They are exceptions to the general rule.

Right now the nations are merely declaring their positions. Many of culture's leading figures and voices are declaring where they stand on key issues, and many are taking a stand contrary to the position of Scripture.

Isn't it interesting that in recent years more celebrities and public figures are vocalizing their opinions on issues without being prompted? For example, when California citizens were battling over Proposition 8 and the state legality of same-sex marriages, it seemed that dozens of major players in Hollywood went out of their way to issue a public statement and urge taxpayers to vote "no on 8" in the name of equality and love for all. As usual, anyone who stood for biblical truth was ostracized and made to look like an unloving, judgmental bigot who wanted to dictate others' lives and limit their freedom.

Celebrities and public figures have always used their clout to push issues, whether they are soliciting donations to animal shelters, raising awareness about starving children in Africa, or discouraging domestic violence. But today these leaders are becoming more strategic about what they stand for and more critical of those who oppose their views. As believers we can expect this activity to increase dramatically in the coming years as culture's most popular figures take a fierce stand in opposition to God's truth.

Today many people are sharing negative views about God's Word, and some are doing it with increasing force. But things will escalate far beyond the mere opinion of sports figures, movie stars, famous singers, well-known actors, and political leaders. Even though their negative opinions have grown bolder in the last five years, they are mild compared to what is to come. These popular figures will soon move beyond voicing opinion to criticizing God's people to fiercely opposing them. Eventually they will use the power of the state to criminalize anyone who stands for biblical truth and to enforce their own ways. A day is coming when it will be considered a crime for a mom and dad to tell their five-year-old child that there is only one way of salvation and that hell is a real place, when parents will be jailed for teaching their children that homosexual marriage is contrary to the Word of God and that the Bible actually calls it a sin (Rom. 1:24–28; 1 Cor. 6:9–10).

Right now we see criticism and ridicule more than outright rage. But when believers look back ten or twenty years from now, we will think the opposition we faced today is mild by comparison. Today the average person is not yet being pressured to take a stand on biblical issues or to bear the stigma of publicly standing for the truths in God's Word. But I assure you, the stakes will continue to increase higher and higher.

The Silent Believers

Unfortunately many believers are already drawing back from the mild opposition and criticism they receive today when taking a stand for the Lord. They are intimidated by the position so many of culture's top leaders are taking against Christ. In fact, many in the church are actually echoing these leaders' stances. These believers do not really know God's Word; they are biblically illiterate, as poll after poll shows. They know some "Jesus language" in that they know how to say grace, they know that God is love, and they may even know some stories that prove Jesus is a cool guy who loves everyone. But they do not know the details of the Word or even the broad strokes of what the Bible says. They cannot explain their beliefs concretely much less "give an answer to every man who asks [them] for a reason for the hope that is in [them]" (1 Pet. 3:15).

So as soon as they hear the cleverly crafted arguments of culture's leading voices or the poignant stories of their favorite pop stars, these believers become bewildered at first then convinced that surely this new way of thinking is truth. They just needed to "open their minds," after all.

Sadly this is the process by which the church arrived at its current condition, with Christians honestly believing it is OK to raise their hands in heartfelt worship at church on Sunday morning and then sleep with their girlfriend or boyfriend that night. Or that God does not mind if we spend two minutes praying for more of His holy presence in our lives and then spend hours upon hours saturating ourselves in godless entertainment. This dichotomy will get more common as the global moral crisis continues to build. It is part of the great deception addressed in the New Testament.

Yet adding to the tragedy, more churches and ministries are staying silent in response to this moral crisis. They refuse to speak out in the public arena, but equally as tragic they refuse to declare the truth to those under their own watch. While the voices of culture get louder and louder and influence these sheep, the shepherds are content to play it safe, lay low so as to not offend too many and push them out the door (after all, the church is in decline, right?), and preach another message on God's grace or the blessings of heaven. They are content to stay silent when it matters most.

Heaven is not silent, though. The Father has strong feelings about what the leaders of culture are saying in defiance of His Son and His Word. The Father has strong feelings about how many in the church are echoing the popular sentiments of culture and about the preachers who tell lies about the Word of God to keep their messages popular, positive, and relevant. And the Father certainly has strong feelings about those who blatantly celebrate the increasing wickedness, perversity, and immorality of our day.

Indeed, God has great emotion about the rising opposition and, as we will discover in the next chapter, will someday respond.

PLOTTING AND MEETING

David describes people groups plotting and kings and rulers meeting together (Ps. 2:1–2). The hatred shared by these leaders will be so great that it will compel them to actually put aside their differences and join together in unprecedented unison. Kings and political figures will continue to scheme and vie for personal position. They will use all their resources—their wealth, their political authority, their favor with people—to promote and push through ungodly agendas.

Again, we have already seen such ungodly agendas promoted in recent years. But the rate at which this is accelerating is something we must not ignore. Many in the younger generation—those twenty years old or younger—do not realize how quickly things have changed because they have grown up in a light-speed world where we get frustrated if our Facebook page does not load in a split second. But those who remember how our culture was thirty, forty, and fifty years ago know that what we are witnessing now is truly unprecedented.

For example, the phenomenon in the last five years of the gay agenda taking center stage in our national conversation—and indeed around the world—was unthinkable only ten years ago. There were whispers of it then, but few could have predicted the agenda would be executed with such precision and perfection in such a short period of time. Think about it: the gay agenda has managed to change public perception of something that for more than two hundred years—dare I say for thousands of years—was universally frowned upon and seen as sin. And all in less than a single generation!

Clearly there are supernatural forces working behind the scenes when evil can accelerate as quickly as that. There is an unholy momentum involved. Yet I believe we have just scratched the surface of the enemy's wicked agenda's advancing. The explosion of heterosexual immorality and pornography in the last five years is equally as shocking as what has happened with the gay movement. Obviously pornography has been around since ancient times. But the global pornification of society in only five years is unparalleled. Pornography has suddenly gone from an industry with limited exposure, most of the products for which were created by a few people in California, to a ubiquitous entertainment alternative that now makes it possible for a five-year-old child to stumble across a neighbor's sex video with one wrong push of a cell-phone button.[2]

In ten years the moral crisis of pornography will escalate beyond anything we can imagine. Already the technology and commercial-sex industries are debating issues such as the rights of online sex workers and whether sexual activity with holograms, lifelike dolls, or even with robots that look human covered with realistic-feeling "skin" constitutes "cheating" on a spouse.

One tech-industry observer tracked current trends and predicted that "with or without mainstream support, the commercial sex industry will move ahead as an established and essential industry because of these technological and societal trends. As a result, sex work is already beginning to move out of the back alleys and onto Main Street. Views towards sex, specifically toward the sex industry, will be debated instead of ignored, stigmatized or generalized."[3] With each advance in technology our culture's insatiable lust for perverted sex expands pornography's cultural presence and availability. And sadly we continue to pollute other nations with our filth.

These advances do not happen by themselves; agendas drive them. I believe these agendas are part of what David refers to when he speaks of people plotting and top leaders meeting together to advance their cause—leaders in fields such as technology, film, broadcast media, education, robotics, marketing, financing, transport of goods, legislation, copyright law, real estate, law enforcement, and so forth. Whether they know it or not, they are working in tandem with Satan's plan to take as many people with him to hell as possible. His sole purpose related to humanity is to steal, kill, and destroy (John 10:10), and to that end he will drive every wicked plan that attempts to thwart God's redemptive kingdom from expanding on the earth.

That leaders from around the world will meet and unite around a single purpose is difficult to fathom. It is tough to imagine such a vast array of dominant personalities being able to agree on anything, much less come up with a solid plan of action. Yet their efficiency in plotting will be demonically driven. And when we take a look at the strategy they come up with, we will understand how a common enemy can make even the wickedest minds align.

A Common Enemy

Verse 2 of Psalm 2 says the kings "set themselves," which means they firmly position themselves in a posture to attack. They take a fierce, offensive-minded stand. Meanwhile the rulers "take counsel together," meaning they come together and meet to discuss their strategy for attack. They will assist one another in an assault, pooling together their resources for the common "good." We get a sense from David's description that these leaders will be consumed with their malicious thoughts and plans for conflict.

Their target of attack is clear: "the Lord and against His

anointed." This is not a generic God. This is not even a generic idea of God. For many years it has been popular in culture to thank "God" at award ceremonies or sports events. When an athlete is interviewed after winning a championship or receiving an award, he will often start with, "First, I just want to thank God for the talents He's given me to play this sport and for helping me win." This type of comment is still fashionable and acceptable. Few are criticized for such expressions because the generic idea of God has no stigma in society. Popular icons of culture can easily "thank God" without offending anyone. After all, the cultural leaders of today do not mind if you mention God, so long as you do not mean Jesus.

The God people love to thank on television is safe, inoffensive, and nonjudgmental. He is a one-size-fits-any-religion God who always comes through when you win the game/race/award/prize but does not need to be mentioned if you do not. He is a pocket-friendly, harmless, yet convenient Oprah God.

Yet Psalm 2 specifically refers to the God of Israel. We know this because the original Hebrew text specifically uses the tetragrammaton, or what we would print in English as "YHWH," meaning Yahweh. Because Israeli tradition forbids Jews from pronouncing or spelling out God's name, *YHWH* was used in the original text. Some English Bible translations translate it by printing "LORD" in all capital letters or small capital letters instead of using the more ordinary "Lord" in upper and lowercase.

The earth's kings and rulers are not meeting and plotting just against Yahweh, the God of Israel. In profoundly prophetic fashion verse 2 points out that they stand against the God of Israel and specifically against *His Anointed*—Jesus.

The word *Messiah* actually comes from the Hebrew word meaning "to anoint." In Greek, *Messiah* is translated as "Christ." So these three titles for Jesus—Anointed, Christ, and Messiah—are practically interchangeable words; they have the same basic meaning.

Some biblical scholars read Psalm 2 as if the term "His anointed" refers solely to David, whom God anointed as an earthly king. They view the entire psalm as addressing Israel's enemies, David's kingship, and the Lord's promise to David that Israel would rule over all other nations. This interpretation does not hold up, though, in light of multiple facts:

- David was not made king of Israel in Jerusalem but in Hebron (v. 6).

- The Lord calls the Anointed His "son" (v. 7).

- The Lord gives Him the "ends of the earth for [His] possession" (v. 8). As vast as David's kingdom was during his rule, it was far from stretching to the ends of the earth. Only one ruler's kingdom will do that, and that is the kingdom of Jesus, the Messiah.

- In the seventeen instances in which Psalm 2 is quoted or alluded to in the New Testament, at least six apply its meaning directly to Christ: Acts 13:32–33; Hebrews 1:5; 5:5; Revelation 2:26–27; 12:5; 19:15.

Psalm 2 is without question about Jesus Christ the Messiah, whom God the Father called the Anointed One as He appointed Him King over all creation. And that is exactly what prompts the nations to rage.

THE SCHEME OF THE NATIONS

The kings, rulers, and peoples of this earth *rage* because they hate Jesus of Nazareth. They hate who He is. They hate His character. They hate what He represents. They hate His authority. They hate that the Father has decreed that Jesus, as the Son of God *and* the Son of Man, will rule all nations from Jerusalem (Ps. 2:6–7). They do not want to be subjected to His leadership. Like a raging bull refusing to be subdued, they will not relent to His kingship over them.

Why are they so fierce in their rebellion? Psalm 2:3 gives us the answer as the kings and rulers announce their strategy for rebellion:

Let us tear off their bonds and cast away their ropes from us.

These earthly leaders detest Jesus's leadership because it means acknowledging that His Word is truth and that His ways are perfect. The pinnacle of humanism is its declaration that man, not God, defines truth. These leaders believe that God's Word is bondage, and that His truth is like cords tying them down. They see the Word of God as that which enslaves them instead of that which liberates them. They see the Word of God as a restraint that limits their human potential.

They want to be freed from God's leadership to explore their independence, their self-reliance, their sexual curiosity, their knowledge, and their lusts and appetites to full capacity. They feel that God's Word limits them from exploring the fullness of their sexuality—which they believe is the core of their identities—and thus from expressing their true selves.

To them, God's Word is old-fashioned, archaic, outdated, and therefore irrelevant. It holds them back from true progress. Their ways are more advanced; after all, they bring equality, peace, and a happier, more pleasure-filled life to all. Their way does not judge anyone but instead allows each person to express himself, herself, or "itself" in "true freedom." Indeed, they want to cast off the restraints of the Word so they can walk in what they imagine is complete "liberty, truth, and justice for all."

Ironically the very thing they seek to get rid of—God's Word—is the very thing that can liberate them and empower them to walk in true, unconditional love. It is the very thing that brings about real justice, peace, joy, and contentment—because it *is* truth. God is love, and through His love we find all these things. Yet the cultural leaders honestly believe they have a superior view of love. They believe tolerance is the key and that true love comes when everyone tolerates and accommodates each other without regard to moral restraints.

Have you ever noticed, however, how tolerance always comes at the expense of someone? Tolerance is a paradox: as soon as a tolerant person has labeled someone else intolerant, it proves he is himself intolerant since he has now not tolerated the "intolerance" of another. Who, then, gets to define what should and should not be tolerated?

This is just one example of the illogical, catch-22 absurdity that humanism brings. Can you imagine the extent of madness that will dominate the world when we continue to claim we have a superior sense of justice, a better definition of peace, and a higher version of truth or love than God does?

Sadly it does not take much to imagine this. We live in a time when such arrogance is not just present; it is increasingly being celebrated. Many of today's cultural leaders shake their fists at God while publicly declaring His ways as archaic. For years they have ridiculed believers who attempt to stand for biblical truth.

Jennifer Lawrence, one of the world's biggest movie stars, recently ranted about "all those people holding their crucifixes, which may as well be pitchforks, thinking they're fighting the good fight."[4] Bill Maher, the outspoken HBO host who routinely calls God everything from a "psychotic mass murderer" to unprintable names, has made a career out of lambasting Christians, whom he regularly refers to as idiots who follow an "imaginary man in [their] head."[5] Comedian Chris Rock took a swipe at believers when he claimed, "A black Christian is like a black person with no memory."[6] And pop star Miley Cyrus has continued to distance herself from her Christian roots with comments such as, "Those people [shouldn't] get to make our laws. That's [expletive] insane. We've outgrown that fairy tale, like we've outgrown [expletive] Santa and the tooth fairy."[7]

Today believers in the public eye—particularly those in Hollywood—are walking targets for these culture-shapers, some of whom actively seek to embarrass anyone who honors God's

Word. When actors Kirk Cameron or Chuck Norris take a stand for a baby's right to live, for example, they are blasted as narrow-minded, chauvinistic bigots. Or when actress Candace Cameron Bure speaks out on biblical submission or modesty, the media calls it a "controversy" and treats her as if she's speaking a foreign language.[8] And in the sports world the mere mention of football player Tim Tebow's name still sparks hate-filled rants about God, Christianity, and abstinence. Though he hasn't played in a regular-season NFL game since 2012, mainstream media still mock Tebow when a girlfriend dumps him because of his God-honoring commitment to stay abstinent until marriage.[9]

THIS MEANS WAR!

Clearly the heat is rising as the movers and shakers in culture show more opposition to Jesus, His Word, and His followers. But we still remain in the early stages of this conflict. The current criticism, mocking, and public ridicule will become full-scale rage in the days to come. The kings and rulers that David prophesied about in Psalm 2 have a defined agenda, and it does not end with an attack against God's commands. No, these leaders will seek to remove His moral boundaries from society, including the sanctity of life, marriage, and sex.

"Let us tear off their bonds," they say, "and *cast away* their ropes from us" (v. 3, emphasis added). They think that if they can remove the Christian conscience from culture, then they can enter into new dimensions of their humanity. They want every trace of God's Word eliminated from the planet, and they will use whatever strength, power, and resources they have to make that happen.

Such an agenda comes from the Antichrist spirit, and you can be assured that Satan's forces will be at work aiding them in their attempts. I mentioned earlier in this chapter how certain evil agendas are now gaining an unholy momentum through demonic assistance. This is why we are seeing agendas that are blatantly against God's Word becoming more popular and gaining traction so quickly. Technology and social media—which have now given everyone a voice—is helping with this, as millions upon millions of people can now participate in the conversation to further these agendas.

The global conversation has already begun, yet it will continue to increase, and Satan will certainly be aided by advancing technology. The masses will first celebrate their newfound "freedom" in resisting the Word of God (which we can already see today), then rage against such godly foundations as the sanctity of life, the sanctity of marriage, and the sanctity of sex.

Eventually, though, this conflict will grow into full-scale war. With Satan's assistance the kings of the earth will war against God and His people using the legal system of governments around the world. Believers will be charged with hate crimes simply for confessing their faith and standing for what the Scriptures say. They will break the law and be thrown in jail when they refuse to teach their children that sex between multiple men is natural or that Jesus was just a good teacher and not the Son of God.

Some believers will be imprisoned for refusing to denounce various truths in God's Word that are unpopular and politically incorrect, and eventually some will face torture and even death. Keep in mind, the cultural leaders and most people will think they are actually doing this in the name of a higher good—that their sense of justice and morality is far superior to those believers who would dare suppress others with their antiquated biblical views.

Eventually this war will go from being a culture war to an actual military war involving all the nations of the world. Revelation 19:19 paints a vivid picture of what this end-times assault will look like:

> I saw the beast and the kings of the earth with their armies gathered to *wage war* against Him who sat on the horse and against His army.
> —EMPHASIS ADDED

The apostle John, who wrote the Book of Revelation, mentions a war in at least four other verses (Rev. 11:7; 12:17; 13:7; 17:14), so we know that as the rage escalates in the coming days, the imminent conflict will usher in the setting for the Antichrist's arrival and an end-times Armageddon showdown.

FULLNESS

When will all this happen? That is typically the first question most people ask whenever the end times are discussed. Though this is not a book on end-times theology, nor will I take the necessary space to cover the sequence of end-times events that the Bible speaks of, I do think it is important in the context of Psalm 2 to discuss when this rage of the nations—and the fullness of war—will occur.

The Book of Daniel is one of the most vivid descriptions in the Bible of the end times. Daniel receives many visions of what is to come as well as divine interpretation for these multifaceted prophetic visions. In chapter 8 the angel Gabriel interprets a vision about the Antichrist and says:

> In the latter time...when the transgressors have reached their fullness, a king shall arise, having fierce features...
> —DANIEL 8:23, NKJV

Gabriel goes on to describe more about the Antichrist, who is the "king" referred to here. But I want to hone in on the brief clause included in this verse: "when the transgressors have reached their fullness." The Complete Jewish Bible phrases it this way: "when the evildoers have become as evil as possible." And I like how the Holman Christian Standard Bible translates it: "when the rebels have reached the full measure of their sin."

Do you know that sin accumulates? Do you know there is a measure of sin, and then there is a "full measure," or a maximum level, of sin that will be expressed on the earth by people? Just as Revelation speaks of the prayers of the saints filling the bowls of heaven (Rev. 5:8)—which indicates that, from God's perspective, there is a quantitative element to prayer and intercession—there is also a measurement of sin. Most believers are unaware that the Bible refers on many occasions to the measurable levels of different spiritual elements such as faith (Mark 6:5–6; Rom. 12:3), grace (2 Cor. 9:8), and love (Matt. 24:12; John 15:13; Phil. 1:9).

Sin is no different, and Daniel 8:23 reveals that there is an hour of history in which sin will reach heights unknown to human history. We think things are bad today, but Scripture declares that sin will intensify and increase.

In fact, we can barely imagine the level of sinfulness that will cover the earth during those days. At that point sin will have reached the end of its course; it literally cannot go any further in terms of its depths of wickedness and depravity. That, according to God's revelation given through Daniel, is when Jesus will say, "Enough is enough!" He will return to the earth, only to find a scene of war in which the nations of the earth hate Him and refuse His leadership.

THE GOOD NEWS IN THE DARKNESS

I have intentionally saved the best for last in terms of what Act I of Psalm 2's divine drama holds. There is a single word David uses in the first verse that I have purposefully not mentioned until now. Without that word it seems this drama could be more than a little depressing. With the entire world despising and raging against Jesus, with wickedness reaching unimaginable levels, we could easily have the mind-set that I have heard far too many Christians express: "Things will get so bad that I just hope I'm not around in those days. I hope the Lord takes me home to heaven before He returns."

Yes, the end times will be undoubtedly difficult for believers. (Though in truth, we must also remember that it will be the church's finest hour. As sin escalates to unprecedented levels, so will righteousness. There will be the greatest outpouring of the Holy Spirit and a great harvest of righteousness flooding the earth even while the darkness of Satan's domain expands across the planet.) But there is a single word that I believe David intentionally uses in verse 1 to set the tone—to establish truth from the start—for this entire prophetic psalm.

Vain.

Everything the kings and rulers plot is in *vain*. David doesn't start this psalm by simply asking why people are so up in arms; he asks, "Why do...the peoples plot in *vain*?" A vain act is one that is literally useless; it produces no results. What the cultural leaders of the end times scheme in their raging against God—indeed, what the leading voices of culture plot now—is to no avail. It is ultimately futile. It will come to absolutely nothing.

It may not seem this way at first. In fact, right now it definitely *does not* seem this way given how quickly those who oppose God have risen in power throughout the nations and how loud their voices have become. The celebration of godlessness is more extensive than ever before, which makes it difficult to believe these wicked agendas will amount to nothing. Many movie stars, business leaders, athletes, politicians, and scientists who publicly defy God are seemingly getting the last laugh as their ideologies and principles grow in popularity. And they may appear to win for a few more years or decades—maybe more, maybe less.

Yet Scripture says otherwise. Not only do we know who wins in the end from books such as Daniel and Revelation, but also David establishes from the very first line of Psalm 2 who comes out on top. Because Jesus is the ultimate victor who will return to the earth to rule as the appointed, anointed King of all, we therefore know that every plan of those who rise up against Him is "a vain thing" (Ps. 2:1, NKJV). Hallelujah!

God is not nervous. His truth and His ways will prevail. His Word will stand forever. In fact, as the curtain for Act I closes, we can already begin to hear Him chuckling as He prepares to respond in Act II.

PART II
THE RESPONSE

Chapter 4

ACT II: THE FATHER'S RESPONSE

He who sits in the heavens laughs; the LORD ridicules them. Then
He shall speak to them in His wrath and terrify them in His
burning anger: "I have installed My king on Zion, My holy hill."
—PSALM 2:4–6

MY FATHER WAS a professional boxer with huge arms of iron, a neck as thick as an oak tree, and a smile brighter than the Olympic torch. At least that's how I saw him as a young child. He was a giant in my eyes.

The truth was not far off, though. Dad had won the international amateur boxing championship in 1951, competed in the 1952 Olympics, and fought professionally throughout the 1950s. Though he weighed in as a lightweight, he gained a reputation as a very tough competitor.

The night before his Olympic fight with eventual gold medalist Aureliano Bolognesi of Italy, he broke his right hand in a bar fight but still went on to compete the next day and even knocked the Italian champion to the mat three times in one round.

I loved my father. When I was small, he and I would play this game that I will never forget. He would stand on one side of the room and, with a childlike gleam in his eye, yell out, "C'mon, son, gimme your best shot! Gimme all you got!" I would then charge at him and, whether with my fists, head, or full body, hit him in the stomach. I remember lunging at him with every ounce of strength I had in me, to the point that I was tired after several attempts. But the results were always the same: he would simply laugh as if

I were tickling him and, when I finally gave up, wrap me in his huge arms and hug me.

The punches of a four- or five-year-old boy, no matter how strong, do not amount to much on a professional boxer. Likewise the wisest, most powerful attacks from the earth's most powerful kings and rulers will not amount to much against an omniscient, omnipotent God. The first verse in Psalm 2 clearly tells us that no matter how much force the nations muster up in rage against their Creator, it will be in vain. Despite a global confederacy of nations empowered by satanic forces, their schemes will come to nothing.

But God does not just sit and take it in the stomach. In the second act of Psalm 2 we find that, just as my father responded to my feeble blows, God responds to the nations' rage by laughing. Simply put, God laughs at their pride. He laughs at the absurd notion that they believe their ways are higher than His. He laughs at their ridiculous confidence that they can overcome Him or even diminish His power in any way.

"He who sits in the heavens laughs" (v. 4). David describes a similar response elsewhere in the Psalms:

> The wicked plot against the righteous, and grind their teeth against them. The Lord will laugh at him, for He sees that his day is coming.
> —PSALM 37:12–13

> But You, O LORD, will laugh at them; You will have all the nations in derision.
> —PSALM 59:8

And in Proverbs, David's son, Solomon, speaks of God in His wisdom laughing at the calamity of the wicked (Prov. 1:26).

We do not often hear of God laughing like this. Typically when we speak of God and laughter it is in the context of His joy; we imagine a God who takes delight in His people (Ps. 149:4) or who sings over us with joy (Zeph. 3:17).

We do not imagine a God who laughs in the face of evil, much less a God who laughs at people's tragedy. But it is important to understand why God responds with laughter as described in Psalm 2:4–6.

God laughs to mock His enemies' challenge and their belief that they can actually pose a real threat to Him simply because they have many nations and such vast resources working together. God's laugh is not evil as we think of this kind of laughter; in fact, it is a holy laugh in the face of absolute pride that presumes that their wickedness can defeat Him. It is the ultimate laugh of triumph, of supreme power amid those who think they are powerful yet have no real authority.

Satan, the face of evil, has forever thought he could somehow defeat God and continues to make every attempt to gain victory. Yet Jesus has already won; Satan is already defeated. The Lord, in His wisdom, is allowing Satan to sift the world until he is ultimately thrown into the lake of fire (Rev. 20:10). Yet even Satan's activity contributes to God's victory. God has included the rage of Satan and his fierce persecution against the church in His ultimate plan to create the optimum environment for the most people to respond to Him in the deepest levels of love. Through the persecution He will purify His people so they are prepared as a bride for Jesus.

So God laughs at any who think He has lost control or that His ultimate plan will not come to pass. He laughs at the audacity of those who think He is somehow weakened by their collective strength in coming against Him. And He laughs because their defiance is the fruit of pride, the fruit of evil, and the fruit of a darkness that He could vanquish by merely speaking one word against them.

PLEASE, KEEP YOUR SEAT

How threatened is God by humanity's collective rage? How worried is He by the nations' plans to attack Him? Here in Psalm 2 we see the kings and rulers mobilizing society and using all the resources at their disposal: media, military, legislation, public opinion. They frantically plot to expose the "truth" that the Jesus of the Bible is not real but is a human myth. Compared to all the great forces in human history, they have built the largest armies, accumulated the most wealth, and gained the greatest support of any rulers before. They are spearheading the most technologically and scientifically advanced movement ever. And they are more globally unified in their wicked purposes than leaders of any prior movement in history.

How does God respond to all this? He does not even bother to stand up!

"He who *sits* in the heavens laughs" (v. 4, emphasis added). The global conspiracy is so pointless, despite the collective fervor of its leaders, that the Father will not even stand to acknowledge it. He simply stays seated.

I love what Matthew Henry says in his commentary on this verse: "Sometimes God is said to awake, and arise, and stir up himself, for the vanquishing of his enemies; here is said to sit still and vanquish them; for the utmost operations of God's omnipotence create no difficulty at all, nor the least disturbance to his eternal rest."[1]

As Act II of this prophetic psalm begins, then, we find a laughing, sitting God. In this posture of rest and confidence the Father has already begun to respond. Yet the verse continues with a frightening phrase: "The LORD ridicules them." The New King James Version translates this as "the LORD shall hold them in derision."

Derision has two elements to it. It is both "the use of ridicule or scorn to shown contempt" and "a state of being laughed at or ridiculed."[2] When God holds these raging nations in derision, He not only ridicules them and makes a mockery out of their futile attempts; He also looks upon them with contemptuous scorn. Both aspects are terrifying when you imagine the God of the universe gazing at you in such a way.

When God laughs at the wicked in their plans to overthrow Him, the results are anything but funny. In fact, I have heard one preacher refer to this laugh of Psalm 2 as the most terrifying laugh of history. It is God saying, "Do you seriously think you can overpower My authority just because you have billions of people working together, or because you have the largest coalition of armies with more money and popular support than any other leader in history? Do you really think you will be successful against Me?"

The Book of Isaiah echoes just how ridiculous this idea is:

> Certainly the nations are as a drop in a bucket, and are counted as the small dust of the balance.... All nations before Him are as nothing, and they are counted by Him as less than nothing and meaningless. To whom then will you liken God? Or what likeness will you compare to Him?
> —ISAIAH 40:15–18

Just a few verses earlier in this passage the prophet points out that God measures heaven with the span of His hand and the waters of the earth in the hollow of His hand (v. 12). He whose hands can hold a vastness larger than our minds can fathom— one that even scientists can only estimate using so many zeros behind a number that it would fill the page—cannot be overcome because He is the very source of all strength.

But let me set the record straight on something. Scripture declares repeatedly that God has no pleasure in the death of the wicked:

> Do I have any pleasure in the death of the wicked, says the Lord GOD, but rather that he should turn from his ways and live?
> —EZEKIEL 18:23

> Say to them: As I live, says the Lord GOD, I have no pleasure in the death of the wicked, but rather that the wicked turn from his way and live. Turn, turn from your evil ways!
> —EZEKIEL 33:11

God does not laugh out of indifference to the ultimate fate of the wicked, nor is His derision fueled by a colossal, out-of-control ego. Think about it: What does God have to prove? Nothing! Absolutely nothing! He has no need whatsoever to validate His authority or His power to anyone because He inherently has those things by His mere existence. God's laughter and derision here in Psalm 2 arise out of His justice, His holiness, His righteousness, and yes, even His love for His own name, kingdom, and people.

Love? In the famous words of Tina Turner, "What's *love* got to do with it?"

In fact, love has everything to do with God's terrifying laugh. The Lord's judgments are *to remove whatever hinders love.* I cannot overemphasize how immensely important this is for each of us to understand. The judgments God releases on the earth against those who oppose Him and oppress His people are not because He is eternally mad or just plain mean. God is actually infinitely glad—not eternally mad or sad, as the world thinks—and He takes unimaginable delight in His people (Ps. 149:4; Isa. 62:4). He will do whatever it takes for His love for us to be unobstructed and to fill the earth (Hab. 2:14), and so that His people, as the objects of His affection, can receive that love in its totality. His deepest desire is for us to enjoy Him and to share in His being. When obstacles prevent that from happening—an obstacle such as rebellion, for example, that brings separation and death—He judges them so as to ultimately remove sin and rebellion from the planet.

This is why He will sit and laugh with scorn at the pride and arrogance of humanity's rage in the end times that they could over-throw Him and His purpose to fill the earth with His glory and love (Hab. 2:14). It is an affront to Him because its sinful core stands in direct opposition to His loving-kindness. The kings' and rulers' resistance to God's glorious purposes for His people and all nations stirs His holy anger. Their rebellious actions, as Psalm 2:5 indicates, lead to His wrath: "Then He will speak to them in His wrath…"

Wrong About Wrath

Is there a more unpopular and politically incorrect subject on the earth today than the wrath of God? Some unbelievers absolutely hate it because they see it as evidence of an intolerant, angry God who sits up in heaven as a moral monster waiting to strike us for our sin. Meanwhile most believers do not want to touch the topic with a ten-foot pole because it seems too controversial and difficult to understand. We would rather focus on how much God loves us, how good and kind He is, and the facts that His faithfulness is everlasting and He has great plans for our lives. Do you know what? All those things are gloriously true, and none of them contradict God's wrath.

Some believers have the wrong idea that the wrath of God was just for the times of ancient Israel. They see it as "an Old Testament thing," much as they see an angry, judging God as "the Old Testament God." "He is different now," they think. Such people are not promoting the biblical view of God. Let me assure you that the God of the Old Testament is the *exact* same God as the God of the New Testament. Whether then or now, His judgments remove all that hinders love.

God has not changed. Culture has changed and people have changed, but God remains constant (Num. 23:19; Mal. 3:6). He is not the problem. His judgments are just and true, which means His wrath is in perfect alignment with His love and mercy (Rev. 19:2). No, the problem is our inability to reconcile God's wrath with His perfect love. We cannot comprehend how these two things go together, and yet I assure you, they are in total unity. The wrath of God exists *because* His love exists. Let me explain.

God's plan for humanity is loving, holy, and just. Because the Lord loves us, He desires to crown us with His glory (Heb. 2:7)—this includes His holiness, love, righteousness, and power. Yet mankind's choosing sin over Him in the Garden of Eden prevented us from enjoying such glory—because sin cannot coexist with God's holiness or with His eternal plan for His people. The Lord determined to remove all that hinders love in His relationship with people and in His created order, including the new heaven and earth. God is holy and just; therefore He cannot overlook sin. He had to pay for it to remove it. Thus Jesus went to the cross to pay the *just* price for our sin to remove it from us in a way that expressed God's justice. The result is that He could then give us salvation as a free gift. Paul taught that God justified us in a way that upheld His own justice (Rom. 3:26). God satisfied all the claims of His justice by sending His Son to take our place of judgment. However, if someone refuses to receive Jesus's gracious gift of salvation, then he is left to pay the price of his own sin by accepting the judgment of it.

From the place of zeal of love and holiness comes God's wrath against persistent rebellion; yet this wrath never contradicts love. You cannot have one without the other.

Again, this is never more evident than at the cross of Christ. Jesus took God's wrath upon Himself so that any who would believe in Him would not have to bear it themselves. Jesus is a perfect reflection of His Father. His death, then, was the purest proof of the Father's love for us—a love offered to us even when we actually deserve wrath. As Paul said:

> God demonstrates His own love toward us, in that while we were yet sinners, Christ died for us. How much more then, being now justified by His blood, shall we be saved from wrath through Him.
>
> —ROMANS 5:8–9

The more we begin to grasp this truth, the more we will understand that our perception of God's justice, anger, wrath, and love falls infinitely short of the truth.

Theologian J. I. Packer, who is one of my favorite Bible teachers, describes it this way: "God's wrath in the Bible is never the capricious, self-indulgent, irritable, morally ignoble thing that human anger so often is. It is, instead, a right and necessary reaction to objective moral evil."[3]

When God speaks to the kings and rulers of the earth "in wrath" as Psalm 2 indicates, then He will speak from a rightful place of His love. He alone can sit in the Judge's seat. His love, holiness, and justice mandate that the nations' rage, pride, and plotting against Jesus—all evil that opposes God's love—be dealt with. Their rebellious plans will stir God's righteous anger, and as an expression of His commitment to love thus, He will "distress them in His deep displeasure," as the New King James Version translates verse 5.

Imagine, then, what the kings and rulers of the nations will experience in the last days when God purposefully "distress[es] them in His deep displeasure." The Lord will respond to their rebellion by shaking the nation that they rule (Hag. 2:7).

Tragically these earthly leaders will bring affliction upon themselves and the nations they lead through their hard-hearted, persistent rebellion. Just as ancient Egypt did under Pharaoh's rule during Moses's time, the nations of the earth will experience God's judgments in part because of their leaders who refuse to submit to Jesus's authority as King. In many cases in the modern world of democracy leaders are voted into office by people who share the same values as they have. So God allows the nations to be ruled by leaders who express the very character of the people in those nations.

BEARERS OF BAD NEWS

David indicates in Psalm 2:5 that the Lord will speak to the earthly leaders in His wrath. But how exactly does God speak to a king or ruler of society? Obviously He can speak to whomever He wants however He wants. God's Word proves that He can get His message across even through a donkey if necessary (Num. 22:22–40). And in a few rare instances in the Bible the Lord spoke directly and audibly from heaven to various leaders. The general rule of Scripture, however, is that God uses His people as His mouthpiece to speak to national leaders.

So who are these people whom God uses?

They are people like you and me. God has chosen to speak to the nations through the body of Christ. In both biblical times and in our generation today God has appointed His servants to communicate His heart and ways to the leaders who shape and influence society—both the believing and unbelieving leaders.

The question, then, is whether we will be faithful to His call.

Scripture highlights many faithful servants who were willing to relay His messages no matter how unpopular the content was.

Think about all the instances in the Old Testament when prophets delivered God's words to people in positions of authority. Many of the messages included pronouncements of judgment as a result of the kings refusing God's repeated warnings to turn from their sin and to embrace His ways.

Do you think the prophets really *wanted* to give those messages? No one wants to be the bearer of bad news. These men and women risked their lives by speaking out on God's behalf. Though what they said was true, it was very likely that they could, like John the Baptist, be sentenced to death for speaking the truth.

God's people are all called to be faithful witnesses of His Word; proclaiming the truth is not something reserved for those with a "prophetic calling." Faithful believers will face some of the same risks the Old Testament prophets did as they speak out the truths related to the end-times fulfillment of Psalm 2. The message of God's wrath will come through ordinary people such as you and me, and we will undoubtedly risk much to communicate it.

I do not know how that makes you feel, but that thought unsettles me. I remember telling the Lord once that I did not want to talk about His judgments because it undoubtedly made people both mad and sad. I did not mind sharing His message of hope or of the Father's love.

In fact, I really delight in speaking on hope and God's love, goodness, and promises. People love to hear about the "good" things of God, especially when they involve personal blessing or favor.

But judgment and *wrath*? The truth is, God's wrath is perfect, which means it produces absolute good. Again, His judgments are an expression of His love. In fact, ultimately they remove everything that hinders love.

Too few are willing to speak out about this unpopular, politically incorrect subject. Indeed, you will not find many pastors preaching on the wrath of God in America today. Worse still, many in the church actually *stand against* the truth of God's judgment. They do not believe that the same God who can offer such eternal love, hope, and mercy could also pronounce such judgments. Even those who accept that there is such a thing as God's wrath believe it is the opposite of His love.

This is a significant error, pure and simple. And such deception will increase as Jesus's return nears, to the point that faithful servants of God will be called intolerant, narrow-minded bigots—both by unbelievers and believers alike—just for mentioning the idea of God's judgments or wrath. Do you remember that Jesus warned us that in the last days there would be many false prophets?

> Beware of false prophets who come to you in sheep's clothing, but inwardly they are ravenous wolves. You will know them by their fruit.
> —Matthew 7:15–16

> And many false prophets will rise and will deceive many. Because iniquity will abound, the love of many will grow cold.
> —Matthew 24:11–12

> For false christs and false prophets will arise and show great signs and wonders to deceive, if possible, even the elect.
> —Matthew 24:24

One primary characteristic of false prophets is that they prophesy *only* blessing to people—even to those people who persistently refuse God's leadership—without ever speaking of His judgments (Jer. 6:14; 8:11; 14:13–14; Ezek. 13:9–10, 16; Mic. 3:5–6). They tickle ears with supposed "words from the Lord" of only favor, peace, and grace, even to some in the church who are walking in deliberate and persistent compromise in their relationships with God. Christ says that we can recognize false prophets by their fruit. One of the "fruits" to look for in the last days is whether a person speaking on behalf of the Lord avoids the topics of God's judgments and speaks only of "good" things all the time, gaining man's applause and favor for such one-sided messages. God has some strong instructions regarding such posturing:

> Do not listen to the words of the prophets who prophesy to
> you. They make you worthless; they speak a vision of their
> own heart, not from the mouth of the LORD. They continually
> say to those who despise Me, "The LORD has said, 'You shall
> have peace'"; and to everyone who walks according to the dic-
> tates of his own heart, they say, "No evil shall come upon you."
> —JEREMIAH 23:16–17, NKJV

It is easier and safer to prophesy blessing over people and over nations without ever mentioning God's judgment. Yet how much more deceptive will it be in the last days to say to the nations that God's message to them is filled with only peace, blessing, and prosperity. Sadly this sort of "sweet-sounding" deception has already begun. There are many leading voices in the church today speaking *only* about peace, revival, power, goodness, and comfort. They declare that *only* good things are coming (and many proclaim this to both believers and nonbelievers). "If you just ask God, He will *only* make everything better and make all your problems disappear; He will remove all the difficulties," they promise. "He will see that you are showered *only* with blessing and comfort. Regardless of how you live, you will be the head and not the tail, the first and not the last!"

The gospel indeed is good news. But Jesus did not die—nor is He coming again as eternal King—so that you and I can avoid all problems in this life, own bigger houses, drive nicer cars, and experience only the winds of ease and blessing. That is a dangerously skewed gospel. We must resist culture's demands for a gospel that is only comfortable and convenient. That was C. S. Lewis's warning when he wrote about our need to have "resistance thinking" against popular trends that seek to make the gospel fit with the spirit of our age. Lewis said that whether we like it or not, the whole, true gospel is one in which there are "elements" that are "obscure or repulsive."[4] If we hope to be faithful to God's call, we must speak the difficult and offensive themes of the gospel as well as the more popular ones.

The church's effectiveness lies in her calling to be against the world yet still for it. As we are led by the Holy Spirit and walk in a spirit of love, we can stand against the moral wickedness of our culture yet still call people to the higher standard and the greater hope found in God. Another teacher who inspires me greatly is Os Guinness. He says that our call is to be both "world-affirming and world-denying at the same time."[5] When the church neglects this dual stance, it results in cowardice, corruption, and decline. Yet when it accepts this posture—refusing to cater to culture's demands for a watered-down, feel-good gospel—it can stand in God's truth and endure to the end.

Jesus said, "He who endures to the end shall be saved" (Matt. 24:13). It is becoming harder to stand strong in proclaiming the whole counsel of God (Acts 20:27), and it will be increasingly difficult. Persecution against Christians will not diminish but continue to rise. Scripture not only promises difficulty in the end times but also speaks of its redeeming nature for the church's growth and God's ultimate plan for expanding His kingdom on the earth. In Daniel 11 we find a key passage on how persecution against believers (what he calls "the people who understand") in the end times will be used in a redemptive way to inspire people to walk in purity:

> And those of the people who understand shall instruct many....And some of those of understanding shall fall [martyrdom], to refine them, purify them, and make them white, until the time of the end; because it is still for the appointed time.
> —Daniel 11:33, 35, nkjv

Though persecution is difficult, God will use it to purify His church. Right now the physical persecution of believers is increasing greatly in various nations, though it is at this time rare in America. At this time persecution of Christians in the USA is mostly limited to being verbally criticized and ridiculed. But I believe physical persecution will come to our nation more in the coming years, however, and my prayer is that it will be a driving force behind a church committed to Jesus and willing to endure anything for Him.

The truth is, physical persecution has always given rise to a church empowered by the Holy Spirit. In his inspiring and eye-opening book *Killing Christians* Tom Doyle says:

> Oppressors over the centuries have never recognized that the persecution of Christians is always a failed initiative. It just doesn't work. To the contrary, killing believers routinely *accelerates* the spread of the gospel and the growth of the church.
>
> For those of us in the West, the threat of [physical] persecution is virtually nonexistent, but statistics show church growth in America—which experiences no persecution—has leveled off during the last twenty years. Why? Because Jesus' message of love and reconciliation thrives in a climate where hostility, danger, and martyrdom are present. Persecution and the spread of the gospel are as inseparable as identical twins. Suffering propels the growth of Jesus movements around the world.[6]

The world is raging more and more against Jesus and those who side with Him. That means those who endure the persecution, who are willing to bear the stigma of His truth—which includes the message of God's love and wrath—"shall be saved" (Matt. 24:13). God's Word remains unchanged; it is still truth. And the truth behind Psalm 2:5 is that God has chosen to use His people to speak to the nations. Those who are faithful will accept this call to speak forth, no matter what the cost.

The Revelation of the King

God's wrath will be deeply offensive to the already raging nations in the end times. But it is not the only part of His message to the global leaders in Psalm 2. At this point in the second act of the psalm the Father has already responded to the kings and rulers of the nations. In verse 4 they have heard His laughter ("He who sits in the heavens laughs") and felt His derision ("The Lord shall hold them in derision," NKJV); and in verse 5 they have faced the reality of His wrath ("Then He will speak to them in His wrath") and sensed His deep displeasure ("…and terrify them in His burning anger").

Now, finally, they will hear of the Father's eternal plan concerning Jesus:

> I have installed My king on Zion, My holy hill.
>
> —PSALM 2:6

The Father's chief message—His primary response to the raging nations—is to exalt Jesus and openly declare and demonstrate Jesus's power as King of the world. The Father will have had enough of the nations' rebelliousness and their refusal to accept His Son. In the context of their rage He announces His commitment to Jesus's rule as King from Jerusalem.

The height of a new father's pleasure is showing off his newborn son. When my first son, Luke, was born, I could not stop bragging about him to everyone I met. "Have you seen my new baby son?" I would ask people, whether they were interested or not. "He's absolutely amazing!" I again did the same with our second son, Paul. I wanted everyone in the world to see them and to know how I felt about them.

God the Father expressed His zeal for Jesus too. First, He announced His Son's arrival in the back side of Judea's country fields with what may have been the world's most spectacular yet least attended concert. In front of only a handful of shepherds in attendance the heavens opened up and the angelic chorus rang out, "Glory to God in the highest, and on earth peace, and good will toward men!" (Luke 2:14). I can only imagine what that celebration must have been like!

Then, years later, the Father once again drew back the curtains of heaven to display His ultimate pleasure in His Son:

> And when Jesus was baptized, He came up immediately out of the water. And suddenly the heavens were opened to

Him, and He saw the Spirit of God descending on Him like
a dove. And a voice came from heaven, saying, "This is My
beloved Son, in whom I am well pleased."

—MATTHEW 3:16–17

During Jesus's transfiguration on the mountain the Father once
again spoke out His profound delight in His Son:

While he was still speaking, suddenly a bright cloud over-
shadowed them, and a voice from the cloud said, "This is My
beloved Son, with whom I am well pleased. Listen to Him!"

—MATTHEW 17:5

In all three instances God was not concerned about crowd size.
Apparently it did not matter how many people heard Him; otherwise the Father would have timed His vocal "appearances" to
be in front of, say, the crowds of thousands who gathered to hear
Jesus speak or to observe when Christ stood before Pilate. No,
in all three of these instances the Father wanted to express His
pleasure with Jesus, and He broke through heaven to express it
publicly.

In Psalm 2:6 the scene is vastly different. Here, God declares
His pleasure in Jesus to every nation of the world and before every
king and societal ruler of every culture. His pleasure sounds very
different to the audience than it did when Jesus first came to the
earth. This time the Father is declaring with ultimate power and
triumph that He has anointed His Son as the King over all. Jesus
is not only Zion's long-awaited King, the Messiah Israel has been
waiting for; He is also the world's long-awaited King—the One for
whom even the rocks cry out in praise (Luke 19:40).

This verse tells of the glorious revelation of Jesus as King. On
the island of Patmos the apostle John had a similar revelation.
He beheld the King whom God the Father will one day manifest
in His splendor, and John fell like a dead man before Him. John
knew Jesus like a brother; in fact, the Living Bible says John was
Christ's "closest friend" (John 13:23). Yet when John saw his friend

Jesus revealed as King, when he saw Him in His glory and His splendor, he "fell at His feet as though [he] were dead" because he had never before seen His majesty (Rev. 1:17).

The nations will have the same response. When the raging, defiant nations see Jesus clothed in His glory and majesty, declared and anointed by the Father as King over all, they will tremble in great fear. At least three times in the Book of Revelation John describes the scene when the little kings—the temporary kings of the nations—are face-to-face with the great, eternal King Jesus Christ (Rev. 6:15–17; 16:14; 19:19, 21). The outcome is never good for those who persistently refuse Him, and David describes how these kings will meet their end at the hands of Jesus:

> He [Jesus] shall execute kings in the day of His wrath. He shall judge among the nations, He shall fill the places with dead bodies, He shall execute the heads of many countries.
> —PSALM 110:5–6, NKJV

This is the King the Father magnifies over all other kings. He is the One exalted by God over all the earth.

FIRST IN HEAVEN, THEN ON EARTH

When the Father says He has "installed My king on Zion, My holy hill" in Psalm 2:6, the Hebrew word for *installed* alludes once again to Jesus's anointing as King. The word connotes a sense of solemnness, as in an inauguration ceremony of a priest (which is why many scholars refer to this psalm as a royal inauguration psalm). The Father is publicly declaring that He has established not just any king, but Jesus, whom He calls "My king."

What is fascinating about the Father's phrase in verse 6, among many things, is exactly where He declares Jesus has been "installed." Zion was the southern hill in the city of Jerusalem. It was the place where David established his throne, and therefore it was also called "the City of David" (2 Chron. 5:2). The Old Testament refers to Jerusalem by the same name because this is the specific place within the larger city of Jerusalem where David brought the ark of the covenant and established an altar to the Lord. Zion was referred to as the "holy hill" (Ps. 2:6), a mount where the Lord Himself dwelt and established His presence (Ps. 74:2). In short, it was God's place of residence, where King Solomon built the temple and where the Shekinah glory dwelt in the holy of holies. Thus all Jerusalem was sometimes referred to as "Zion."

But the Bible also refers to Zion as a heavenly city. Hebrews 12:22 says, "You have come to Mount Zion and to the city of the living God, the heavenly Jerusalem." In this sense Zion also speaks of the New Jerusalem. We know that Jesus currently sits in heaven at the right hand of the Father. As David described in another prophetic psalm in which He saw a glimpse of God's government:

> The LORD said to my lord, "Sit at My right hand, until I make your enemies your footstool." The LORD shall send your mighty scepter out of Zion; rule in the midst of your enemies.
> —PSALM 110:1–2

After Jesus was resurrected from the dead and ascended to heaven, the Father positioned His Son as King to sit at His right hand. Through His sacrifice Jesus gained the "keys of Hades and of Death," meaning He now as a Man has all authority over death itself—which was the ultimate triumph of sin—and hell (Rev. 1:18). Most believers know about these keys, as Jesus's resurrection and victory over death is at the core of our faith.

But did you know that Jesus also possesses another key? In Isaiah and Revelation Jesus is said to possess what is called the "key of David":

> The key of the house of David I will lay on his shoulder. Then he shall open, and no one shall shut. And he shall shut, and no one shall open.
> —ISAIAH 22:22

> These things says He who is holy, He who is true, "He who
> has the key of David, He who opens and no one shuts, and
> shuts and no one opens."
> —REVELATION 3:7, NKJV

The verse in Isaiah, though initially applying to God's servant Eliakim, is a Messianic foreshadowing, as indicated by the context. And although the verse in Revelation references this same verse, it clearly and directly refers to Christ. Like the keys to death and Hades, this key represents total authority; even the verses indicate that whoever holds this key has the power to keep people in or out. But what does David have to do with this?

Jesus was often called the Son of David because He was the complete fulfillment of the covenant God had established with David. In that covenant, recorded in 2 Samuel 7, God promised the king that the Messiah would come through his family line and establish a kingdom that would never end. Jesus indeed came through David's lineage, but that was just part of the fulfillment. As Israel's greatest king, David established a united kingdom like none other in the nation's history. Jesus's kingdom dwarfs David's—or that of any other king, for that matter. As prophesied in Luke 1:32–33:

> He will be great, and will be called the Son of the Highest.
> And the Lord God will give Him the throne of His father
> David, and He will reign over the house of Jacob forever,
> and of His kingdom there will be no end.

Jesus has the key of David because He was the rightful heir to all of David's territory. This key indicates that Jesus rules from His position at the right hand of the Father, with all authority over both the heavenly Jerusalem and the earthly Jerusalem.

Obviously He is not yet openly ruling over the earthly Jerusalem. But one day Jesus will return to reclaim the city of David as the site of His earthly throne, from which He will be seen by all the nations as ruling forever in the millennial kingdom and then on the new earth. And this is why Psalm 2 offers powerful insight to our understanding of Jesus's true authority as King over the earth. In Psalm 110 David emphasizes Jesus's kingship over the earth while sitting in heaven at the Father's right hand, but in Psalm 2 he highlights Jesus's kingship on the earth while sitting on the throne in earthly Jerusalem. How do we know? How do we know Psalm 2 is not referring to Zion in just the heavenly sense?

It does not take a Bible scholar to answer this question. The Father specifically uses the phrase "Zion, My holy hill" rather than just saying Zion. We know that there are no hills in the heavenly New Jerusalem. The word *hill*, then, refers specifically to the Jerusalem of this earth, just as it did in David's time. Jesus will be openly established on the throne to rule over all the earth just as He now rules in heaven. The Father first declares His Son's kingship in heaven (Psalm 110), and then He declares His Son's kingship over the earth openly for everyone on the planet to see (Psalm 2).

With this declaration concluding an impassioned response from the Father to the nations' rage, the curtain of this divine drama begins to close again, ending Psalm 2's second act. But as the curtain descends, we are left to ponder what we have just seen and heard.

Do we really know who this King is? Even though we call ourselves followers of Jesus, do we truly know whom it is we serve? Do we realize how mighty He is and what kind of power and authority He wields? Even more, do we recognize how troubled the Father is that our culture is standing more and more against His Son? The Father is not neutral about the negative things going on in culture today. He is not indifferent to what is and is not being said about His Son and His Word—both inside and outside the church. He is not ambivalent. As David so succinctly prophesies in Act II of Psalm 2, the Father will respond with passion, particularly when it comes to declaring His Son's authority over all.

Will we respond with the same passion?

Chapter 5

ACT III:
JESUS'S RESPONSE

I will declare the decree of the LORD: He said to me, "You are My son; this day have I begotten you. Ask of Me, and I will give you the nations for your inheritance, and the ends of the earth for your possession. You will break them with a scepter of iron; you will dash them in pieces like a potter's vessel."
—PSALM 2:7–9

As ACT III OF this prophetic drama begins and the curtain rises, the spotlight shines brightly and solely on Jesus. This reveals some of what He is zealous for. With the nations raging against Him, this is the context the Father chose to show the world who He really is. Yet in typical manner Jesus immediately turns the attention to His Father—or more specifically, to His Father's words. Just as He did throughout His life on the earth, Jesus uses His time in the spotlight to say only what He has heard the Father say (John 5:19; 8:28; 12:49; 14:10).

From the very first statement of this third act we learn that a decree has been issued. And more importantly it is the Father who has made this decree about Jesus.

We rarely use the word *decree* today. A decree is simply an official order, edict, or decision that has the force of law adding weight to it.[1] It is one thing for a government official to make a pronouncement, proclamation, or declaration; for instance, governors can declare a state of emergency for a city, state, or region, or a president can pronounce that the Olympic Games have begun.

But when a king or ruler issues a decree, the matter is taken to another level. Not only does it become official by nature of its being written down, but also whatever is in that decree suddenly becomes law over the entire land.

This is exactly why the Father *decreed* the statement that Jesus quotes in Psalm 2:7–9. It is not a suggestion; it is law—it is final. And not only is it law for one state or country; it is law over all of creation!

So what was decreed? First, the Father proclaims to the world through this decree that Jesus is indeed the Son of God: "You are My son; this day have I begotten You" (v. 7). Questioning Jesus's divinity has been a common practice in the world ever since Christ walked the planet. From the moment Jesus revealed Himself on this earth as the Son of God, every human is in only one of two categories: believer or unbeliever. Those who doubt His divine sonship have often used the faithless crutch that Jesus never existed but is merely a fictional character. Yet verse 7 shows us that the propaganda that has been strategically marketed world-wide throughout the ages—that Jesus is just a man-made myth—is refuted with a single statement by the Father: "Jesus is My Son."

When the master of the universe declares something to be true, it is difficult to say otherwise. And I can only imagine what this does to the world's kings and rulers when the message of Jesus's kingship is declared in the power of the Holy Spirit by God's anointed messengers. This is in context to the kings having already declared their hatred for Jesus. They continue to fume in rage toward Him. And it is specifically with these societal leaders in mind that the Father decrees that the nations are His Son's inheritance. He pronounces that the ends of the earth "belong to King Jesus"; thus they do not belong to the earthly kings—these will be fighting words in the eyes of vain kings. This, of course, makes the kings and rulers even more determined and fierce in their rage, for the truth has been proclaimed: they are subject to this Jesus, and the One they hate so fervently now has total authority—as given by the Father—over them.

A JESUS RARELY MENTIONED

What follows the Father's decree is not just bad news for these royal rebels; it is a terrifying promise. The Father issues a statement that His Son will "break them with a scepter of iron" and "dash them in pieces like a potter's vessel" (Ps. 2:9). The "scepter of iron" alludes to governmental authority and power. Scripture is clear on how Jesus will wield this scepter against His enemies:

> He shall strike the earth with the rod of his mouth, and with the breath of his lips he shall slay the wicked.
> —ISAIAH 11:4

> Out of His mouth proceeds a sharp sword, with which He may strike the nations. "He shall rule them with an iron scepter."
> —REVELATION 19:15

In Revelation 1:16 John also spoke of a "sharp two-edged sword" coming out of King Jesus's mouth. The sword and the scepter of iron both indicate Jesus's powerful rule over His enemies, which means sure destruction for them. Jesus will annihilate these evil enemies and remove them from power as He acts out of a righteous judgment that removes every hindrance to His love. Speaking of the terrible Day of Judgment, Scripture says His garments will be stained with the blood of His trampled enemies (Isa. 63:1–6). In another psalm David wrote, "He shall strike down kings in the day of His wrath. He shall judge among the nations; He shall fill them with dead bodies; He shall scatter heads all over the land" (Ps. 110:5–6).

You don't often hear that preached on a Sunday morning, do you?

Indeed, this is a Jesus we do not hear much about in today's world—both in the church and outside it. We like the peacemaker Jesus, not the Jesus who confronts rebellion. I have heard many popular preachers explain away these verses by saying they are all figurative, that because Jesus's kingdom is one of peace rather than violence—which His earthly ministry proved—then His means to victory will also be a peaceful opposition that the nations will not expect. They believe He will slaughter His unrepentant opponents with kindness, compassion, forgiveness, and love.

It is true that Jesus is all those wonderful things and more. But I find it hard to believe, especially after years of studying the more than 150 chapters in the Bible that are mainly about the end times, that Jesus will use passive resistance and nonviolence to defeat the league of nations partnering with Satan to stand against Him. Far too many scriptures use graphic, violent, and bloody descriptions for me to believe that this epic, final showdown will in any way feature a passive Jesus. Based on the Father's decree in Psalm 2 alone, we can see that Jesus's victory over His enemies is not described with figurative, poetic language. There will be an actual war, and Jesus will emerge as the great Warrior King and Conqueror, crushing His enemies with a force unmatched in history.

This is the sense we get when Jesus mentions the Father's decree that He will "dash them in pieces like a potter's vessel" (Ps. 2:9). When eastern kings went to battle in ancient times, they often smashed clay jars in a ceremonial ritual before heading off to fight, symbolizing the utter destruction of their enemy. As the Father has decreed, Jesus will smash the opposing nations that are in allegiance to the Antichrist and are filled with rage against Him. He will obliterate them into nothing as easily as a rod of iron can smash a clay pot into pieces.

THE GREAT PRAYER OF PSALM 2

It would be possible to end our reading of Psalm 2's third act at this point. Jesus has repeated the Father's declaration, which definitively decrees Him as victorious King over His enemies and rightful Ruler of the earth. End of act, right?

Wrong. In fact, if we stopped there, we would miss out on one of Psalm 2's most profound messages—particularly in how it applies to us today.

I have briefly mentioned how Jesus responds to the nations'

rage against Him by simply *saying what the Father had already said to Him.* This is intercession in its simplest form. Telling God what He tells us to tell Him is foundational to prayer. We speak God's promises back to Him, and this becomes the foundation to our dialogue with Him.

In Psalm 2:7–9 Jesus not only models for us how to pray but also shows us that He, as the Great Intercessor, is the greatest Prayer Warrior of all. Jesus is not quoting His Father in these verses because Jesus does not have anything to say. He is repeating the Father's words because that is exactly what He does in dialoguing with Him—He speaks back to God what the Father has spoken to Him. So when the Father tells Him, "Ask of Me, and I will give you the nations for your inheritance, and the ends of the earth for your possession" (v. 8), Jesus does what His Father commands—He asks!

Many people make prayer out to be a complicated, exclusive discipline that only a select few über-spiritual individuals can accomplish. Do you know that prayer is actually one of the simplest gifts God has given us? In fact, it is so simple that anyone can do it. Sadly that is the same reason why so few actually do!

The best definition of prayer I have found is also the simplest, and it is this: talking with God. That's it. God invites us into conversation with Him. He loves us so much and has such a desire to be with us that He created prayer as a direct channel between Him and us. Through this wonderful gift we have the privilege of speaking one-on-one with the Creator of the universe—with His full attention, mind you. Through prayer we can release the power of God's heavenly kingdom to the earth—complete with supernatural elements of healing, prophetic words, signs, and wonders. Through prayer we can change the spiritual atmosphere in a city or nation, bind the darkness, and cast out demons. Through prayer we can change the world. But maybe most important of all, through prayer we can know and experience God in a deeply personal way.

We do not get to know God well just by only talking to Him, however. There is a big difference between talking *to* God and talking *with* God. Many people approach prayer as a religious duty, so they spend their time talking *to* a God who, in their eyes, never responds but still expects them to pray. Is it any wonder they eventually tire and give up? No one wants to be in a conversation in which one person does all the talking. That is not a conversation; that's a monologue. When we approach prayer as simply talking *to* God, then we miss out on the gift of a two-way dialogue of friendship and partnership.

God invites us into a conversation with Him. He listens to what we have to say, no matter how insignificant we might think it is, and He wants us to listen to what He says back to us by His Word and His Spirit.

But even for those of us who are just beginning this journey of talking *with* Him, He has made it profoundly easy to start: we simply tell Him what He has already told us. We speak His promises back to Him with confidence (faith) and affection (love). And if we are wondering what He has already said, there is no better place to start than in His Word.

For a model of how to develop a life of prayer, we need look no further than Jesus. Each time we find Him praying in the Gospels, we get a better sense of His relationship with the Father—which is the foundation of prayer. The love shared between the Father and the Son is profound. And in Psalm 2 we get a sneak peek of what this love looks like and what it sounds like in Jesus's response. In verses 7–9 it is as if we are eavesdropping on a Trinitarian conversation between the Father and Son (with the Holy Spirit participating in some way, I'm sure).

Jesus essentially starts by saying, "I will declare the decree of My Father, and this is what My Father has said..." He responds to the Father by declaring back to the Father what the Father has declared over His life. This is the primary principle of *intercession*: we tell God what God tells us to tell Him. Of course, there are more elements to intercession than this. Intercession includes "standing in the gap" for someone, something, or some situation

(Ezek. 22:30). It involves intentionally petitioning God according to His promises, so as to release and enact His will on the earth.

Here in Jesus's response we see that, though He is fully God as well as the rightful human King over all creation, Christ still chooses to engage in intercession with His Father. Take a moment to think about that: this is Jesus, the only One in all of creation who is fully God and fully man, yet He lives forever to be an Intercessor (Heb. 7:25). He spends His time and energy asking the Father for that which has been spoken to Him by the Father, and yet the Father has said He will not release anything except in partnership with Jesus and in response to His church's asking Him. What an incredible picture of humility, submission, obedience, partnership, and love—and yet what a remarkable reality!

This relational picture of Psalm 2 does more than show us the Father-Son relationship. It also gives us a blueprint for how Jesus will rule the nations upon His triumphant return. Jesus could reveal Himself as anything at this pinnacle moment in which the Father publicly decrees His authority. The nations are watching. The arrogant leaders who have hated Him so passionately and plotted obsessively against Him are now reeling in utter anger, humiliation, and defeat. This is His time to show Himself as the mighty Warrior, the Healer of the nations, the triumphant King, the anointed Priest…you name it. And yet of all these descriptions Jesus emphasizes Himself here as the Great Intercessor.

Why would He do this? Wouldn't He present Himself better with a more powerful title? I believe the reason is inherently connected with the deep affection He has for His bride, the church, and His desire for partnership with her via intercession.

LEADING THE BRIDE

By showing Himself as engaged in intercession amid the endtimes conflict, Jesus once again models—just as He did during His ministry on the earth—the profound importance and power of prayer. Through His example we see that prayer is not merely rote words; it is the Spirit-empowered language of heaven. By declaring what the Father declares and partnering with His Holy Spirit, the church engages in a spiritual war in which the victor and the victory are already assured.

The need for prayer explains why it is alarming that more people in the church are not interested in it. It is rare to find believers who are passionate about it and who place it as a priority. Isn't it amazing how quickly we place things above spending time talking with God? We would rather watch another rerun on TV, play another video game, or spend even more time hanging out with friends. Even among more "spiritual" activities we would rather read another Christian book, study another book of the Bible, attend another conference... *anything* but actually pray!

If I just hit a nerve for you, don't worry—you are not alone. Many believers today spend more time talking about prayer than actually praying. I have attended more prayer meetings and conferences than I would like to admit in which the leaders talked about how great it is to pray and how privileged we are to be able to pray. Then they spent time teaching on what prayer does and how we can do it. And finally they even mentioned what things we specifically needed to pray for. By the time they were finished, there were mere minutes left for actually praying!

My experience is not unique. Leaders pray less often than we would like to admit. In fact, I believe it is one of the enemy's subtlest strategies to keep the body of Christ distracted with talking *about* prayer rather than actually doing it. For far too long the bride of Christ has been content to prepare herself for the Bridegroom without paying enough attention to what He told her to do and how He showed her to do it. We must follow the leading of our Lord!

Jesus modeled how simple prayer is. The Father is looking for conversation with His children. It is truly remarkable that God values communication with us. In fact, He values conversation with us more than we value conversation with Him. Think about it: Jesus is the most interesting Man who ever walked the earth, but for some reason He is fascinated by talking to us.

Why? Because He is incarnate love. God is the fullness of love.

And He is looking for partnership with His people. At the core of His being He desires partnership and relationship with weak and broken people. That's us! Most kings would not be interested in talking to us. Yet the King of kings who rules in heaven is continually pursuing us to have a longer conversation, simply because He enjoys our presence so much.

Conversation with God is called prayer. And when we consider how much He desires it, how can we say no?

A Global Movement Underway

Jesus's strategy for manifesting His victory on the earth in the end-times war is the same today as it was when David wrote Psalm 2: He will lead the church in prayer. As the Great Intercessor He will be at the forefront of a massive, global prayer movement of holy dialogue with the Father.

Here is the incredible news, though: this movement has already begun. In what may already be the greatest prayer movement in history, the church is rising up to finally become the praying bride.

Volumes of books could be written about the prayer movement covering the earth today. But to give you a sense of just how global this is, let me offer you some snapshots of God's movement around the world.[2]

Asia

- One of the most significant events that jump-started the current prayer movement was the first International Prayer Assembly in Seoul, South Korea, in 1984. At least six hundred thousand believers (half of those Koreans) attended what would become a pivotal launching pad for many of the prayer strategies and initiatives seen today. For example, in 1984 the number of 24/7 houses of prayer in the world was fewer than twenty-five; today there are more than ten thousand, with the majority of that growth occurring in the last ten years.

- South Korea began leading the global prayer movement even before the 1984 gathering. In 1973 David
  Yonggi Cho, founder of the world's largest church,
  Yoido Full Gospel Church, established Osanri
  Prayer Mountain, which has held 24/7 prayer for
  more than forty years. For the last twenty years
  almost ten thousand people have filled the sanc-
  tuary every day for prayer. Osanri has also inspired
  hundreds, if not thousands, of other prayer mountains and houses throughout the world. In addition,
  Boaz Park leads a house of prayer in Seoul in which
  prayer meetings led by a worship team have continued 24/7 since 2009.

- It is almost impossible to number the houses of
  prayer in China due to countless believers' "unoffi-
  cial" faith there, yet we know they are at least in the
  thousands. A recent report from Colorado-based
  missions organization Every Home for Christ claims
  there are currently more than five thousand "walls of
  prayer" that host 24/7 prayer chains.

- In Indonesia, the world's most populous Muslim
  nation, more than nine thousand intercessors
  gathered in 2012 for an historic event that openly
  declared Jesus Christ as Lord over the nation.
  For almost fifteen years houses of prayer—many
  offering nonstop day-and-night prayer—have continued to emerge around the nation. And recent
  reports indicate that more than five million local
  intercessors are currently standing in the gap for
  specific believers and churches in more than five
  hundred cities across Indonesia.[3]

- Tom Hess, leader of the Jerusalem House of Prayer
  for All Nations, estimates that God has already raised
  up more than one hundred million intercessors in

India, Malaysia, Singapore, Philippines, Vietnam, Thailand, Myanmar, Bangladesh, and Pakistan.[4]

Africa

- Equally as remarkable as God's movement among Korean prayer warriors is the rise of a praying Africa. In Nigeria monthly all-night prayer meetings can often draw a million people. More than four million people attended an all-night prayer meeting led by E. A. Adeboye in 2001—after which a Christian president was elected the following month.[5]

- Each year, through the South African–led Global Day of Prayer, more than one hundred million believers gather on Pentecost Sunday in more than two hundred nations to pray for a global outpouring of the Holy Spirit.

- Thousands of 24/7 prayer rooms have been established in townships and cities throughout South Africa, with many ministries working together to build a more united front in prayer.

- Rwanda's Zion Temple in the capital city of Kigali launched day-and-night prayer and worship in 2000 and has continued 24/7 ever since.

- Since 1995 World Trumpet Mission and Watchman Intercessors Network have helped to establish twenty-four-hour prayer watches in forty-three districts in Uganda. Many strong prayer ministries also exist in Zimbabwe, Tanzania, Kenya, and Ethiopia.

The Middle East

- The house of prayer Hess leads is one of eight in Jerusalem currently organizing 24/7 prayer.

An additional half-dozen prayer rooms exist in other parts of Israel, while several monasteries throughout the country conduct prayer meetings many hours each week, some hosting 24/7 prayer.

- Kasr El Dobara Church in Cairo, Egypt—the largest evangelical church in the Middle East—hosts a Monday night prayer meeting attended by two thousand people that is broadcast on TV and the Internet to additional thousands throughout the region.

- Prayer watches, many held 24/7, also exist in Kuwait, Algeria, Sudan, Dubai, and Turkey. And despite ongoing war and unrest, Syria and Iraq have houses of prayer in operation.

Europe

- What began as a single prayer room in the south of England in 1999 has since spread around the world. Under Pete Greig's leadership the 24/7 prayer movement is now operating in nonstop day-and-night prayer in twenty-eight other countries.

- In Germany the Watchman's Call Initiative organizes twenty-four-hour prayer chains covering more than three hundred cities. There are more than ten houses of prayer throughout the country, including the Augsburg House of Prayer, which has functioned in 24/7 prayer since 2011 and currently has one hundred staff members and several thousand visitors each year.

- Eastern Europe continues to see a growing prayer movement combined with a greater emphasis on prayer within the larger church. Twelve cities in Poland hold twelve-hour, citywide solemn assemblies once a month, in addition to the houses of prayer established in Warsaw and Wrocław. Russia and Ukraine both have multiple ministries hosting daily prayer gatherings—including some that have drawn fifty thousand people in the last three years—and there are houses of prayer being established in at least half a dozen other Russian-speaking countries.

North America

- More than four hundred houses of prayer exist in the United States, in addition to prayer rooms on one thousand university campuses. This does not include the countless churches and prayer ministries that operate prayer rooms, prayer watches, prayer gatherings, and solemn assemblies.

- Canadian prayer ministries are on the rise, including several ministries conducting solemn assemblies, mass prayer gatherings, and weekly prayer meetings in every city hall across Canada. In all, the country has nearly fifty houses of prayer, some going 24/7, and an additional twenty-five houses of prayer that operate on university campuses.

- Mexico currently has more than 170 houses of prayer in operation.

South America

- While the revivals in Argentina and Brazil are well documented, the rise of the prayer movement throughout Latin America, though equally dramatic, has remained somewhat under the radar. In the last ten years Brazil's prayer and worship movement has seen millions gather at times for all-day worship events. More than thirty-five houses of prayer have been established in Brazil during that time, including several that operate 24/7. Among those is a new house of prayer in Florianópolis pioneered by Dwight Roberts that continues many hours each week and is led by worship teams.

- In Peru, one of a handful of South American countries that has experienced dramatic social changes since revival came, prayer gatherings can draw more than one hundred thousand believers. And prayer leaders are currently establishing more houses of prayer in Colombia, Bolivia, and Venezuela.

The evidence is clear: More and more people are accepting Jesus's invitation to partner with Him in prayer at this time in history. He is truly preparing His church to be a praying bride who enjoys conversation with the Father as much as He does. What an honor that we get to be alive during this exciting period of time!

Jesus is indeed the Great Intercessor, and it is profoundly significant that He reveals Himself as such in David's prophetic picture of Psalm 2. Yet if Jesus sees prayer as so important that it is the first thing He wants to be known for in front of the nations and the main way He will lead them as their King, then how can we possibly relegate prayer to a five-minutes-a-day duty?

We must begin to see talking with God as the incredible, powerful gift it is. It is our lifeline to the Father. It is, as Jesus proves by the close of the third act of Psalm 2, the greatest work we can engage in. As Oswald Chambers said, "Prayer does not fit us for greater works; prayer *is* the greater work."[6] Let us grab hold of this truth and partner with Jesus in prayer.

Chapter 6

ACT IV:
DAVID'S EXHORTATION

*Now therefore, be wise, O kings; be instructed, you judges of the
earth. Serve the LORD with fear, and rejoice with trembling. Kiss the
Son, lest He be angry, and you perish in the way, when His wrath is
kindled but a little. Blessed are all those who put their trust in Him.*
—PSALM 2:10–12, NKJV

DAVID BERNAYS AND Charles Sawyer were enjoying the
climbing expedition of a lifetime through the Peruvian Andes
in the summer of 1962. An electrical engineer from Florida, twenty-
nine-year-old Bernays was an avid mountain climber who had
scaled some of the world's greatest peaks. Sawyer, twenty-five, was
completing his graduate studies in geophysics at the Massachusetts
Institute of Technology. Throughout the summer they had joined
other thrill-seekers to climb several peaks through the Cordillera
Blanca range, including the first ascent of the 18,986-foot Mount
Tullparaju. It was a dangerous climb, in part because only the
previous January the edge of a nearby glacier had broken off and
caused an avalanche that killed more than four thousand people.[1]

While spending weeks traversing through the range of twenty-
thousand-foot peaks, Bernays and Sawyer had a close-up view of
the same glacier and noticed that it still posed a serious threat.
In fact, because of loose bedrock under the melting glacier, they
believed another avalanche could trigger at any time and cause
even greater damage than the previous one.[2]

Upon their descent, the mountaineering pair warned authorities of the imminent threat. Local leaders did not take their report too seriously, but that changed when a newspaper in a nearby town called Yungay caught wind of the Americans' words and ran a front-page headline that read, "Dantesque Avalanche Threatens Yungay." News spread to the regional papers, then a national one, and soon the young adventurers were described as "scientists" with a "dramatic revelation that a gigantic avalanche three times larger than that of [the previous one] threatens to dislodge, putting in danger" several towns in the valley.[3]

Instead of heeding the warning, however bloated at this point, area authorities saw the Americans' report as more of a nuisance than a legitimate concern—especially with the media hype surrounding it. They quickly denied its validity, told Bernays and Sawyer to retract their story or face prison time, and went so far as to threaten anyone who furthered the Americans' findings with criminal charges for "disrupting public tranquility."[4] The official announcement encouraged locals with the following words: "Return to your homes with your faith placed in God."[5]

Unfortunately that faith did not prevent disaster from impacting the 25,000 inhabitants of Yungay. On May 31, 1970—almost eight years after Bernays and Sawyer warned the Peruvian authorities—an earthquake set off what has now been called history's deadliest avalanche. At 3:23 p.m., while most locals were watching the Brazil-Italy World Cup match, an 8.0-magnitude quake struck the nearby coast and caused more than 350 million cubic feet of ice, rock, and snow to break off from the same glacier the Americans had warned about. The avalanche came racing down the valley at speeds of more than 120 miles per hour and within seconds buried the village—and another nearby one—in almost 200 feet of muddy rubble. Only 350 people survived.[6]

Back in the United States, Bernays and Sawyer were grieving from the news yet undoubtedly thinking, *If only they had listened…*

The Last Word

As the curtain rises for Psalm 2's final act, there is a similar heaviness in the air. Tragedy is about to strike. Unlike the story about the avalanche in Peru, however, this story has yet to conclude. The death toll remains to be seen, as does the last of who will be counted among those swept away by this end-times avalanche of God's judgments upon the persistent rebellion against King Jesus.

David stands alone onstage, the spotlight solely his. He does not speak but instead soaks in the silence. No one in the audience dares to move, for this is a somber moment, one in which the only fitting response is to reflect upon what has transpired onstage and consider the weight of what lies ahead.

David has delivered a drama of epic proportions. The kings and rulers of the earth have raged against their Creator. Nations have risen in defiance. The Father has answered in wrath and declared His Son's glorious exaltation and rightful rule. And Jesus has declared His Father's words of ultimate authority and turned them into intercession. Clearly the Lord has had the last word.

Yet, somehow, the Lord now allows David, the kingly scribe of this prophetic psalm, to—at least technically—have the last word.

After what seems like an eternity David finally speaks. The heaviness and urgency of his words go far beyond two young mountaineers warning Peruvian townspeople of an imminent avalanche. No, this king's warning applies to the whole world and will still resonate three thousand years after it is spoken. Its stakes are as high as they come; indeed, all of creation must heed this warning.

If only they would listen...

Wisdom for Kings, Instruction for Judges

Psalm 2 ends with a warning that is simultaneously ominous and open-ended—the latter simply because we are only now seeing this end-times prophecy start to unfold. David begins by exhorting world leaders to heed the earlier responses of the Father and the Son: "Now then, you kings, be wise; be admonished, you judges of the earth" (v. 10).

Stated another way: *Don't say I didn't warn you.* Warn them of what? Of everything the Father and Son have said in verses 4 through 9. That is why David starts with the phrase, "Now then...," or "Now therefore..." in the New King James Version. The word *therefore* points back to verses 1 through 9, yet the warning is clearly given through the responses of the Father and the Son in verses 4 through 9. As the writer of the psalm, David is acting as the host of this prophetic drama, and his concluding remarks essentially begin with, "In light of what the Father and the Son have just said..."

David's warning is first to the kings, calling them to the way of wisdom by which they will align with Jesus and His leadership rather than foolishly standing opposed to Him. The psalm's second and third acts have already depicted what will happen to those who rage against the Lord; verses 4, 5, and 9 clearly reveal how Jesus's enemies will be pulverized. There is no hope for those who refuse to yield. Therefore David urges them to be smart enough to seek God's friendship to avoid experiencing His wrath.

David is speaking to the senior political authorities of the nations—kings and judges—including presidents; prime ministers; senators; governors; top financial leaders; prominent people in sports, entertainment, and the arts; as well as leaders in education, science, and the military who are highlighted in the media; and more. These are the men and women who shape society by their ruling authority. And his words are what God wants this specific group of leaders to understand.

David specifically calls out the "judges of the earth" (v. 10).

Judges are those with senior judicial or legislative authority. They interpret laws and enforce justice in society, and they carry the weight of differentiating between right and wrong, between truth and lies. If kings are the leaders who determine the laws for a nation, then judges are the leaders who make application for the execution of those laws.

The original word that David used for the phrase "be admonished" in verse 10 means to chastise or correct in the spirit of exhortation. It is those who enforce justice who often most need the correction of the Lord. They must learn directly from Him if they hope to understand how to rule with true justice.

David's twofold warning goes deeper than just a suggestion. It is, in fact, a sentence upon those who, according to verses 1 through 3, vehemently stand against the Lord. These are the kings, rulers, and judges who hate Jesus and His commands. In their rage they want to eradicate the Word of God from society. In time they will enact laws that make it a hate crime to take a stand for various truths in the Word of God. They will use the judicial system—what should be a means for ensuring justice—to release their vitriol toward the Lord and His followers. And they believe that through such ruling they will have the last word.

In verse 10 David tells these kings and judges that they are sadly mistaken. They will not have the last word. Only Jesus, the great King and Judge who sits at the right hand of the Father, has the final word. "So beware," David warns them, "if you criminalize being faithful to the Word of God. Know that you will surely stand before the great King and Judge one day as a 'criminal' against His kingdom and people, and to the same degree that you have determined and executed a false 'justice,' He will execute His true justice against you. To the same degree that you have mocked justice and truth itself, He will mock you. For rest assured, in the end, God will not be mocked."

David charges the kings, rulers, and judges of the nations throughout history—but particularly those leaders in the generation in which Jesus returns—to be wise and be instructed. It is as if he is simultaneously pleading with them to "humble themselves...and turn from their wicked ways" (2 Chron. 7:14) while also declaring their stubbornness as the reason they are now being "instructed" or sentenced.

LOVING WITH ALL OUR HEARTS

After offering a harsh warning, David then turns to what may be his favorite subject: the loving God. At first glance, though, verses 11 and 12 seem far from that topic.

God called David a "man after My own heart" (1 Sam. 13:14; Acts 13:22). That means David responded to God in a way that was consistently in agreement with God's heart. Through David's understanding of living all of life as a continuous act of love and worship to God, he became a theologian on the love of God. Of course David understood other aspects of God's character; his psalms prove that he could marvel at His majesty (Ps. 8), unending mercy (Ps. 86), righteousness (Ps. 11), forgiveness (Ps. 51), faithfulness (Ps. 143), and many other attributes of the Lord. And yet no man or woman in the Old Testament had greater revelation of the love of God than David. He probably experienced intimacy with the Lord as no one else did before Jesus walked on the earth.

This is why we must pay close attention to these two remaining verses. Using minimal words, David gives us the practical details of what it means to love God with all our hearts. Moses was the first to teach, "You shall love the LORD your God with all of your heart" (Deut. 6:5). That was around five hundred years before David was born.

In the Psalms David emphasized enjoying a close, loving, and intimate relationship with God. Here David once again emphasized the command to love God—our first command—and he applied it more than any other man in the Old Testament.

Here in Psalm 2 David gives us practical details about how to walk out loving God with all our hearts, even in the context of the growing global crisis. For those still willing to listen—including those kings and rulers willing to repent—he offers further instruction. Here is how the New King James Version translates it:

> *Serve* the LORD with fear, and *rejoice* with trembling. *Kiss* the Son, lest He be angry...
>
> —PSALM 2:11–12, EMPHASIS ADDED

David's words apply to more than the hard-hearted kings and cultural rulers of his time and any since then. They are wisdom for all people of all generations. David exhorts us with three distinct directives: *serve, rejoice,* and *kiss.* As we engage in each of these, we discover a different element of loving God with all our hearts. In addition, each directive includes a sobering yet critical reminder that involves our trembling with fear before God—yes, even as we grow in intimacy with Him. (I will explain shortly how this is possible.)

Remember, David was writing under the inspiration and guidance of the Holy Spirit. We must understand that in verses 10 through 12 he is giving insight on what the Holy Spirit will say to the church in the generation in which the Lord returns. These three main directives have many implications that could fill books as they are three profound dimensions of loving God. Let's take a relatively brief look at exactly what each one means.

Serve

At first glance you could easily think David's first item on his three-part list—to serve—is either a mistake or a complete anomaly since it seems to be nothing like the others. Rejoicing and kissing—the second and third directives from David—sound upbeat, delightful, intimate, and full of love. They seem naturally connected to the heart. But *serving?* Why would David's first directive on how to love God with all our hearts involve serving—something that often can be reduced to a robotic, dare I say *loveless,* action?

For us to serve the Lord speaks of fully engaging with what He is doing in our generation. Many believers have drawn back from diligently engaging in prayer, outreach, and discipling younger believers and are content with a passive Christianity that mostly chooses personal comfort with regard to investing money, energy, and free time. These believers are not engaging with Jesus by actively serving people and building up His kingdom.

Jesus linked serving to following Him. He said:

> If anyone serves Me, he must follow Me. Where I am, there
> will My servant be also. If anyone serves Me, the Father will
> honor him.
> —John 12:26

To serve Jesus means to follow Him and be where He is. It
means to engage with Him fully with real actions.

Those who serve will love, and those who love will serve.

The truth, then, is that David's first directive is anything *but*
loveless. In fact, it is the exact opposite! We serve God because we
love Him. We seek to do His will because we delight in Him, we
desire to please Him, and we want to pour out our affections upon
Him and to bring honor to Him. In God's kingdom servanthood
is inherently linked with the love of God.

Soon after washing His disciples' feet, Jesus repeated the same
phrase three times in the same teaching:

> If you love Me, keep My commandments....He who has My
> commandments and keeps them is the one who loves Me.
> And he who loves Me will be loved by My Father. And I will
> love him and reveal Myself to him....If a man loves Me, he
> will keep My word. My Father will love him, and We will
> come to him, and make Our home with him. He who does
> not love Me does not keep My words. The word which you
> hear is not Mine, but the Father's who sent Me.
> —John 14:15, 21, 23–24

If we claim to love God, then we will keep His words and obey
His commandments, which includes serving His purposes. Our
love for Him will compel us to find ways to serve Him by serving
others, placing them above ourselves, and finding a way to meet
their needs.

... with fear and trembling

All this begs the question, though: If serving God is such an
intimate, loving thing, then why does David tell us to "serve the
Lord with fear"?

The fear of the Lord is an important theme in the Bible, yet many believers rarely consider it, much less treat it as one of the cornerstones of their faith. Most Christians come to know God through the concepts of His love and forgiveness. We hear John 3:16 and learn that God's love is so great that He did whatever it took to restore us to relationship with Him, and from this revelation we surrender our lives to Him. Only later do most of us stumble upon the idea that God is to be greatly respected or "feared," and even then we typically leave this as one of those tough topics we will ask God more about when we get to heaven.

The fear of the Lord, however, is a foundational element of our faith. Without it we serve and love God with a limited view of who He really is. That sounds extreme, but it is true not only because of God's revealed character but also because of the numerous times in both the Old and the New Testaments that we are commanded to fear Him. In fact, the Bible uses the word *fear* more than three hundred times in reference to God.

To fear God means to be in profound awe of His majesty and beauty and to have utter respect for His authority. David was calling us to serve God *on His terms*, not on ours. Fearing Him means giving Him the honor He is due, and that includes serving Him in the way He says to serve Him, even if it means not receiving recognition and not seeing things done the way we prefer. In other words, some are happy to serve, but *only* on their terms.

When we fear Him, we acknowledge that He is great and powerful, He holds the universe in His hands, and He sees everything that we do and think. From that sense of reality we develop a "holy fear," as it is often described. As John Bevere writes in his book *The Fear of the Lord*:

> Holy fear is the key to God's sure foundation, unlocking
> the treasuries of salvation, wisdom, and knowledge. Along
> with the love of God, it composes the very foundation of
> life!...We cannot truly love God until we fear Him, nor can
> we properly fear Him until we love Him.[7]

To fear God does not refer to fear in the negative sense, as in the fear of being rejected by Him. It is not the same fear of rejection that is cast out by perfect love (1 John 4:18). It is instead the awe of God that empowers us toward "perfecting holiness," as Paul said (2 Cor. 7:1). The fear of God should be a healthy, ever-present motivator behind our approach to serving Him.

When we serve the Lord with this kind of fear or respect, we serve Jesus, knowing He is no ordinary King. He is the great King with all authority, the eternal God who is over all. Often we get so involved in kingdom activities that we forget who we are serving and talking to. Yes, Jesus is our Brother and our Friend, but He is also the King of all kings, and the One whom all creation looks to as Lord.

Serving in the fear of the Lord does not mean that we are afraid of being rejected by God. It means we serve Him with a sense of His greatness and awesomeness, being careful to serve Him on His terms, knowing He is watching all that we do. Because He is, there is no reason for us to attempt to get away with secret compromises. The Lord sees everything!

This is good news for those committed to serving God with "fear and trembling" (Phil. 2:12)—both aspects of our wholehearted love for Him that David highlights in Psalm 2:11. God does not see only the negative; He does not note only when we mess up. First John 1:9 says the Lord "is faithful and just to forgive us our sins" if we ask Him. So we have no reason to fear being judged or rejected for sins that we have confessed with genuine repentance. Praise the Lord, for He is faithful to forgive us of these compromises, and He sees the positive as well as the negative.

Did you know that Jesus has seen *every* cup of cold water you have ever given someone in His name? He remembers *every* time you reached out to those who were naked and clothed them, or visited those in prison who were lonely, or fed those who were hungry (Matt. 25:31–46). He sees *every* conversation you have to encourage a lonely person or to help in even the smallest ways. This is an important aspect of fearing the Lord—to grasp that He is watching and esteeming our smallest acts of obedience. And the exchange rate on these actions is unbelievable. Even the slightest act of compassion in Jesus's name during our seventy-or-so years on the earth results in rewards that last forever in eternity. What a deal!

When we serve the Lord with fear, we do not serve just to get something back, however; we serve because He has told us to obey Him. And because we love Him above all, we will obey Him at any cost.

Rejoice

The word *rejoice* is not used much in today's world outside the church. I believe part of the reason is that there is an overwhelming lack of joy in the world today. With a spiritual enemy who is committed to stealing our joy, it is no wonder we have a global epidemic of depression, anxiety, and fear. This is exactly why Paul encouraged us in Philippians 4:4, "Rejoice in the Lord always. Again I will say, rejoice!"

To rejoice in the Lord means to have confidence in Him. Rejoicing blends confidence with gratitude. It entails much more than just being happy during a worship service. I like being happy in a service as much as the next believer. I like songs that make me reflect on His goodness in my life. But rejoicing in the Lord goes far deeper than a momentary surge of feel-good emotions.

When we rejoice in God, we have confidence in the sure victory of who He is and what He has promised to do throughout the earth. We know His kingdom will triumph and His reign will be openly seen by all in due time, no matter how seemingly powerful earthly kingdoms become. This confidence compels us to not draw back in fear as powerful leaders of society threaten us. We can rejoice because we have a certainty of victory already in our hearts. We need not fear the kings and rulers of this earth because our King has already won. Period.

Our sure victory in no way means we are immune to persecution, pressure, or difficult circumstances. Those in the persecuted church can attest to this. Yet their underlying cry remains the same as the great martyrs of generations past: "You may kill my body, but I will have a resurrected one that reigns with Jesus for billions of years to come!"

Such confidence is part of our rejoicing. It is the opposite of defeatism and fear—two tactics of the enemy that attack our confidence. Revelation 12:10 reveals that the devil stands before God accusing us day and night. He does not stop assaulting us with condemnation as he attempts to overwhelm us with guilt before God. This could easily wear us down were it not for God's command for us to rejoice in Him. How can we rejoice in the face of such attacks? Because through Christ Satan's accusations are struck down every time! We rejoice because we can take confidence that although we stand before God in our weakness and brokenness, yet we still find favor with the ultimate Judge. He forever rules in favor of His people because of the blood of Jesus!

Many believers lack holy confidence because they remain preoccupied with their failure. I have known ministers who focus their preaching on how bad they are and how they always seem to mess up despite their best intentions and efforts. Though they acknowledge that Jesus has saved them from themselves, they develop a message that highlights their failures far more than pointing anyone to Christ, yet their approach attracts those in the audience because their message is supposedly "relatable" and "real."

Allow me to give you some good news if you have not already heard it: you are a new creation in Christ Jesus (2 Cor. 5:17). In fact, you have become the very righteousness of God in Christ (v. 21)! How's that for a radical transformation? How's that for the *real* truth?

We have every reason in the world to rejoice because of our new, permanent status in Christ Jesus. He has made a provision for you and me to stand with confidence even in our weakness. We are now partners with Him because of the Lord's remarkable generosity. He has treated us with kindness and mercy when we deserved judgment and punishment. That means we no longer have to live under the unbearable weight of our sin. Some

Christians live filled with shame and condemnation, and they erroneously believe they are walking in humility. True humility is acknowledging with confidence our position in Jesus. We can take confidence that the blood of Jesus is sufficient for us to stand before God, even in our weakness.

We can also rejoice because the Lord sees even the smallest acts of obedience that no one else notices. This gives our lives great relevance. I mentioned in the last section that God sees all and that the eternal rewards He gives His people change our outlook on the small things we do in this life. They not only give us incentive to do everything "as for the Lord" (Col. 3:23) but also help us realize we can rejoice that He truly sees and remembers our efforts to do His will. You may never be recognized or honored before a crowd of people. You may never be thanked in the spotlight or invited onstage for recognition. Yet you can still rejoice knowing that "as you have done it for one of the least of these brothers of Mine, you have done it for Me" (Matt. 25:40).

Rejoicing speaks of having gratitude for the privilege of being allowed to know and serve the Lord even when we aren't recognized—this can be more difficult than it sounds. The devil wants to convince you that people have mistreated you by not appreciating your efforts. He wants you to be preoccupied with what you have not received and how much others have overlooked you. "You didn't get the recognition you deserve," he'll whisper. "You could have done better if that person had only given you more resources and cooperated more. It's her fault you didn't succeed; she never bothered helping you because she doesn't value what you do."

Satan knows that the more you dwell on thoughts like these, the less chance there is of gratitude settling in your heart. And he will fight hard to gain a stronghold in your thought life because he knows the power of gratitude. Gratitude for His kindness toward us awakens love and dedication in our heart. It empowers us to endure hardship and pain. This is also why one of the enemy's subtlest tactics in this area is to plant seeds of resentment in your thoughts about God. If Satan cannot get us feeling bitter toward or overlooked by others, he will go down swinging in an attempt to get us feeling these things toward the Lord. "God has overlooked you," the enemy will whisper. "If only God had healed you, then you would have seen more people come to Jesus." (Wow—talk about cunning!) Or how many times will Satan try to use negative thoughts about church leaders to impact our view of God. "If that pastor had only honored your outreach ministry or prophetic gifting more, people would have been set free and revival would have come to the church. Why would God put such a spiritually clueless man in that position anyway?"

Can you see the progression of thoughts Satan tries to build? As the enemy of your soul he will do whatever it takes to stir up internal strife and conflict. Yet we can prevent his lies from gaining hold on us by simply rejoicing out of a spirit of gratitude. Satan's attacks are thwarted when our hearts are filled with gratitude because gratitude energizes our love for Jesus and His people. Things may not go as we thought they would. But that is no reason for us to abandon the truths we know about God. We have the privilege in our unique assignments to partner with Jesus. We have the honor of serving and loving Him, of standing with Him rather than being crushed under His authority. Because of this, we can look in the face of whatever the enemy tries to throw our way and still rejoice.

... with trembling

As with David's directive to serve, his exhortation to rejoice comes with an unusual partner. Rejoice... *with trembling.* It's not exactly a pairing you would expect to find among the keys to loving God with all our hearts. And yet David reiterates the same fundamental principle as he did in establishing the concept of fearing God—namely that we must keep the truth of God's whole character in mind as we love Him wholeheartedly through service and rejoicing.

David's exhortation comes with a subtle warning given to all but specifically to the kings and judges he addressed in verse 10.

He warns them that they must learn to tremble before their Maker—to do things His way, knowing He has far greater power.

Think about it: kings are accustomed to seeing the people of their nations tremble before them because of their authority; judges are also accustomed to having people shake before their decisions or verdicts. Neither kings nor judges are used to trembling before others, yet here David is charging both groups to tremble before another whose power is infinitely greater than theirs.

He also warns them that they should tremble because this high King is coming soon and will not tolerate their raging arrogance in making laws that resist His written Word. They must yield to the true King and embrace what He values and says instead of following the popular voice of the culture.

If anyone knew this posture of complete, trembling submission, it was David. As the greatest ruler Israel had ever known, David served as both king and judge. By all appearances he had reason to boast in his power and to do things his own way. Yet He submitted to the authority of a far greater King and Judge, and he understood what it meant to lead people from this humble position of submitted authority.

Even those of us who are not leaders can glean from this profound warning, for it does not apply just to those shaping culture. We will delve more into this idea of trembling in chapter 8 and look at why it is so important, but for now simply realize that every person on the earth, no matter what his societal position, will be given the opportunity to see the Lord in His majesty and glory, and the fitting response—even for those rejoicing in their intimacy with Him—always contains an element of trembling.

Kiss

Since the origins of the British monarchy subjects have sworn their allegiance to the ruling king or queen with a kiss to the hand. Yet recently the nation watched with its collective jaw dropped when Jeremy Corbyn, leader of the United Kingdom's Labour Party, knelt down before Queen Elizabeth II, kissed her hand, and pledged his loyalty to Her Majesty. The reason for their astonishment? Corbyn is a lifelong anti-monarchist who has spent years campaigning to replace England's monarchy with an elected president. He has even tried to rally support multiple times to evict the queen from Buckingham Palace. By all accounts, he is not a fan of the queen. Yet when given the opportunity to join one of the top councils in the kingdom, apparently Corbyn had a change of heart. And to the surprise of all, he swore that he would be the queen's "true and faithful servant" by kissing her hand.[8]

Such kisses that promise loyalty with affection have been a staple for kings and queens since the earliest times. There is nothing romantic or sensual about this act; it is a symbolic gesture expressing affectionate loyalty, and its meaning carries great significance.

David understood this truth, both as one who received countless kisses of allegiance from subjects of his kingdom and as one who knew what it meant to humble himself and "kiss the son" (Ps. 2:12). The son referred to in this verse is, of course, the same Son the Father has openly declared as King before the entire world: Jesus (v. 6). David has watched the nations rage against this King, and he has been moved by the Father's and Son's responses. Now, in one of his last statements, Israel's king urges his fellow kings and rulers of the world to do more than offer lip service; he advises them to pledge their allegiance in complete submission and with loyal affection.

The beauty of this call, however, is that it speaks of more than just dutiful service. To "kiss the son" here means to give ourselves to the King in loyal, obedient love *with all our hearts*. Anytime the heart is mentioned, strong emotions are not far away. This is a sense of affection with loyal love and service that Jesus is so worthy of.

In our King's presence we can come boldly to say, "I love You, Jesus, and I want to be near You." This is service that flows out of deep relationship filled with affection. We love who Jesus is, we trust His leadership, and we will dedicate ourselves to serving this mighty King for the rest of eternity.

The first time I read Psalm 2:12, I did not understand what "kiss the son" meant. It actually made me uncomfortable, as I was sure God was not calling all of us—men and women—to literally kiss Jesus. Over time I came to understand what this phrase actually means regarding our relationship with Him. To "kiss" Jesus means we lean further into Him in reliance, confidence, and loyal, loving obedience as we continue to receive more of His love. Rather than staying distant from Him, we respond to His first loving us (1 John 4:19) by pouring out our sincere affection upon Him as we serve Him. As we grow in intimacy with God, He continues to fill us with a greater capacity to love Him than we ever thought possible.

...lest He be angry

Once again David couples a beautiful concept—kissing the Son—with a seemingly harsh reality. In verses 4 and 5 we learn of the Father's wrath against the raging nations ("The LORD ridicules them. Then He will speak to them in His wrath and terrify them in His burning anger"). In verse 9 we hear of what Jesus will do to His enemies ("You will break them with a scepter of iron; you will dash them in pieces like a potter's vessel"). The Father and Son are alike in their terrifying potential, and here in verse 12 we are reminded of Jesus's righteous anger.

Too often believers and unbelievers alike think of Jesus only as a soft, hippie-like pacifist who goes around singing songs such as "Give Peace a Chance" and "All You Need Is Love." It is easy for us to picture a wrathful God because, after all, we are familiar with a glimpse of the angry side of God from a few Old Testament stories. Some think that Jesus, on the other hand, is nothing but peace, love, butterflies, marshmallows, and happiness.

Wrong. In fact, those who still buy into this belief in the last days will be rudely awakened. Jesus's love and anger flow in complete unity with His kindness and purity. As I have stated before, the Lord will do whatever it takes to remove any obstacle that hinders His love. In chapter 4 we looked at how His wrath expresses His love. That means His righteous anger and His fierce love go hand in hand. They are neither opposite nor separate.

That also means Jesus, as the perfect reflection of His Father, is not the good cop to the Father's bad cop. Our God is not a Jekyll-and-Hyde God. The Father and Son are in perfect unity. So when David warns the kings and earthly rulers to serve *in fear*, to rejoice *with trembling*, and now to kiss the Son *lest He be angry*, he is reminding us of the breadth of this mighty God. Some see these characteristics as separate—wrongly concluding that fearing God cannot coexist with rejoicing in Him, much less being intimate with Him. Yet God is loving *and* just; He is whole in His holiness *and* wrath. He is simultaneously awesome in His majestic splendor and terrifying in His beauty and greatness. This is why we both love and fear Him and why we both rejoice and tremble before Him.

Some Christian communities skew to only one or two sides of this threefold reality. Some focus almost exclusively on reverential awe for Him. Their services and liturgy are dominated by themes that attest to how great He is and how small we are; therefore we must approach Him with reverential fear. Although such holy fear is essential for us, we must also understand how to love Him and rejoice in Him.

Other ministries or churches focus almost entirely on rejoicing in God's blessings. They exclusively emphasize enjoying His goodness and receiving His blessings in their circumstances, but they never really call people to tremble before His majesty. Still others concentrate on the intimacy of our friendship with God while neglecting to consider God's greatness. When we do not allow all three dimensions of loving God to thrive in our relationship with Him, we miss out on the heights of what He intended for us. He designed us to serve in awe, to rejoice in gratitude and confidence, and to kiss Him in intimate allegiance.

The kings and judges whom David directly addresses in Act IV, of course, have not considered this. They truly believe they can outwit and overpower God. They do not want intimacy with Jesus, and they certainly do not intend to rejoice in Him. But to their own detriment and destruction they have also forgotten exactly whom they are dealing with.

Because of their rejection of Jesus, David essentially warns these cultural leaders that they should throw themselves at the Son's feet "lest He become angry." Those of us who will kiss the hand of the King can rejoice in the privilege of our service. We can remain confident and grateful because we are in close relationship with this beautiful King.

But for those who have raged against Him, who have spent much of their lives plotting (albeit in vain) against His authority, and who have tried so desperately to abolish His Word from every corner of society...for those David seems to present a last-second glimmer of hope. Throw yourself at His feet, he says. Throw your life in His path. And with your head bowed low, reach for His hand. Take it and kiss it until it is covered in kisses, each one asking for mercy. Lay down your crowns, your pride, and your raging defiance, and pledge your allegiance to the one true King. Shower Him with heartfelt repentance blended with utter adoration. Maybe then you will avoid His righteous anger. Maybe then you will avoid "perish[ing] in the way, for His wrath kindles in a flash" (Ps. 2:12). Then surely you will live.

THE FINAL BLESSING

After such a sobering message—both to the wicked end-times leaders and to people of every generation—David offers a more upbeat reminder to conclude this dramatic psalm. His final words, though simple, ring like an ageless anthem of assurance: "Blessed are all those who put their trust in Him" (Ps. 2:12, NKJV).

This is not directed toward just an elite group. It is not just the "good guys" who can latch on to this promise. Blessed are *all*...

Kings and paupers.

Rulers and subjects.

Young and old.

Rich and poor.

Black and white.

Thankful and ungrateful.

Healed and wounded.

Spiritual and heathen.

Free and bound.

Blessed are *all those* who do one thing. What is this thing? It is easy yet difficult. Simple yet profound. Unconditional yet limited. But it is one single thing that brings all these people into a safe haven of blessing:

Trust in Him.

Today it may seem harder to trust Jesus as the crisis of our times grows in both reach and intensity. Believers may find it more difficult to stand for the truth of His Word. Our faith is being criminalized, and it will not be long before many more who profess to follow Jesus will face persecution, prison, torture, or death. This will not be an isolated ISIS, Middle Eastern, or North Korean thing; it will be global, affecting every culture. Psalm 2 is not limited to Israel or the Middle East but is a drama set on a worldwide stage.

As believers, then, how are we to serve and respond to Him in the growing crisis? At the very core of our response is trusting His leadership—especially in the context of the growing crisis in the nations, along with our personal trials, struggles, and failures. If we trust that He is good, that His eyes are on us, that He will cause all things to work together for our good, that He is in control, and that His eternal promises are true, then we will have the frame of mind to persevere through all the difficulty and disappointment we face in the growing crisis that unfolds before He returns in glory.

We will answer the question about how we are to respond more fully in the next few chapters. For now, we can start at the very place David ended, with the reminder of what it means to trust Jesus. Our great King is trustworthy. He is faithful. His Word will emerge victorious over every force of opposition. And for these and countless other reasons we can rejoice that as we trust in Him, we will be blessed.

Blessing may not come the way we think it will. It does not make us immune to persecution or death. This is why the

Bible—particularly the New Testament books written to a young, New Testament church—repeatedly exhorts us to be strong amid the storms of our time:

> Yes, and all who desire to live a godly life in Christ Jesus will suffer persecution.
>
> —2 TIMOTHY 3:12

> You will be hated by all men for My name's sake. But he who endures to the end will be saved.
>
> —MATTHEW 10:22

> For I consider that the sufferings of this present time are not worthy to be compared with the glory which shall be revealed to us.
>
> —ROMANS 8:18

> But even if you suffer for the sake of righteousness, you are blessed. "Do not be afraid of their terror, do not be troubled."...For it is better, if it is the will of God, that you suffer for doing good than for doing evil.
>
> —1 PETER 3:14–17

> Beloved, do not be surprised at the fiery ordeal that is taking place among you to test you, as though some strange thing happened to you. But rejoice insofar as you share in Christ's sufferings, so that you may rejoice and be glad also in the revelation of His glory. If you are reproached because of the name of Christ, you are blessed, because the Spirit of glory and of God rests upon you. On their part He is blasphemed, but on your part He is glorified....Yet if anyone suffers as a Christian, let him not be ashamed, but let him glorify God because of it....Let those who suffer according to the will of God entrust their souls to a faithful Creator, while continuing to do good.
>
> —1 PETER 4:12–19

> Do not fear any of those things which you are about to suffer. Look, the devil is about to throw some of you into

prison, that you may be tried, and you will have tribulation
for ten days. Be faithful unto death, and I will give you the
crown of life.

—Revelation 2:10

Those who side with King Jesus are given the privilege of
sharing in His sufferings (2 Tim. 3:12; Rom. 8:17; Phil. 3:10; 1 Pet.
4:13). This is a promise associated with great reward. And though
what we experience on the earth may not seem like victory, yet
we are certain to experience it in eternity. We are assured that
even in the small, everyday, mundane things we do—the things
nobody sees—we are eternally rewarded because God sees and
is moved by even our smallest acts of obedience (Heb. 6:10). So
we *can* rejoice! We can take confidence in the King who greatly
rewards those who endure to the end. We can enjoy the intimacy
of kissing the Son who, despite wielding a terrifying wrath stored
up for enemies, shows us favor. Those who put their trust in Him
will indeed be blessed.

PART III
THE CALL

happen if one day your coworkers, friends, or even family members report you for hate speech just because you shared biblical truth with them? What will you do when your career is at stake if you refuse to sign a document that says you approve of gay marriage? How will you react if you are threatened with losing your job or even going to prison if you share the gospel with someone in public?

I am not trying to be an alarmist. Some of these things may not happen for another few decades in America, but I can assure you that at the rate we are going now, a few of them will take place within the next five to ten years in our nation. Regardless of the timeline, we know, both from our study of Psalm 2 and from countless other biblical texts and developments in the culture, that *these things will happen.*

Between now and then the church faces a critical juncture. This is not a season for believers to sit on the sidelines and see how things pan out for others before going "all in." In fact, "sitting this one out" is not an option. We are facing a defining moment for the American church. Either we stand up and declare the truth of Jesus, or we get washed away with the cultural tide of compromise.

We need only to look to Europe to see what our future looks like. Within only a few generations the European church went from being the center of global Christendom to being a shell of itself. Today in Britain, France, and Germany approximately 1 percent of the total population attends a weekly church service (though 70 percent still claim to be Christian). Out of 211 million people in those three countries, only 2.4 million are committed believers. In fact, there are more atheists in Germany than in the United States, even though its population is roughly one-fourth the size of America's. And in Britain four times as many people attend a mosque on Friday as a church service on Sunday.[2]

Barring a miracle, this is where America is headed—fast. The crisis is at hand. Culture has already determined which way it is going. The real question is: How will the church respond? And how will *you* respond?

A Psalm to Prepare

During the American Revolutionary War a British spy arrived at the Trenton, New Jersey, headquarters of a Hessian commander carrying an urgent message. (Hessians were German mercenaries serving in the British army.) Despite the gravity of his report, the British spy was denied a personal meeting; the commander was busy playing poker, he was informed. Frustrated, yet still committed to his mission, the spy wrote his message on a piece of paper: George Washington and the Continental Army had secretly crossed the Delaware River and were on their way to Trenton. When the note reached the commander, he stuffed it into his pocket, unread, and continued playing his game. He was still shuffling the card deck when his watchmen scrambled to load their muskets upon spotting Washington's army. With no time to prepare, the Hessian soldiers were easily captured.[3]

The church has been given ample warning. We not only have seen this crisis coming for years but also have watched the enemy build his army and, one by one, assault different areas of society. We have witnessed the rise of animosity toward God's Word. And we have sensed a change in the spiritual atmosphere of our nation.

Indeed, the storm is approaching, and the body of Christ must be prepared for the coming deluge. This is not something to take lightly. We do not have the luxury of playing games or even "playing church." The days we are living in are critical.

I get asked all the time, "Mike, what do you think the Holy Spirit is saying to the church right now?" The answer is clear—maybe as clear as it has been in years.

Psalm 2.

The Holy Spirit is definitely highlighting Psalm 2 in this hour. The importance of the Davidic drama has been emphasized in the past, as evidenced by Psalms being the most referenced Old Testament passage in the New Testament. But today I hear of more and more people around the world drawn to the prophetic picture of Psalm 2, and that is not by chance. The reason is simple: the Holy Spirit is leading the church to this blueprint for end-times activity; He does not want us to be offended or overwhelmed by what is to come. If we do not realize what lies ahead for believers, then we will take offense at the arrogance of worldly leaders and will be shocked by the level of sin, immorality, and wickedness celebrated by the masses. We will become discouraged by the supposed decline of the church, as proven through the rising godlessness of cultures around the world. We will be fearful of the increase of terrorism and persecution against believers. And some of us will feel as if God has abandoned His people. The resulting sense of rejection will lead to doubt, bitterness, and eventually abandoning the faith.

But the Holy Spirit does not desire that we fall prey to any of these emotions. No, the Holy Spirit wants us to be ready for the looming crisis, and He is using Psalm 2 to prepare the body of Christ.

God's Twofold Calling

During this critical time God is calling His people to stand in His truth. To do so is costly, and He is fully aware of the cost. He never said it would be easy, but He did promise that His presence, strength, and grace would be with us. And His call remains the same.

Here in Psalm 2 David highlighted two primary activities for God's people to engage in—to proclaim the Father's message (v. 5) and to partner with the Son's intercession (v. 8).

God is calling messengers and intercessors to rise up in these last days. Both are essential to His end-times plan, and both are key to the bride of Christ's being prepared for the Bridegroom's arrival.

What is the Father's message? Let's review what we covered in chapter 4.

In Psalm 2:4–6 the Father responds to the rage of the nations by pronouncing His wrath against the kings and rulers and by openly declaring His commitment to exalt Jesus's kingship across the whole earth, which will result in a great revival in the nations. His response—or His message—is one of both judgment and revival. And *that* is what He wants us to proclaim throughout the nations.

Most of us do not mind publicly stating that Jesus is King and that the Father is committed to exalting His kingship before all the nations. We understand that it is not a popular message, but we can stomach a few rejections or even insults thrown our way that label us as foolish to believe in a God-Man who is pouring out His Spirit, who is one day returning to rule the world, and who will bring to an end all those who oppose Him. Although that is considered hate speech to some even now, we can accept that this is the message God has asked us to deliver.

But judgment? Wrath? Who wants to deliver *that* message? Regardless of how we feel about it, God has called His people to be His mouthpiece and to declare the truth about His coming wrath. We do not have to approach this calling like an angry, out-of-balance, fire-and-brimstone sidewalk preacher wearing a billboard and shouting through a megaphone, but ultimately we must deliver a similarly unpopular and politically incorrect message.

Proclaiming the message goes beyond merely taking a stand for the truth about immorality or abortion. It is more difficult than forming a prayer chain or conducting a prayer walk around a state capitol building. God wants to anoint His people to speak out a Psalm 2:5 message—to use His church to "speak to them in His wrath" and proclaim that He will "distress them in His deep displeasure" (NKJV). Who are the "them" in this verse? Though it can apply to all people, I believe the "them" are specifically kings and rulers!

Indeed, God has commissioned His people to tell local and national leaders—presidents, kings, prime ministers, judges, CEOs, university presidents, sports stars, Hollywood producers, and so on—that He will distress the nations in His wrath. He is deeply displeased with the passing of laws directly opposed to His truth. He is deeply displeased with how glamorized immorality continues to pollute the entertainment airwaves of America. He is deeply displeased with companies fostering injustice for financial gain and using unethical systems to keep the poor enslaved.

And we are the ones who get to relay this message.

SPEAKING OF HIS WRATH

I definitely prefer to communicate only the "softer" side of the message of God's exalting Jesus in the nations. After all, verse 6 is the heart of Psalm 2: "I have installed My king on Zion, My holy hill." We like that message; it is far less judgmental and offensive to simply say that one day God will exalt Jesus as King. It would be tempting, then, to skip verse 5 and just focus on the primary message of Jesus's being exalted in verse 6. We know that when Christ is exalted, God's power will be revealed even more and the greatest revival in history will cover the globe. Yes!

But we are to be faithful to the message of verse 5, not just that of verse 6. And there are several reasons God wants His servants to speak the message of His wrath.

First, the very proclamation of God's wrath will result in a stigma on the church that will be one means of purifying the church. Some believers will be so offended by the message of God's judgment that they will go so far as to rail against it and its messengers and will do everything in their power to discredit specific messengers. Many will call the messengers narrow-minded, old-fashioned, and irrelevant; but others will go so far as to say they are unbiblical. This is how pervasive the distortion of God's Word will be in the church in coming years.

Yet God will use conflict within the church to purify the body of Christ. Those willing to stand uncompromisingly on God's whole truth—not just the parts of the Bible that are easier to accept—will inevitably endure hardship and attacks. God will use this to cleanse the bride of Christ from compromise and distortion.

The second reason God has called us to speak this message of wrath is that it will give unbelievers a chance to be saved. God will shake the nations (Hag. 2:7), and the shaking process will result in some turning to Him as the one true God. Rather than succumbing to the popular rage against Jesus, some will be awakened by God's judgments to the reality that He is the eternal God who is all powerful.

Though it sounds odd, many will be saved by hearing about God's judgments.

This will not be the first time God's judgment has resulted in turning men's hearts. Isaiah 26:9 promises, "For when your judgments are in the earth, the inhabitants of the world will learn righteousness." Indeed, some of the church's greatest seasons of revival, awakening, and reformation have come through people's hearing about the Lord's judgments.

Jonathan Edwards lived at a time when the church in New England had grown cold with much compromise. In 1729 Edwards began crying out to the Lord to awaken believers throughout the area from their spiritual stupor. Eleven years later British preacher George Whitefield spoke at Edwards's parish in Northampton, Massachusetts, and ignited a move of God. Many in the church repented and were saved. Edwards was among those moved, and soon afterward he preached in many churches throughout Massachusetts and Connecticut as the Great Awakening swept through the American colonies.[4]

One church in Enfield, Connecticut, remained hardened to the call to repent. Edwards spoke there on July 8, 1741. On that day he gave what has widely been known as America's most famous sermon, "Sinners in the Hands of an Angry God." Edwards expounded on Deuteronomy 32:35, wherein—in his words—"is threatened the vengeance of God on the wicked unbelieving Israelites." He described how these unbelieving ones—who appeared to be God's people but were not—stood on the edge of slipping into eternal destruction. He spoke of God's judgment awaiting them and told them, "Unconverted men walk over the pit of hell on a rotten covering, and there are innumerable places in this covering so weak that they will not bear their weight."[5]

Pressing his point, Edwards declared, "The use of this awful subject may be for awakening unconverted persons in this congregation. This...is the case of every one of you that are out of Christ—that world of misery, that lake of burning brimstone, is extended abroad under you. There is the dreadful pit of the glowing flames of the wrath of God; there is hell's wide gaping mouth open; and you have nothing to stand upon, nor any thing to take hold of; there is nothing between you and hell but the air; it is only the power and mere pleasure of God that holds you up.... The God that holds you over the pit of hell... is dreadfully provoked: his wrath towards you burns like fire....O sinner! Consider the fearful danger you are in: it is a great furnace of wrath, a wide and bottomless pit...that you are held over in the hand of that God....You hang by a slender thread, with the flames of divine wrath flashing about it, and ready every moment to singe it, and burn it asunder; and you have no interest in any Mediator....Let every one that is yet out of Christ, and hanging over the pit of hell...now hearken to the loud calls of God's word and providence....Therefore, let every one that is out of Christ, now awake and fly from the wrath to come."[6]

Edwards's sermon was interrupted over and over again with people crying out, "How can I be saved?" As he spoke of hell, some people clung to the pews for fear that they would slide right into the mouth of hell.[7]

Why did Edwards represent God this way? Did he not see God as a God of love? In fact, we know from his other writings that Edwards delighted in the love of God, and "Sinners in the Hands of an Angry God" was somewhat of an anomaly for him in its graphic depiction of God's wrath and judgments. Yet Edwards found that there were times when it was not enough to speak only of the love and mercy of God. He understood that there were times when we need to speak of the anger of God toward the unrepentant and the judgments of God that await them.

The Holy Spirit used Edwards's sermon to change a church in Enfield and continue an awakening that swept America in the 1740s. I believe He is waiting for God's people today to be willing to be equally as bold in pronouncing His message. I also believe that, as a result of hearing this message of judgment, some of the kings and rulers that Psalm 2 mentions will be saved. We cannot know which rulers will be fixed permanently in their rebellion or which ones will have open hearts even though they will be surrounded by such rage. But we can infer from David's final warnings to these leaders that there will still be some who can be saved. (Otherwise, why would David emphasize exhorting them to turn back to the Lord?) As the church we must contend for these souls in prayer, even during times when they are the very ones who are persecuting believers. May we pray in more Sauls of Tarsus!

Finally, God has called His people to speak forth His wrath because He is a God of justice. That means that in perfect fairness He requires that His judgments be announced before they are released—again, giving people a chance to turn from their wickedness and repent. Amos 3:7 says, "Surely the Lord GOD does nothing without revealing His purpose to His servants the prophets." He will announce His judgments through the prophetic voices among His people.

God's people must sound out His judgments *before* they come. And even then His mercy is so great and unending—yes, even as His justice prevails—that He does not will "any to perish, but all to come to repentance" (2 Pet. 3:9). Even in the eleventh hour, in the face of His judgments, He desires them to turn and be saved.

DISTORTION IN THE CHURCH

God will purify His church amid the growing deception that causes many believers to fall away. In chapter 2 we talked about this increasing deception within the church. This was a primary focus of Jesus's warnings for the end-times church. Unfortunately we can already see how part of this deception is expressed by the dismissing of God's message of judgment.

When an audio signal is distorted, the original sound waves that comprise it are altered during transmission. What is intended to be transmitted gets changed; certain parts (frequencies) get exaggerated while other parts are diminished. This results in distortion, and the outcome is different from what was originally created.

We see this same effect at work in churches all over the world today. The message God originally sent through His Word is altered—certain parts such as grace, forgiveness, God's intended blessings for believers, or the role of faith are overstated with exaggeration or understated by being totally ignored. Meanwhile other truths such as God's judgments, the seriousness of sin, or the importance of purity are downplayed. You would think that in a noisy world filled with clamoring voices, the church would be the very place a message from God would find clarity, yet the truths of God's Word are increasingly being distorted and watered down among believers today. Chief among these is the biblical view of the gospel of grace.

Today Bible teachers are perverting God's grace by reducing it to only a matter of receiving forgiveness and blessing without calling sinners to repentance. They justify ongoing sin and empower compromise and passivity by teaching that God continually smiles on us no matter what we do or continue doing. They present His love and grace in a distorted way—a way that differs from how Scripture teaches these glorious truths. Twisting certain passages and taking others out of context, they insist that in light of their version of God's grace, nothing we do will ever alter His look of favor upon us.

The entire Book of Jude warns us of Bible teachers who bring such deception. Speaking of the church, the author says, "Certain men have crept in unnoticed…ungodly men, *who turn the grace of our God into lewdness* and deny the only Lord God and our Lord Jesus Christ" (v. 4, NKJV, emphasis added). The true grace message inspires us to deny lust and gives us power to walk godly. As Titus 2:11–12 says, "The grace of God that brings salvation has appeared to all men, teaching us that, denying ungodliness and worldly desires, we should live soberly, righteously, and in godliness in this present world."

Unfortunately some of the largest and most popular ministries today include false teachings presented with some biblical language. They sell hundreds of thousands of books, and millions of people tune in to their TV programs. They quote Scripture and use their God-given charisma to speak only on popular themes defined as "relevant" messages. But their favor with people does not change the fact that what they teach does not line up with sound doctrine and the full counsel of God's Word (Acts 20:27).

> I did not keep from declaring what was beneficial to you…testifying to both Jews and Greeks of repentance toward God and faith in our Lord Jesus Christ….I am innocent of the blood of all men. For I did not keep from declaring to you the whole counsel of God.
>
> —Acts 20:20–21, 26–27

I love the biblical message of grace. I believe it needs to be preached with greater clarity and consistency, as the health and destiny of the church depend on this glorious message. It manifests the very riches of God's glory. And on a personal level I depend on God's grace every moment, as it is one of the foundational elements of my life and is essential to my walk with God. But I also seek to interpret the truth of God's grace through the lens of the entire Bible—through the lens of the first and most important commandment to "love the Lord your God with all your heart, and with all your soul, and with all your mind, and with all your strength" (Mark 12:30).

The gospel of grace is perverted in two ways: first, by seeking to earn God's love and forgiveness; and second, by responding halfheartedly to receiving God's grace. Either way involves receiving "the grace of God in vain" (2 Cor. 6:1). This means we accept it in a way that produces neither confidence in God's love and power nor a desire to respond with wholeheartedness.*

I believe there is no spiritual battle more significant in the church today than contending to keep the grace message faithful

---

* There is much more to say on this topic, but this is not a book on grace. If any of this is new to you, however, or if you feel as if you are being pulled into either extreme of grace, I highly encourage you to dedicate yourself to learning the truth about this key area of your faith. We have several free resources on the topic available at mikebickle.org, and there are also some great books that have been written about the subject, including *Hyper-Grace* by Michael L. Brown.

to Scripture. Over the last few years I have seen an explosion of distorted grace teaching within the body of Christ, and much of it has gone unchecked and, as Jude says, "unnoticed" (v. 4, NKJV). Satan would like nothing more than to use what seems to be an "innocent," biblical message to cause countless believers to stumble into deception—a deception that can result in many falling away from their faith with eternal consequences.

KINGDOM MESSENGERS

As glorious and life-changing as God's grace is, the truth is that the gospel of the kingdom involves more than just the message of God's forgiveness. It also calls believers to, and equips them for, the privilege, power, and delight of embracing Jesus's heart and leadership and walking in His purposes for their generation.

But being a messenger at this time demands a cost. Are we willing to accept that cost? Are we willing to preach the whole counsel of God and take on the cultural stigma of Jesus—by speaking on both His kingship *and* His judgments?

We should preach about revival. Most believers want to hear about the glory and power of God and a harvest of souls in which millions, maybe even a billion, come to know Jesus.

But who will preach about the coming crisis? We currently have a serious spiritual crisis in America; anyone committed to the truth of God can see that. It is the crisis of Psalm 2:3, in which God's Word is not only challenged but also increasingly removed from society. Soon this crisis will escalate into a national and an international one, and the message of Psalm 2:5, including God's judgment, will also need to be openly pronounced.

We cannot have one part of the gospel without the other. We cannot preach the positive themes but ignore the difficult ones. Crisis without revival is not the full message. Likewise revival without the coming crisis is not the full message. Jesus was explicit when He talked about allowing the wheat and the weeds—the good and the bad—to rise up side by side:

> Let both grow together until the harvest, and in the time
> of harvest I will say to the reapers: Gather up the weeds
> first and bind them in bundles to burn them, but gather the
> wheat into my barn.
>
> —MATTHEW 13:30

The last days will simultaneously feature a great revival (wheat) and a great measure of sin and apostasy (weeds). We cannot ignore the dual nature of these days.

Today many ministers dumb down the Word of God and make it primarily about being happy and getting blessed. I appreciate being happy and getting blessed in my present circumstances, but this is not the primary message of the gospel. In fact, we inadvertently lead people into a wrong understanding of the gospel of grace if that is the only message we pronounce. We are called to be messengers of His full gospel and of "the whole counsel of God" from His Word (Acts 20:27).

PARTNERING IN INTERCESSION

As stated earlier in this chapter, David highlighted two primary activities for God's people to engage in—to proclaim the Father's message (Ps. 2:5–6) and to partner with the Son's intercession (v. 8).

Psalm 2:7–9 shows us the importance Jesus places on intercession. Jesus enters the Psalm 2 drama presenting Himself as the Great Intercessor. Jesus chose to respond to the nations' rage by simply declaring the Father's words back to Him. This is pure intercession—telling God what He has told us to tell Him. We speak the words He has given us to say to Him. How easy is that? And yet it is profound enough that it is the greatest weapon ever formed and the same strategy with which Jesus will rule the world as King. By giving intercession such priority in His own response, Jesus modeled for us how much priority we must give it in our own lives.

God has invited us to partner with Jesus in this profound privilege of intercession. In fact, we have received a personal invitation to rule and reign with Him, under His leadership, in His new kingdom on the earth. Second Timothy 2:12 says, "If we endure, we shall also reign with Him." And Revelation 20:6 says specifically we "shall reign with Him a thousand years," speaking of Jesus's millennial kingdom.

Is this too good to be true? In case you missed it, let me recap: the Father makes known what we are to say *to the nations* (Ps. 2:5), and then Jesus makes known what we are to say *to the Father* (v. 8). Joining Jesus in speaking to the Father somehow changes everything. This is one practical way in which we rule and reign with Jesus.

In Psalm 2 David described two of the most significant activities of the forerunner ministry—*proclaiming a message* related to the coming King and *praying to release power* to confirm the message.

THE FORERUNNER MINISTRY

A forerunner is simply someone who goes ahead to prepare the way for something or someone else. Forerunners pave the road, remove obstacles, clear the path, and make various preparations for the arrival of an event or person.

In ancient times heralds and messengers would often be sent ahead to alert the people that certain royalty or aristocrats would be visiting the area. They would "prepare the way" for a king, queen, duke, or duchess by announcing their coming.

Although there are other examples of forerunners in the Bible, John the Baptist is the most well known, as He prepared the way for Jesus's first coming (Isa. 40:3; Luke 1:11–19; John 1:23). In foretelling John's birth, the angel Gabriel described him as one who "will go before [Jesus] in the spirit and power of Elijah…to make ready a people prepared for the Lord" (Luke 1:17).

Gabriel was quoting Isaiah's prophecy about John, which came seven hundred years earlier. In that prophecy Isaiah described John as:

> The voice of him who cries out, "Prepare the way of the LORD
> in the wilderness, make straight in the desert a highway for
> our God."
>
> —ISAIAH 40:3

John indeed cried out in the wilderness, preparing the way for Jesus so that the people would see Him as the promised King and more readily accept Him. John "made straight...a highway" for the Lord by declaring a message of repentance and partnering with God in prayer for His kingdom to come.

John's message of repentance from sins was not always a welcome one. He was considered an outcast, declaring an unpopular message. In fact, many in Israel concluded that John's ministry was demonic: "For John came neither eating nor drinking, and they say, 'He has a demon'" (Matt. 11:18).

The forerunners' assignment—their ministry—is to prepare people for the Lord's coming. John prepared the way for Jesus's first coming. Of course, John stands alone in history in a unique category as the one primary forerunner in that hour. After John, the apostles functioned in a forerunner spirit as they went two by two to cities preparing people for Jesus to come to their city in that day.

> [Jesus] sent messengers before His face. And as they went,
> they entered a village of the Samaritans, to prepare for Him.
>
> —LUKE 9:52, NKJV

John the Baptist and the apostles were examples of first-century forerunners. They announced Jesus's coming to various cities in Israel while winning souls to the kingdom and making disciples by teaching converts to pray, fast, and live righteously (Matt. 9:14; Luke 3:3–18; 11:1–4). These first-century forerunners give insight into the ministry of forerunners in the end times.

Isaiah prophesied about end-time forerunners who would prepare people by lifting a "banner message to the ends of the earth" that declares the full manifestation of Jesus's salvation and glory when He returns to the earth as the great King.

> Prepare the way for the people...lift up a banner for the
> peoples [the nations]! Indeed the LORD has proclaimed to
> the end of the world: "Say to the daughter of Zion, 'Surely
> your salvation is coming; behold, His reward is with Him.'"
> —ISAIAH 62:10–11, NKJV

Just as the first-century forerunners proclaimed the first coming
of Jesus ahead of time, so also the end-time forerunners will proclaim the second coming of Jesus ahead of time.

I believe that the Lord is even now beginning to prepare a mul-
titude of forerunners from many different streams in the body of
Christ worldwide. These forerunners will proclaim the message
of Jesus's glorious coming as evangelists, pastors, teachers, media
missionaries, artists, singers, musicians, actors, writers, and marketplace leaders. Like John and the apostles they will evangelize
and make disciples (by leading small groups in their churches,
universities, or workplaces). Some homeschooling moms will
function in the forerunner spirit as they teach their children
about Jesus's coming and its implication.

The forerunner ministry is not reserved for some elite group—
it is a calling available to any who are willing to embrace the message and engage in prayer with a view to the coming of Jesus the
great King. Forerunners emphasize Jesus's second coming while
also proclaiming the benefits of His first coming as they win the
lost, heal the sick, help the poor, and walk in love and holiness. By
doing this they prepare people spiritually to respond rightly to the
great King of Psalm 2 in light of His imminent return.

That may sound like a task for only the super-spiritual faith-
giants of the world, yet it is anything but. Forerunners are simply
"messengers" or faithful witnesses who function with a specific message from God in different spheres of life. They may be
preachers, musicians, salespeople, actors, teachers, writers, dis-
ciplers, doctors, construction workers, moms, and dads. (In fact,
moms and dads are some of the most important forerunners on
the planet.) Ultimately a forerunner can be anyone who will set

his heart to understand the message related to the Lord's return and fearlessly proclaim it.

As messengers, forerunners proclaim now what the Holy Spirit is soon to emphasize in a universal way to the body of Christ related to the unique dynamics that will occur on the earth in the generation the Lord returns. Imagine one generation in which godly living and God's power are manifest beyond any time in history; now imagine that in the same generation wickedness and Satan's power will also be manifest beyond any time in history. The release of an unprecedented measure of God's glory as well as an unprecedented measure of sin and demonic activity in the same generation will create unique dynamics for the people living in the generation of the Lord's return—these are components of what forerunners proclaim. They announce what the Holy Spirit is about to openly stress so that people can respond rightly to Jesus in faith and obedience.

Why is this necessary? Because people who do not understand what is going on will be more vulnerable to fear, offense, deception, confusion, and compromise. Forerunner messengers declare the gospel of the kingdom and prepare people spiritually by proclaiming Jesus as Bridegroom, King, and Judge and by helping them to understand what the Scripture says about the unique dynamics—positive and negative—that will occur related to Jesus's bringing in a harvest of souls, raising up a victorious church, and judging oppression and wickedness in the generation in which He returns. God's people must be prepared with understanding so that they will not yield to deception, fear, compromise, or offense at God's leadership but will instead be filled with clarity, peace, purity, and confidence in it. The gospel of the kingdom will be preached in all nations before Jesus returns (Matt. 24:14). The kingdom message has a personal application as individuals freely receive salvation, and a global, cosmic application as all the nations receive Jesus as their King when He returns.

Simply put, forerunners make God's plans known so people can make sense of what will happen before it actually happens. This is why the Holy Spirit is highlighting Psalm 2 to many around the world in this time. He is calling forerunners to declare the Father's message of Psalm 2:4–6 *and* partner with the Son's intercession of Psalm 2:7–9. It is a twofold call. In fact, the Father's message and the Son's intercession are the essence of the forerunner ministry. The two together prepare the way of the Lord. We do not just share the message; we also join with Jesus in intercession. And both are essential to setting the stage for His coming.

SHOUTING IN THE STORM

In the 1990s FBI agent John O'Neill became known as an expert on global terrorism as he investigated incidents around the world such as the 1993 attack on the World Trade Center buildings and the 1998 bombings of the American embassies in Kenya and Tanzania. Although O'Neill was not the first person in the FBI to discover Osama bin Laden, he was relentless in tracing al Qaeda's extensive network and pool of resources, and he quickly understood what a serious threat the terrorist group was to the United States. His predictions of future attacks were largely ignored, however, as the Clinton administration was mired in scandal and the agency seemingly had more pressing priorities to tend to.[8]

Still, O'Neill would not be quiet. The more he uncovered about the bin-Laden-led terrorist network, the more he warned anyone who would listen that al Qaeda's previous attacks merely scratched the surface of their plans to cause major harm to America—yes, even on US soil. O'Neill was brash, however, and though he was respected for his tireless work ethic and extensive knowledge, his larger-than-life personality often got in the way, particularly with the FBI's top leaders.[9]

In August 2001 O'Neill left the FBI to become head of security at the World Trade Center. His repeated warnings had gone unheeded, particularly by a new Bush administration that was unconcerned at the time, despite the fact that some of O'Neill's former colleagues were now raising red flags concerning al Qaeda. When O'Neill took his new post, a friend jokingly said at least he did not have to worry about the towers being bombed again since that had already been done.[10]

"They'll probably try to finish the job," O'Neill replied with a straight face.[11]

Indeed, on the same day he began his new job at the World Trade Center, the FBI was informed that two suspected al Qaeda terrorists were in the United States. A few days later these two were among those executing the 9/11 attacks. O'Neill survived the damage caused by the planes that flew into the north and south towers, but he later died, apparently while attempting to rescue others as the buildings crumbled.[12]

O'Neill is one of countless examples of men and women who have refused to "soften" their message just because it was not popular or well received. He spent much of his career warning the nation's leaders of a coming storm of homeland terrorism. Whether he envisioned the full extent of what has happened since 9/11 or not, he remained true to his message.

Will we do the same? Our message is infinitely greater—and more pressing—than O'Neill's, as horrific as the damage on that tragic day was. Indeed, what will transpire in the season surrounding the Day of Judgment will dwarf any terrorist attack, for God's final judgment will involve every person on the face of the earth.

My prayer is that more and more people will be spiritually prepared for this time of great trouble (Matt. 24:21–22) and that they will heed the warnings of those committed as forerunners to pronounce the Father's message of judgment. But exactly how many respond depends on those willing to take up the forerunner's call and not only declare such judgment but also partner with Jesus in intercession as He prays for the nations to turn to Him—yes, the very nations and peoples that rage against Him in utter hatred.

Chapter 8

ENGAGING IN A JOEL 2 RESPONSE

Duː URING THE LAST two years I have had the opportunity to meet with various governors, senators, congressmen, and congresswomen. Providentially situation after situation opened up for me to sit down in private, heart-to-heart conversations with a few well-known public officials in America.

I discovered quickly that these men and women love Jesus. They desire to lead in a way that honors the Lord. They realize that it is becoming increasingly difficult to do so, especially because they are among the small percentage of politicians who do more than just use God's name as a means to gain more votes. They are born-again believers who truly follow Jesus and seek Him for answers. Several have stood boldly for God's Word even when their counterparts said that was career suicide. Some have even stepped out and, despite backlash, called for days of fasting and prayer because they are so troubled by the current state of affairs in the United States.

On several occasions when I met with these political leaders, they asked me the same question: "Mike, what do you think God is doing right now?"

My answer was the same each time. I shared with them the very message set forth in this book. I walked through Psalm 2 with them and pointed out that they were actually mentioned in it.

"What do you mean?" they asked.

"Well, governor, take a look at verse 10."

They read it again: "Now then, you kings, be wise; be admonished, you judges of the earth."

"See, that's you!" I said. "You are right there in verse 10. As a governor, you are one of the 'kings' specifically mentioned by David."

They then asked what I thought they should do in response, and I told them: *the Psalm 2 crisis requires a Joel 2 response, resulting in an Acts 2 outpouring of the Spirit.*

Psalm 2 is about a crisis that begins as a serious spiritual crisis and quickly escalates to a global crisis that affects every area of life. Joel 2, as we will see, is about sounding the alarm and calling people to prayer and fasting in the face of such a growing crisis. And Acts 2, as most believers know, is about the promised outpouring of the Holy Spirit that is in response to God's people crying out, as described in Joel 2.

I repeat: *the Psalm 2 crisis requires a Joel 2 response, resulting in an Acts 2 outpouring of the Spirit.*

In each passage referenced above, there is a dual fulfillment of the Scripture. All three passages have been fulfilled to an extent in the past, yet a complete and total fulfillment will come in the future. For example, we know that the Holy Spirit *was* poured out on the Day of Pentecost—this is how the church began. Yet before Christ returns, we know the Holy Spirit will also be poured out "on all flesh" (Joel 2:28; Acts 2:17) in such a way that the body of Christ will walk in unprecedented power while God releases "wonders in heaven above and signs on the earth below" (v. 19).

The timing of the fulfillment rests on God's people responding in a way that is described in Joel 2. Many believers love to quote from this key chapter in Scripture, particularly the verses that highlight the outpouring of the Spirit mentioned above. Yet Joel 2 provides more than just a hopeful message that has been partially fulfilled in the past and will be completely fulfilled in the future. It actually gives us God's blueprint for responding to the growing crisis today *so that* we can one day see such an outpouring. If we are experiencing the Psalm 2 crisis today (which we are) and desire an Acts 2 outpouring of the Spirit (which we do), then we would do well to look closely at God's guidelines for how the church is to respond, as described in Joel 2.

Individual Response vs. Corporate Response

It is one thing to know that the current crisis will continue to increase; it is another thing to know how to respond to that crisis.

We have spent most of this book identifying different aspects of the spiritual crisis—how it has already begun in its early stages, what and who will be affected by it, and how quickly it will accelerate within our culture. We have looked at Psalm 2 verse by verse and examined the responses to this crisis from the Father, the Son, and even David. As we understand the relevance of Psalm 2 and discern the times, we know that God has called us as believers to respond to the crisis in the way that He has set forth in Scripture.

But how do we actually respond as the collective church?

In Psalm 2:10–12 we find the individual response God desires. Even though these verses feature David speaking specifically to kings and judges, the message applies to all: we are to turn to God with all our hearts. David explained that we do this by *serving* the Lord with fear, *rejoicing* before Him with trembling, and paying homage to Him as the great King by *kissing the Son* or expressing our loyalty and devotion to Him.

As we saw in chapter 6, this is the individual expression of our response to the crisis. He wants us to turn to Him with all our hearts because He turned to us with all His heart. He wants us to love Him with all our soul, mind, and strength (Mark 12:30) because He first loved us with His all (1 John 4:19). This is our individual response.

Yet God has called us also to respond corporately as the body of Christ. That means there is both an *individual* and a corporate expression of turning to Him with all our hearts. The individual response is important—God looks at the heart. But there is also a *corporate* turning to God. God often responds with power and blessing when people come in unity and turn to Him. As Psalm 133:1, 3 says, "Behold, how good and how pleasant it is for brothers to dwell together in unity!...For there the LORD has commanded the blessing, even life forever."

This is where Joel 2 comes into play, as it is one of the key scriptures where God lays out the blueprint for this corporate response. We would do well, then, to examine this passage in detail.

Keep in mind, our response to the coming crisis is not only individual, or only corporate. It is not an either-or calling but a both-and. God desires *both* the individual turning of Psalm 2 *and* the corporate turning of Joel 2.

Up to this point we have looked extensively at the Psalm 2 individual response, so now let us take a closer look at the corporate response of Joe 2.

THE JOEL 2 CORPORATE RESPONSE

The major theme in the Book of Joel can be summed up in a single phrase: the Day of the Lord. Stated simply, the Day of the Lord refers to the unusual events—positive and negative—that will escalate dramatically in the three and a half years just before Jesus returns and will culminate with what happens afterward. The twofold nature of this time is seen in the great blessing it releases on those who call upon Jesus and in the great judgment for those who refuse Him. Joel 2:11 sums up this sentiment: "For the day of the LORD is *great* and *very terrible*; who can endure it?" (NKJV, emphasis added).

It will be a great "day" to those who call on Jesus's name because they will experience the greatest outpouring of the Holy Spirit in history, resulting in the greatest harvest of souls and leading to Jesus's second coming (Joel 2:28–32). In this unprecedented revival the Spirit will release miracles as seen in the books of Acts and Exodus but combined and multiplied on a global scale.

For the rebellious, however, it will be a "day" worse than terrible. Because of their continued defiance toward God, they will experience the most severe outpouring of His judgments in history—called the Great Tribulation. It will occur in the last three and a half years of this age:

> For then will be great tribulation, such as has not happened since the beginning of the world until now, no, nor ever shall be. Unless those days were shortened, no one would be saved. But for sake of the elect those days will be shortened.
>
> —Matthew 24:21–22

Jesus's intense, unprecedented comment about this time period—that "unless those days were shortened, no one would be saved"—should cause our hearts to tremble. Though no one knows precisely when the Day of the Lord will begin, many Christians believe that the crisis that leads to this global end-times drama is imminent.

As part of our corporate response to the current and increasing crisis, Joel starts to unfold the blueprint from the very first verse of his second chapter:

> Blow the trumpet in Zion, and sound an alarm in My holy mountain! Let all the inhabitants of the land tremble; for the day of the Lord is coming, for it is at hand.
>
> —Joel 2:1, nkjv

In ancient Israel the trumpet blowing Joel refers to had two purposes, as indicated in Numbers 10. First, it was for sounding an alarm to *alert* people of a coming disaster. More specifically, it was to notify people of a military invasion from an outside force. Throughout the land trumpets would blow to alert people of an attack so they could prepare.

The second purpose for the trumpet blowing was to *gather* God's people to the tabernacle or the temple. At the trumpet's sounding, all Israel would come together and stand before the presence of the Lord. Then they would respond to Him and hear His Word.

The Angel With the Trumpet

In September 2005 I was alone at home when I had a dramatic encounter with the Lord. It was about two o'clock in the morning, and I was in my bedroom. For some reason I could not go to sleep, so I was awake, praying and meditating on the Lord. Suddenly, with my eyes wide open, I looked straight ahead and saw what appeared to be an angel in front of me. I sat up, rubbed my eyes, and looked to the right and the left, but he remained there, as real as the furniture in my room. I was stunned.

This kind of thing does not happen to me very often. In more than forty years of ministry I have had only five to ten supernatural encounters with the Lord, and none of them were like this one. This was certainly the only time that I have seen an angel face-to-face. So obviously I was paying close attention.

What I saw was relatively short and simple. The angel did not look at me, nor did he speak to me. He held a large trumpet in his hand, and I watched him raise his face toward heaven and lift the trumpet as if he was going to blow it. He slowly brought the instrument to his mouth, but it never touched his lips.

Then he was gone.

I sat there in utter bewilderment. I could not seem to shake two thoughts: First, "I just saw an angel!" Second, "What in the world just happened?!" I had no idea what this meant or why I had seen an angel. But as I lingered in shock, he reappeared to me.

Again he held a trumpet. Again he brought the trumpet to his mouth. And again the trumpet never touched his lips. Then he disappeared again.

This time I was even more perplexed. I looked around the room and wondered what was going on. What was the Lord trying to tell me, and what was His message in sending a trumpet-wielding angel?

Soon after the angel appeared a third time and did the same thing. Once again the trumpet never touched his lips.

Obviously I did not go to sleep anytime soon after that. In fact, the presence of the Lord rested on me for another hour or two. As my thoughts became clearer, He reminded me of Numbers 10 and of the dual purpose of trumpets being sounded in Israel's time. Again, the trumpet had two functions: to warn people that disaster is coming and to call people to gather at the temple to pray. Keep in mind that in Scripture the temple is also called the "house of prayer" (Isa. 56:7).

The meaning of what I saw became crystal clear: the Lord is warning us of great trouble coming to America. It will be a time of unrest that most people never thought possible in our land. And the Lord is sounding this alarm to let the church in particular know that turmoil is coming. Yes, revival will come, but so will trouble.

Yet the Lord is also sounding the trumpet as a rallying call to gather believers to pray. This is not just an individual calling; He is summoning the church to assemble to pray. He is blowing the trumpet to rally intercessors across the land. They will at times fill stadiums, high school auditoriums, church sanctuaries, and marketplace offices. God is beckoning those who will gather for solemn assemblies with prayer and fasting.

The good news is that this has already begun. I think of the ministry of Lou Engle, which is a helpful picture of God's raising up individuals as a "trumpet" to call people for the purpose of gathering and crying out to the Lord for mercy in a time of increasing crisis in our nation. For more than fifteen years the Lord has greatly used Lou to host large gatherings for prayer and fasting in fields, arenas, and stadiums. On April 9, 2016, he held his most recent—Azusa Now in Los Angeles—at which seventy thousand people came together in the pouring rain for fifteen hours to ask God to send another revival on the scale of the Azusa Revival of the early 1900s.[1] I believe God is raising up more trumpets like him today as a statement of His grace upon the United States.

SOUND THE TRUMPET

The charge to sound the trumpet is part of the forerunner calling. And for those heeding this call, God is asking the same question: *Will you sound the trumpet on My behalf?*

Remember, a forerunner simply goes ahead of something or someone with a message to prepare the way for others to respond. In the context of our Joel 2 response to the coming crisis, these forerunners can also be called "Day-of-the-Lord messengers" because their message is specific to His end-times purposes. God will anoint these Day-of-the-Lord messengers to alarm people of both the spiritual crisis (Ps. 2:3) and the natural crisis (vv. 5, 9).

The Lord wants His people to blow a trumpet and sound out His twofold message: that great trouble is coming (i.e., the Father's message of wrath in Psalm 2:5) and that we must gather in prayer (i.e., the Son's call to intercession in Psalm 2:7–9). We are to sound the alarm and rally God's people to turn to Him with all our hearts so that He will release His Spirit in the greatest outpouring in history.

You may never speak with a microphone to hundreds of people, but you can still sound the trumpet in your own sphere of influence, however big or small. You may alert only your family, your Bible-study group, or a few coworkers. Or you may alert tens of thousands who follow you on social media. Whatever the scope of your influence, the Lord is calling you to sound the trumpet. He wants you to use your time, money, resources, and influence to blow the trumpet and alert people to the coming trouble so they can respond to the Lord in the way He desires.

Notice that Joel 2:1 says to "blow the trumpet *in Zion*" (NKJV, emphasis added). Zion represents the people of God, which means the primary focus of this exhortation is not to the unbelieving world but to believers. Those who are walking in covenant with Jesus are the ones who are to cry out to God to make a spiritual difference in their businesses, schools, churches, cities, or nations. The only hope we have begins in the place of prayer. True change begins as the church cultivates a culture of prayer, and it is the blowing of the trumpet that will call the people of God.

The Lord said that if His people will repent and cry out, He will heal their land (2 Chron. 7:14). This scripture has been at the forefront of God's call to the church in America for many years, but particularly as we have witnessed the dramatic shift in our culture over the past few years. And God continues to raise up people willing to sound the trumpet to remind His people of this call to turn to Him in prayer. For example, I am blessed by Bob and Darla Vander Plaats' national prayer initiative that is called simply "If 7:14." A movement of renewal and revival based on 2 Chronicles 7:14, it is aimed to help people answer the call to pray for revival. The ministry developed an "If 7:14" app that helps remind people to pray each day at 7:14 a.m. and 7:14 p.m. (Visit if714.org for more information and to download the app.) I encourage everyone to join with others across the nation to stop for a minute at these times and to humble themselves, pray and seek God's face, and repent of sin in their own lives.

A CORPORATE TREMBLING

The church's first response to the coming crisis is to blow the trumpet and sound the alarm. We are called to do this in such a way that it causes those who hear to tremble.

> Let all the inhabitants of the land *tremble*; for the day of the LORD is coming, for it is at hand.
>
> —JOEL 2:1, NKJV, EMPHASIS ADDED

For many, this sounds absurd. They understand the purpose of blowing the trumpet. It is a noble thing to warn others of impending trouble. And it is even more honorable to call people to corporate prayer. But what is the purpose of speaking in a way that causes people to *tremble*?

We are accustomed to hearing Sunday sermons that inspire us to receive more blessing. I love speaking the Word of God in a way that brings faith for blessing to God's people. I also love preaching that warms or tenderizes my heart because it focuses on God's love. One of my favorite messages is on Jesus as the Bridegroom King. Oh, how I love to share that message with people and watch their hearts melt before a tender, loving God!

But there is another type of preaching that makes the heart tremble. When was the last time you heard a message that made you tremble? You may never have heard one because unfortunately this type of sermon has almost disappeared in the body of Christ in modern times. Preaching that makes people tremble is not popular, and it is not seeker-sensitive. In fact, if you are a pastor looking to grow your congregation in size, you may want to shy away from giving too many messages that make people tremble.

Why? Because a "trembling message" reminds people of the certainty of God's wrath and judgments. It tells the truth about this God who, while infinitely loving, is also perfectly just, holy, and righteous. When our preaching causes people to tremble with sobriety, we have reminded them of how truly majestic, powerful, and "terrifying" our God is and how zealous He is for His people and His purposes on the earth. This kind of preaching is necessary, just as preaching on God's joy and His love is necessary.

We cannot offer only messages that make people rejoice in the Lord or have tender affection for Him. Just as David's words in Psalm 2:10–12 included an element of trembling before the Lord, so we need to include in our messages the whole counsel of God, not only a limited part. But part of the reason Joel 2:1 says "Let all the inhabitants of the land tremble" (NKJV) is that the Holy Spirit, who inspired the prophet to write these words, knew that in the end times God's awesome power and judgments would be taken for granted. He knew that amid the growing deception in the church—including the distorted grace message and an overemphasis on personal blessing—the church would lose sight of the reality of the Lord's wrath amid the end-time distress that will come to the nations.

We must keep the entirety of God's character and purpose in mind. One of the ways we can do this is to meditate on Joel 2:11. Verse 1 already indicated why God's people should corporately tremble—"for the day of the LORD is coming, for it is at hand"; verse 11 expands on the reason when it describes this time as "great and very terrible" (NKJV).

The Day of the Lord will usher in the greatest revival ever seen. That is, of course, glorious news! But the Day of the Lord will also usher in a time of tribulation that will culminate with Jesus's return. There will be seasons of national and international crisis before the great and final end-time crisis. I believe what we are currently experiencing is the early days of this season of increasing trouble in the nations.

One day in November 2008, when I was wide-awake, I saw an open vision that was like a three-by-three display movie screen on my wall. I saw a massive number of tanks going across America— through streets, hills, cities, and countryside. I was not sure what it meant; I think it speaks of a time when martial law will be called in America. But I sensed that this was worse than martial law, and it was difficult to imagine that this was the same America where I lived. This was the only open vision that I have ever had, and it shook me. I could not help but respond with increased fervency in prayer and intercession for our nation.

Beloved, we need to be shaken in the same way. We must tremble in a healthy yet holy fear of the Lord. We must have seasons of sobriety as we realize God's awesome power and what He will do to those who continue to oppose Him during His great "day." From that balanced place that includes rejoicing in Him, loving on Him, and trembling before Him, we can do what comes next in Joel's blueprints for our corporate response: we can turn to Him with all our hearts.

TURNING TO GOD

In Joel 2:12 the Lord gives a clear directive for responding in the face of crisis:

> Yet even now, declares the LORD, return to Me with all your heart, and with fasting and with weeping and with mourning.

We can do this individually. In fact, part of the forerunner's message is to call individuals to repent of sin and compromise. Many people stop short at understanding repentance when they define it as simply "turning from sin." They believe that turning away from such things as pornography, lying, bitterness, jealousy, and covetousness is enough. But true repentance involves a change of mind and heart that results in not only turning *away* from something but also turning *to* God. As we change our minds and hearts and turn toward God in the spirit of true repentance, then our actions change too. As Paul says in Acts 26:20, "I preached that they should repent and turn to God and demonstrate their repentance by their deeds" (NIV).

We turn to God individually through true repentance. Yet turning to God with all our hearts is not only an individual thing; it applies also on a corporate level. In fact, more happens when God's people turn to the Lord in unity and within the context of being a corporate family.

We collectively turn to God by corporately gathering and together calling on His name. We respond to His love as the body of Christ by loving Him, and one way we express that love is through corporate repentance, fasting, and prayer. In His faithfulness God will respond as a Father hearing the cry of His beloved family.

I believe an environment of corporate wholeheartedness in obedience and faith is the safest place on the earth, and that is especially true in a time of God's judgment. I want to be in the midst of a people who are developing a corporate, long-term history in wholeheartedly turning to God. As we turn to Him with all our hearts and respond in this way to Jesus's work on the cross, we can walk in God's favor, protection, and provision even in a time of judgment.

CORPORATE FASTING

Joel 2 shows us specifically how we are to respond in the face of crisis. It starts by sounding the alarm ("blow[ing] the trumpet") and alerting people of the coming disaster (v. 1, NKJV). Though our message may not be popular among the masses, we are to warn believers specifically of the coming trouble to the degree that we understand it. We also blow the trumpet to assemble the people so that they will turn to God—personally and collectively—with all their hearts.

In Joel 2:15–17 we find further instructions for how to respond by gathering together as the corporate body of Christ in our cities:

> Blow the trumpet in Zion, *consecrate a fast, call a sacred assembly*; gather the people, sanctify the congregation, assemble the elders....Let the priests, who minister to the LORD, weep between the porch and the altar.
>
> —NKJV, EMPHASIS ADDED

As we gather, we are to "consecrate a fast," which simply means we set apart specific periods of time for corporate fasting.

In Joel's time Israel was absolutely helpless and once again needed God's intervention to deliver them. Their crisis was twofold. First, they were experiencing an agricultural crisis due to the swarms of locusts and severe drought that were crippling the farming industry, which led to severe economic problems throughout the nation (Joel 1). Second, the mighty Babylonian army was crouching at their borders, preparing for a military invasion (Joel 2).

Joel—and probably most Israelites—knew that God had allowed both crises as a form of judgment, so the prophet encouraged the people to throw themselves at His feet and, through fasting and prayer, to cry out to Him for mercy so that He might spare them from the coming judgments.

Corporate fasting in the face of a national crisis is demonstrated elsewhere in the Bible through such examples as the sinful Assyrian city of Nineveh, where residents humbled themselves through fasting and repented before God upon hearing Jonah's preaching regarding His judgment. The result was that the Lord spared their city (Jon. 3:3–10).

People at various times throughout history other than biblical times have responded to crisis as the Ninevites did. The people of Britain are a good example. They proclaimed a national fast when Spain's "Invincible Armada" (1588), Napoleon's army (1805), and Hitler's Nazis (1940) threatened to invade England—and in each instance the British experienced improbable victories that even unbelievers still call "miraculous."[2] Likewise several American presidents have declared national days of prayer and fasting throughout our country's relatively young history.

These leaders all understood the need for their nations to fast and cry out to God for His salvation when there was no other answer. Fasting increases our capacity to respond wholeheartedly to the Lord. It positions us to receive more from Him. It is, ultimately, an outward sign of an inward desperation for God.

We do not fast to earn His favor; we fast instead to position ourselves in God's grace to receive more of the Holy Spirit's activity on our hearts. When we fast, it is as if we position our cold hearts before God's burning fire, asking Him to set us ablaze with tender love for Him.

Fasting also positions us to cooperate with the Lord in changing circumstances in history. We become agents of change for the Lord's agenda—His plans for towns, districts, cities, regions, nations, and beyond.*

In chapter 2 I mentioned how in May 1983 the young adult church I was pastoring went on a twenty-one-day corporate fast. We met together to pray for many hours each day while we fasted. Though the fast did many things, one of the most profound results was that the Lord spoke powerfully with a promise that one day He would move in our midst and enable us to establish 24/7 prayer led by full worship teams. This became one of the most significant assignments and promises the Lord gave us, and more than thirty years later it still rings true. Yet it is important to note that this came in the context of a corporate time of prayer with fasting and turning to the Lord with all our hearts. The Lord honors our times of corporate prayer with fasting, even though we usually feel weak while engaging in them together. We may not think much is accomplished through our times of praying and fasting together, but God sees and measures things differently.

Fasting and prayer should always go hand in hand. As South African pastor Andrew Murray wrote, "Prayer is the one hand with which we grasp the invisible; fasting, the other, with which we let loose and cast away the visible.... Prayer is the reaching out

---

* For more on fasting, I encourage you to read my book *The Rewards of Fasting*, which goes into far greater detail on the topic than I do here.

after God and the unseen; fasting, the letting go of all that is of the seen and temporal."[3]

Combining fasting and prayer is not a magic formula, as if we could wave a magic wand at God and—*poof!*—His supernatural power is released as He suddenly responds to our requests. It is not the actual act of fasting and prayer that moves the heart of God; it is the wholeheartedness of our deep agreement with God's heart. This is a key point for us to keep in mind because some people assume that they earn God's favor by fasting, and in doing so, they end up overemphasizing fasting and missing the main point of Joel 2:12–17.

God desires us to fast and pray because He is ultimately after our hearts. Fasting and prayer are expressions of wholeheartedness. Fasting leads to our hearts being tenderized before God. And as our hearts are moved with greater tenderness and faith that is in agreement with God, then with increased tenderness and faith we in turn touch God's heart. When we fast and pray, we intensify our agreement with God because our hearts become more aligned with His and the connection between them more enriched.

Remember, God is after intimate relationship with His people. He has chosen to use prayer and fasting as a way to partner with us through relationship. He is not after merely increasing His workforce or getting us to prove our sincerity to Him through extended times of prayer and fasting; He desires our friendship. And as we gather corporately to fast, we collectively express our wholehearted friendship with Him. What a genius plan He made!

Solemn Assemblies

Another way we respond to the growing crisis is by gathering in solemn assemblies. We assemble God's people for corporate prayer and fasting—referred to by Joel as solemn (or sacred) assemblies. Twice in the first two chapters of Joel the Lord declares that in crises He not only wants but also *requires* that His people gather in solemn assemblies.

A solemn assembly takes place when people join together to

repent and fast and pray for the intervention of God's power and mercy. It accomplishes more than what a lone ranger intercessor can accomplish in prayer, though God values individual prayer. He wants His people to be in unity together, laboring together. He is not just the captain of an army who wants only soldiers; He is a Father who wants a family that operates together. He says to us, "I want you to gather together."

"Well, Lord, I don't really like the way that group does things. I'm not into their style, and to be honest, Lord, I think some of their theology is a bit off."

"That's OK," the Lord says. "Just put that aside and gather before Me."

I find it intriguing that so many believers have never considered God's command to gather for solemn assemblies. I have met many mature believers over the years—people who have walked with the Lord for decades—who have never been part of a solemn assembly. Yet the encouraging truth is that these types of gatherings are springing up all over the earth in this hour of history. People are responding to God's clear instructions in Joel 2.

The response God requires is the same today as it was in Joel's generation. A solemn assembly is called "solemn" because it is so. I appreciate the Modern English Version's use of the term *sacred assembly* in verse 15 because this gathering needs to be approached as a sacred, holy, "set-aside" meeting that is anything but business as usual. However, I think the term *solemn assembly*, used in many other Bible translations, such as the English Standard Version, is more descriptive and fitting. At times we must approach prayer in a solemn spirit because of the seriousness of the crisis building in our nation.

There are times for rejoicing, and there are times for crying. And when we stare straight into the face of national and global crisis, we are to be solemn and *weep*. In verse 12 God tells the Israelites to turn "with fasting and with weeping and with mourning." And in verse 17 He tells the priests to weep "between the temple porch and the altar."

We are a nation that, in the aftermath of any tragedy, would rather pick ourselves up by reminiscing about the past or making bigger and bolder plans for the future. And in the face of imminent tragedy, many people become more defiant. Yet God tells His people to weep. To consider both the gravity of the nation's sin and the intensity of the coming crisis. To stop and grieve over the culture's celebration of immorality. To meditate and mourn over just how far we have fallen into our unbelief and disregard for the Lord.

As we weep and mourn, the Lord says to also "rend your heart, and not your garments" (v. 13). To rend something means to tear it violently, and in ancient Israel people would show grief by rending or tearing their garments. Tearing their clothes indicated the depth of their grief. It was a symbolic demonstration of how much pain they were experiencing.

Our timeless God says the same thing to us today as He did to the Israelites in Joel's time: "Don't bother tearing your clothes—I'm more interested in your heart condition. I don't want a symbolic demonstration or just a public show of grief. I want you to tear your heart in such a way that you radically confront the issues in your heart that aren't in agreement with My heart."

Rending our hearts is challenging. It requires tearing ourselves away from everything in our lives that quenches the Holy Spirit. Many people want the Spirit to instantly free them from their sinful patterns and relationships without their having to make personal choices that might involve tearing their hearts. But Jesus showed that following Him not only costs something; it also requires radical obedience that involves a "tearing."

In Matthew 5:29 He said, "If your right eye causes you to sin, pluck it out and throw it away. For it is profitable that one of your members should perish, and not that your whole body to be thrown into hell." Obviously He was speaking figuratively. Similarly, when He says "rend your heart," He does not mean a literal tearing. Yet the point remains: we must weep and mourn over our sin to such a degree that we are willing to do whatever it takes to remove it from our lives.

We tear our hearts knowing that Jesus tore His heart when He went to the cross for us. Our hearts are rent knowing that the Father's was also when His only Son hung on the cross. He tore His own heart in His pursuit after us. By this He has proven that He does not love us in a detached, distant way. And He calls us to fully enter into this love, even when it requires that our own hearts be torn.

Solemn assemblies are indeed solemn because we return to God in a posture of prayer, knowing He is our only hope. For those of us who trust in the Lord and who will humble ourselves before Him, we throw ourselves at His feet, seeking His mercy even when we do not deserve it. We are solemn before the Lord because we recognize that the only way out, the only thing that can save us from our sinful ways, is God and His mercy and goodness.

A FOUNDATION OF PRAYER

The Joel 2 response to a Psalm 2 crisis is multifaceted, as we have seen. It involves several elements in the corporate context—from sounding the alarm to gathering for solemn assemblies—yet there is still one common thread that, while not spelled out directly in Joel 2, remains foundational to every expression.

Prayer.

This may seem obvious or even trivial to mention, and yet because Joel 2 does not specifically mention the word *prayer*, some can overlook the necessity of it while still attempting to respond as God wants. Yet prayer is intricately tied to each element we have looked at so far.

- We sound the alarm to alert people of impending trouble and to call them to pray.

- We tremble because we recognize the severity of the coming crisis and God's awesome power, and thus we are compelled to pray for mercy.

- We turn to God in prayer, crying out to Him for help in our time of need.

- We fast so that our hearts will be softened and aligned with His in prayer and so that we can partner with Him in prayer to change history.

- We gather in solemn assemblies so we can pray, seek His face, and collectively cry out for His mercy and provision.

As we see Psalm 2 becoming more of a reality in our time, and as more and more people in America grow in their defiance toward Jesus, we are helpless to find a remedy without crying out to Him, discovering what is on His heart, and engaging with Him in prayer.

Remember that prayer is, at its core, telling God what He has told us to tell Him. He gives us words to pray, and we repeat those words back to Him. It is literally that simple—so simple that many do not do it because it sounds too elementary. Indeed, prayer offends our minds. The notion that God would use such a simple method to change everything—His creation, our circumstances, laws, leaders, all of eternity—is foreign to our natural, logical mind-set.

If prayer is simply telling God what He has told us to tell Him, then in many people's opinion it is, to put it bluntly, foolishness. Yet as Paul says:

> God has chosen the foolish things of the world to confound the wise. God has chosen the weak things of the world to confound the things which are mighty.
>
> —1 CORINTHIANS 1:27

People may see prayer as foolish and weak, but, in fact, through it God releases His strength because it expresses our reliance on Him. Remember, the Lord wants partnership. He desires authentic relationship with Him, not robotic service. And prayer reflects our wholeheartedness to Him. The Lord, in His incomprehensible wisdom, has chosen to use prayer as the means by which He releases

His power on the earth. It is the channel through which we feel His presence the most and receive His love, which changes everything.

This is why He calls us, His people, to a corporate Joel 2 response. The Joel 2 response is built on the foundational element of prayer. It is one thing to individually "return to the LORD" (Joel 2:13); God certainly honors that. But when we come as a collective unit, corporately turning to Him with all our hearts (v. 12) by obeying the commands He has given us, then we enter into a new arena. Then we shift into the second half of Joel 2, in which the Lord responds to our prayers. Then we move into the wondrous things believers like to focus on: an end-times outpouring of the Holy Spirit that, like the one described in Acts 2, dramatically changes the world. I will say it again: *the Psalm 2 crisis requires a Joel 2 response, resulting in an Acts 2 outpouring of the Spirit.*

Chapter 9

CONTENDING FOR AN ACTS 2 OUTPOURING OF THE SPIRIT

JOEL 2 GIVES US a blueprint for how the church is to respond to the growing crisis. It describes elements that God desires us to engage in corporately and with all our hearts so that we will find His blessing, protection, and provision even in a time of judgment. Yet the outcome that both we and God ultimately seek is described clearly in the last verses of that chapter. After telling us to "blow the trumpet in Zion; consecrate a fast; [and] call a sacred assembly" (v. 15, NKJV), the Lord paints this prophetic picture:

> And it will be that, afterwards, I will pour out My Spirit on all flesh; then your sons and your daughters will prophesy, your old men will dream dreams, and your young men will see visions. Even on the menservants and maidservants in those days I will pour out My Spirit.
>
> —JOEL 2:28–29

What happened when this picture first became a reality? Acts 2 records what it was like during the first "installment" of Joel's prophesied outpouring of the Holy Spirit. What happened on the Day of Pentecost changed human history by igniting Spirit-empowered believers to walk in supernatural power for the sake of expanding God's kingdom on the earth. In the process people were healed, souls were saved, and the gospel persevered in the face of harsh opposition. Even then this "both-and" condition existed for the church: while believers faced horrible persecution, still "the Lord added to the church daily those who were being saved" (v. 47).

Isn't it interesting, then, that the very first explanation of what happened on the Day of Pentecost points directly to Joel 2? In the original text the prophet Joel stated, "And it will be that, *afterwards...*" (v. 28, emphasis added). At Pentecost Peter quoted a slightly different variation of verse 28 by replacing the word *afterward* with "in the last days":

> "In the last days it shall be," says God, "that I will pour out My Spirit on all flesh."
>
> —Acts 2:17

Though subtle, the difference is significant for us today. Peter indicated that his generation was living in "the last days," and to him the outpouring of the Holy Spirit confirmed this belief.

We are still waiting for the complete fulfillment of this prophecy—an even greater outpouring of the Holy Spirit than what happened at Pentecost, one in which "*all flesh*" will be affected. Indeed, the complete fulfillment of this prophecy involves an outpouring and revival that will dwarf all others.

Peter and the rest of Jesus's followers embraced one of the necessary conditions that Joel emphasized. It was reiterated by Jesus when He "commanded them, 'Do not depart from Jerusalem, but wait [in prayer] for the promise of the Father,'" which was the Holy Spirit (Acts 1:4).

As was the case in Peter's time, there is a conditional aspect to the greater outpouring of the end times, and it centers on the single word that Peter replaced: *afterward.*

The total fulfillment of Joel 2:28–32 will come *after* there has been a Joel 2:12–17 response of corporate prayer and waiting on God. This is precisely what the 120 on the Day of Pentecost in the Upper Room were in continual prayer for:

> When they had entered, they went up into the upper room, where they were staying: Peter, James, John, and Andrew;

> Philip and Thomas; Bartholomew and Matthew; James the
> son of Alphaeus and Simon the Zealot; and Judas the son of
> James. These all continued with one accord in prayer and
> supplication, with the women and Mary the mother of Jesus,
> and with His brothers.
>
> —Acts 1:13–14

God wants to pour out His Spirit in an even greater measure today as we face an increasing global crisis of Psalm 2 proportions. The Lord has promised that this last-days outpouring will affect *all flesh.* But He has also called His people to turn to Him with all their hearts, "with fasting and with weeping and with mourning" (Joel 2:12). He wants us to rend our hearts and return to Him (v. 13). He has called us to "blow the trumpet in Zion; consecrate a fast; [and] call a solemn assembly" (v. 15, NKJV).

This, as we saw in the last chapter, is the Joel 2 response we are called to as the bride of Christ. And *after* that happens—after we have responded in the way He has asked—then we will see an Acts 2 outpouring as promised. Remember, the Psalm 2 crisis *requires* a Joel 2 response, which *then* results in an Acts 2 outpouring of the Spirit.

Our Role and God's Sovereignty

If the end-time outpouring of the Holy Spirit in history is in context to the response of God's people to God, then we must begin to respond right now. Knowing that He requires this prayerful cooperation with Him changes how we live our lives, what we prioritize, and why we do certain things. In essence, it changes *everything.*

Yet many people balk at the notion that God's people somehow can affect God's actions during the last days—both His judgments and His blessings.

They think that because He is sovereign, omniscient, and omnipotent, responding to the prayers of His people instead of acting independently from human response would limit Him. After all, what kind of god would be so weak as to wait upon men and women to respond? The answer is—a God who deeply values relationship with His people.

Obviously God *is* sovereign. He *is* omniscient and omnipotent. He does not *have* to wait on anyone. But if we are serious students of His Word, we will notice that Scripture repeatedly presents "if-then" statements in which God sovereignly determines to "limit" the degree of His response according to the actions of His people:

> Now therefore, if you will faithfully obey My voice and keep My covenant, then you shall be My special possession out of all the nations.
>
> —Exodus 19:5

> It will be, if you diligently obey My commandments which I am commanding you today, to love the Lord your God, and to serve Him with all your heart and with all your soul, then I will give you the rain of your land in its season, the early rain and the latter rain, that you may gather in your grain and your wine and your oil. I will provide grass in your fields for your livestock, that you may eat and be full.
>
> —Deuteronomy 11:13–15

> See, I am setting before you today a blessing and a curse: the blessing if you obey the commandments of the Lord your God, which I am commanding you today, and the curse, if you will not obey the commandments of the Lord your God, but turn from the way which I am commanding you today, to go after other gods which you have not known.
>
> —Deuteronomy 11:26–28

> If My people, who are called by My name, will humble themselves and pray, and seek My face and turn from their wicked ways, then I will hear from heaven, and will forgive their sin and heal their land.
>
> —2 Chronicles 7:14

If you have faith as a grain of mustard seed, you will say to this mountain, "Move from here to there," and it will move. And nothing will be impossible for you.

—MATTHEW 17:20

If you remain in Me, and My words remain in you, you will ask whatever you desire, and it shall be done for you.

—JOHN 15:7

For if you live according to the flesh, you will die, but if through the Spirit you put to death the deeds of the body, you will live.

—ROMANS 8:13

These verses merely scratch the surface of all the conditional statements contained in the Bible. Surely God does not lack anything. Isaiah taught the Lord waits to hear the prayers of His people:

Therefore the LORD will wait, that He may be gracious to you....Blessed are all those who wait for Him....He will be very gracious to you at the sound of your cry; when He hears it, He will answer you.

—ISAIAH 30:18–19, NKJV

He is not limited in His ability by our actions. He does not need to wait for people to "do their part" before He does His. Why, then, do we find so many "if-then" scenarios in Scripture linked to God's actions?

Herein lies the mystery of God's sovereignty: He *does* wait for us, and He *does* limit His actions based on our response. Why? Because He is a God of relationship.

He wants to partner with us in what He does on the earth. He wants to rule and reign in His kingdom *with* His people. He is a sovereign God who is also a Father, and Jesus is a Bridegroom King. He is a not just a God of power *over* His people but a God of desire *for* His people. Yes, He is a God of relationship.

In the context of an Acts 2 outpouring that depends on a Joel 2 response, God wants to release His power as we respond to Him in relationship. He wants us to know that the way we respond to Him really does make a difference.

That their response matters is difficult for many believers to accept because they have a wrong idea about the sovereignty of God. They think that because God is sovereign, He will do whatever He wants regardless of what His people do. No! In fact, the opposite is true. *Because* God is sovereign, He has *chosen* in His sovereignty to limit His actions so that He can partner with His people. His people are not just passive observers but active participants with His heart and His kingdom purposes. What we do makes a difference to what He does in our nations or businesses or families or ministries. Partnering with Him is a remarkable privilege!

Some believers are content to stand back passively and "trust God's sovereignty." To do so is to misapply the biblical truth of His sovereignty, and this will yield bad fruit in our lives. We will miss out on the fullness of what God has in store for us because we never seize the opportunity He has given us to partner with Him in His activity on the earth.

If God's people are active participants with Him in expanding His kingdom on the earth, then they have a role in determining in part how the end times will unfold. Granted, God's Word already declares the final results of the main events. We know Jesus will win; we know He will cast Satan into prison; we know that the Antichrist will be defeated, along with every other opposing force; and we even know some of the facts along the way (such as the scale of global damage inflicted by each of the seven seals, seven trumpets, and seven bowls mentioned in the Book of Revelation). However, we do not know how many people will be saved before Christ returns, nor do we know what geographic areas will experience a greater measure of God's glory or which will receive a greater intensity of His judgments.

Amid the strongest global opposition to Jesus, humanity's deepest moral depravity, and the most widespread falling away of believers in history, there will also be the greatest outpouring of the Holy

Spirit. This will occur in various places *after* God's people turn to Him with all their hearts (Joel 2:12–13) and *before* the Lord's second coming (v. 31). As believers become equipped with the understanding of Psalm 2 and respond with Joel 2 commitment, then we are positioned by grace—despite our personal weaknesses and brokenness—as partners with God in the unfolding of this great end-times harvest of souls related to the Joel 2 outpouring of the Holy Spirit. In God's sovereignty He has based some of what happens on the actions of His people.

I don't know how you respond to that truth, but it leaves me in awe. It gives our lives tremendous purpose, and it means that our choices to obey Him really matter.

"WHO KNOWS?"

The astounding truth of God's sovereignty means we also influence the timing and intensity of both His end-times *blessings*—the greatest outpouring of His Spirit—and His *judgments*. It is natural for us to focus on the blessings of this outpouring and the greatest harvest of souls in history. We like that. But what about God's judgments during this era? What role does the church play in those?

The answer is given in two short words in the heart of Joel 2:

> *Who knows?* He may turn and relent and leave behind a blessing.
> —JOEL 2:14, NIV, EMPHASIS ADDED

Who knows? The New King James translation continues the question by asking, "Who knows if He will turn and relent?" Who knows if our prayers, our solemn assemblies, and our gatherings to cry out to Him for mercy will indeed cause the Lord to withhold His judgments and instead release greater blessing?

I am sometimes asked if certain disasters can be stopped through prayer. Inevitably the question leads to a series of others that attempt to understand God's seemingly unpredictable response to our prayers. Why does God answer some prayers to avert His judgments but not others? Why does He seem to delay in answering some prayers for the outpouring of the Holy Spirit while others are answered much faster?

Who knows? Certainly none of us.

Is it possible, however, that we are focusing on the wrong question? We often do not know the why behind some of God's response. But what we do know is that God *may* answer our prayers to avert judgment and to pour out His Spirit in a greater measure, and it *may* be when we ask. I believe this is essentially what the prophet Joel meant in chapter 2 when he used the phrase "Who knows?" We do not know if or when God will relent from His judgments on a certain place, people, or situation. Nor do we know if instead He will decide to extend mercy and "leave behind a blessing" (Joel 2:14). Joel essentially says that we never know when the Lord will break in with a greater measure of blessing, nor do we know when He will delay, thwart, or even stop impending trouble.

Trouble comes in different forms, different measures, and different time frames. Sometimes trouble will come to a nation in the economic realm but may disturb only part of that nation. Meanwhile another part of the nation may be experiencing agricultural troubles via droughts or storms. Still another region may be completely at peace during this time yet only months later see major civil unrest with riots in urban areas and uprisings against local law enforcement. Who knows *when* trouble will come to a nation, *how* it will come, *where* it will come, *whom* it will come to, *why* it will come, or *what* will actually come?

Who knows but God?

By the same token, who—other than God—knows when the Lord will delay such trouble? He may postpone trouble for ten or twenty years. He may minimize a catastrophe that was to originally head a nation's way. Or He may even cancel the calamity entirely. Which is it, then?

Joel gives the same answer: *Who knows?*

Even prayer warriors and intercessors who regularly hear God's voice—those who spend extensive time talking with Him in prayer—ask the Lord for insight regarding trouble. "Lord, which part of my nation will be shaken? What will happen? When will it happen, Lord? Will it be this year or in ten or twenty years? Will You protect my city from trouble—fully or partially? Will You protect my family from this disaster?"

The same is true with blessing: "When will You touch the businesses in our area with greater economic blessing, Lord? When will You send a mighty revival? God, when will You raise up leaders to reverse the laws of abortion? When will You establish houses of prayer in every city of our state?"

These are all great questions to ask, especially when the intent is truly to contend in prayer for God's kingdom purposes to break through. Naturally we want to know the details of how and where and with what measure the Lord will break in with greater blessing if we cry out to Him. But the Lord does not give us all those details regarding what types of blessings He will release or to what measure they will be released or where they will be released. He simply says, "Repent, cry out for mercy, and trust Me with the details."

I have since learned the Lord rarely tells us in detail what will happen in our nation or city. He may provide bits and pieces of information, but He does not give His people all the specific details of what measure of blessing He will leave behind in a particular region.

Why would the Lord do this? Why would He withhold information? After all, doesn't He want relationship?

In fact, that is exactly why He does *not* reveal all the details. The Lord does not want His people putting their hope in the specific details of a breakthrough. He wants us to trust in Him as we repent and return to Him with all our hearts. He leaves us simply with the knowledge that His desire is to relent from judgment and instead grant blessing.

The Lord delights in releasing blessing and finds no pleasure in judgment. As 2 Peter 3:9 says, the Lord "does not want any to perish, but all to come to repentance." And in Ezekiel 18:32 the Lord says, "I have no pleasure in the death of anyone who dies.... Therefore, repent and live." God's desire is to turn "would-be disaster zones" on this earth into "revival centers of blessing." He wants cities, states, regions, and nations to turn to Him so He can bless them and transform their societies with His blessings.

Though we want to know the details of those blessings, what He wants is for us to know His heart and to trust it. We can have confidence in knowing that He is gracious and extremely kind, and that His leadership is trustworthy.

PREVENTING JUDGMENT

Knowing the truth about how God feels about people—His heart for us—is essential to understanding His blessings and judgments. Conversely, not knowing this is one reason why some will fall away from their faith in the end times. They will not know the truth about how God feels tender compassion for them or toward the people who live around them, and as a result they will take offense at Him when He does not respond in the way they think He should. When we do not trust God's heart and His leadership, it is virtually impossible to develop true relationship that can stand strong through trials. And no generation in history will experience as many pressures as the generation in which the Lord returns.

In the Book of Zephaniah we find the prophet dealing with a national crisis, just as Joel did. The people of Judah faced a time of judgment. Like Joel, Zephaniah tells the people to return to the Lord by gathering themselves for solemn assemblies of prayer. Notice how often Zephaniah calls the people to gather *before* the increased trouble starts. He emphasized this by using the word *before* four times in this short passage.

> Gather together, yes, gather together, O shameless nation, *before* the decree takes effect, *before* the day passes like chaff, *before* the fierce anger of the LORD comes upon you, *before* the day of the LORD's anger comes upon you. Seek the Lord, all you humble of the land, who carry out His

judgment. Seek righteousness, seek humility. *Perhaps you
will be hidden* on the day of the LORD's anger.
—ZEPHANIAH 2:1–3, EMPHASIS ADDED

Once again God calls a small group of godly people—"all you
humble of the land, who carry out His judgment" (v. 3)—to seek
Him in prayer and intercession on behalf of the nation. It is the
same for us today as we face a looming end-times crisis. The size
of our gatherings is not what matters most; they may be a family
meeting in the living room, a gathering of leaders of a church (or
churches), or an outreach ministry in a university. It does not
have to be thousands of people coming together; sometimes there
may be only five or ten people gathering after work.

What matters is not how many gather but *how* we gather. Much
happens when we come united in a spirit of repentance and trust
before the Lord. Of course it is good to turn to the Lord in private, but God is moved when we turn to Him corporately with
our brothers and sisters in the Lord in a unity that expresses His
very heart.

It is imperative that we recognize another biblical principle
behind God's judgments and His instructions to "turn to Me with
all your heart" (Joel 2:12, NKJV). When we turn to God with all
our hearts, the Lord may minimize, delay, or even cancel a judgment that has already been decreed in heaven. Stated another way,
it is possible for God to issue a judgment in the court of heaven
and yet, in response to our prayers, change the intensity or measure of that judgment before it actually reaches the earth. That our
prayers affect God's judgments is a remarkable truth!

We see this principle revealed in part in Zephaniah 2, which
offers a glimpse of how prayers, decrees, and judgments (or blessings) are "processed" in heaven. Zephaniah distinguishes between
the moment when "the decree [of judgment] takes effect" *in heaven*
and the moment when "anger of the LORD comes upon" people
on the earth (v. 2). This means there is a period of time—a "gap"—
between these two things. We see this gap principle throughout the

Old Testament as God repeatedly delays the release of His judgments on the earth even though they have been "issued" in heaven.

The Lord decrees a judgment from the courts around His sovereign throne in heaven. Yet just because a decree is issued in the heavenly realm does not mean God has released it into the natural realm yet. Thus when God's people—those in a covenant relationship with Him—gather to cry out to Him before the heavenly decree is released on the earth, there is still a chance God will relent and change the course or measure of that decree. In fact, this is exactly why Zephaniah was encouraging the people of Judah to gather together in prayer.

Just as Joel asked "Who knows?," which related to the possibility of God's relenting, Zephaniah says that when God's people gather together to return to the Lord, *perhaps* something different happens than what was decreed in heaven. The New King James Version uses the phrase "it may be" (Zeph. 2:3). In other words, there is still a possibility. When we gather together in prayer and intercession, crying out to God to have mercy on our land, *perhaps* God will not only hear our cries but also in response minimize, delay, or even cancel His judgment even though it has already been decreed in heaven. Who knows? It may be!

HIDDEN FROM JUDGMENT

Zephaniah 2:3 reveals yet another important principle for believers to remember as we respond in prayer to the impending crisis. The prophet mentions, "Perhaps *you will be hidden* on the day of the LORD's anger" (emphasis added).

We can actually pray that we will be hidden or protected in the midst of a time when God releases His judgments. As believers we know there is no greater protection from trouble than to be hidden in the Lord. Yet this remarkable truth, combined with Zephaniah 2:3, means that if the Lord releases a judgment over a nation, those who turn to Him may still be hidden or find protection in the time of that crisis.

Even if we live in a nation or among a people group who are

facing such judgment, it may be that we can experience what I refer to as "pockets of mercy." These pockets of mercy keep people "hidden" under the shadow of the Lord's hand even while everyone everywhere else faces His judgment. Like the Israelites during the first Passover, we may be hidden or protected as the Lord allows angels of judgment to bring His just consequences upon the earth.

This is not an assured promise. God may have a greater plan for us in standing strong amid the increasing troubles of His judgments. But the Bible is also full of examples of how God's people were often "hidden on the day of the LORD's anger" (Zeph. 2:3), which gives us hope and a reason to press on in prayer for Him to have mercy.

For example, Israel's greatest disaster, as described in the Old Testament, was the destruction of Jerusalem and the burning of the temple in 586 BC by the mighty Babylonian army. God had repeatedly warned the Israelites not to worship demons and other gods, yet they refused to turn to the Lord. As a result, He raised up the Babylonian king Nebuchadnezzar and allowed the majority of Israelites to endure judgment because He loved them and wanted them to turn to Him.

Prior to this disaster God commissioned angels to "go through the midst of the city, through the midst of Jerusalem, and set a mark upon the foreheads of the men who sigh and groan for all the abominations that are done in its midst" (Ezek. 9:4). The Lord literally marked for protection those who, despite the godlessness of their surrounding culture, remained faithful in crying out to the Lord. These men were the few who likely gathered together to pray for God's mercy, and they were protected in the midst of a terrible judgment in Jerusalem.

The Lord did not relent from sending judgment on Jerusalem by the Babylonians, but He certainly hid the faithful remnant who prayed. Amid Jerusalem's total destruction—including the slaughter of women and children, young and old—God told His angels to spare anyone who cried out for His righteousness in that city (Ezek. 9:5–6).

As God's people cry out to the Lord in the face of future judgments, *perhaps* the Lord would have the same mercy on those who faithfully seek Him, so that we too would be hidden or protected amid His righteous judgment.

PRAYERS THAT CHANGE THE COURSE OF A NATION

We can be assured that God is ultimately in control of where, when, and from whom judgment is withheld and mercy and blessing are given instead. He alone makes it rain on one city while withholding rain from another in a time of drought (Amos 4:7). In fact, one of the most remarkable elements of God's mercy in the context of His judgment is that at various times in history the Lord has changed the fate of an entire nation due to the prayers of godly believers.

If you do not think your prayers matter, think again—they do! And as you consider this truth, take a look at just three of the many cases the Bible records of those whose history-changing prayers made the difference between blessing and judgment.

King Josiah

Josiah lived in the same generation in which Babylon destroyed Jerusalem. Both his father and grandfather were wicked kings of Judah, yet Josiah "did what was correct in the eyes of the LORD" (2 Chron. 34:2). Despite Josiah's own godliness, the people he ruled still worshipped other gods and refused to turn to the Lord. As a result of their persistent sinfulness, the prophets told Josiah that trouble was coming and that Jerusalem would be razed to the ground.

Josiah's response revealed his true colors, which so moved the Lord that He said this to the king:

> Because your heart was tender and you humbled yourself
> before God when you heard His words against this place
> and those who dwell here, and you have brought yourself
> low before Me and torn your clothes and wept before Me, I
> have heard you, declares the LORD. I am bringing you to be

with your fathers, and you will be brought to your grave in peace, and your eyes will not see all the disaster that I am bringing on this place and on those who dwell here.

—2 CHRONICLES 34:27–28

Because of Josiah's commitment to the Lord and his lifestyle of crying out to God on behalf of his nation, the Lord actually delayed His judgments against Judah. This one man caught God's attention to such an extent that He altered history on his behalf. Following God's assurance that Josiah would not see Jerusalem destroyed, the king successfully brought the people of Judah and Israel back to a posture of truly worshipping God and walking according to His covenant—"to walk after the LORD, and to keep His commandments and His testimonies and His statutes with all [their] soul" (v. 31).

Amos

God called a shepherd named Amos to warn God's people about the judgment they had brought on themselves due to their idolatry and sinfulness. Though he was from the southern kingdom of Judah, Amos traveled north to Israel to deliver his prophetic message, part of which is shared in Amos 7. The Lord revealed two visions to the prophet, both of which involved Israel's being overrun by disaster.

The first vision showed the Lord sending locusts upon the crops (Amos 7:1–3). The resulting destruction of crops would create an agricultural disaster, which would lead to a national economic catastrophe. Though just one man, Amos pleaded with the God of the universe to forgive the Israelites and save them from sure ruin. Because of his cry the Lord showed mercy and relented from sending the locusts.

In the second vision Amos saw the Lord sending a terrible fire that "was consuming the great deep and was devouring the fields" (v. 4). Though this could be a literal fire, scholars believe it could also describe a massive drought affecting the entire Middle East. Undoubtedly such a "fire" would have crippled Israel agriculturally and economically. Once again Amos cried out for God to have mercy on Israel, "for he is small" (v. 2). And once again God relented because of the cry of one man—a shepherd, no less.

Moses

On several occasions Moses vented to God about the Israelites' stubbornness, and the Lord reassured him of His plans for His people. Yet in Exodus 32 we find the tables slightly turned after the Israelites made a golden-calf representation of God and began to worship it and make sacrifices to it. The Lord was so enraged that He told Moses, who was meeting with Him privately atop Mount Sinai, "Let Me alone, so that My wrath may burn against them and I may destroy them" (v. 10). The Lord planned to wipe out the Israelites and start over with just Moses.

Despite his frequent frustration over the hard-heartedness of Israel, Moses pleaded with God to change His mind. "Turn from Your fierce wrath," Moses asked the Lord, "and relent of this harm against Your people" (v. 12). Once again God listened to the prayer of one of His servants. He spared Israel from the judgment they deserved (v. 14), even though He knew how often they would eventually turn from Him.

WHERE DOES THAT LEAVE US?

Each of these examples reveals the extravagant compassion of our God—a kindness that goes far beyond what is deserved. Today we live in an era of extravagant mercy and grace. Given our nation's growing defiance of the Lord and His ways, God's justice and righteousness could demand judgment—we certainly deserve it. And yet God continues to show mercy. As King David wrote, the Lord is "full of compassion and gracious, slow to anger, and abundant in mercy and truth" (Ps. 86:15).

The Lord remains compassionate by giving those who rage against Him more time. To use a cliché, we as a nation are truly living on borrowed time, just as the Israelites were in each of the examples above. Why are we living under such extreme mercy? Because God does not delight in releasing a severe judgment upon America or any other nation; He wants restoration of our nation and He desires for all to be saved. Likewise He is waiting for the nations to turn to Him in repentance. Even the wickedest nation has an opportunity:

> At one moment I may speak concerning a nation and con- cerning a kingdom to pluck up, and to pull down, and to destroy it. If that nation against which I have spoken *turns from its evil*, I will relent of the disaster that I thought to do to it.
> —JEREMIAH 18:7–8, EMPHASIS ADDED

Not only is God waiting for nations to turn to Him, but also He is actually *seeking* intercessors who will pray these nations into His kingdom. This is how badly God wants people saved; He is *actively looking* for those who will "stand in the gap" and contend in prayer on behalf of even those wicked nations that hate Him and rage against Him (Ezek. 22:30). What an amazing God!

The Lord desires to see an Acts 2 outpouring of His Spirit more than we do. His purpose for humanity has always been for us to be His family so that we can experience His glory in relationship with Him. And in the days to come He has promised to cover the earth with His glory (Hab. 2:14). He wants as many people as pos- sible to be part of this glorious time. For this reason He is willing to minimize, delay, or even cancel any of His judgments that have been decreed in heaven and to release His blessings instead.

But I believe He is also waiting for His people to some degree to step up and do their part of the partnership. We often act as if it is only about us waiting on God. But the truth is that the bal- ance of the nations is somewhat in the hands of the people who are in covenant with the King of kings. The greatest outpouring of God's Spirit will happen just as promised but only in response to His people *contending* for it in prayer.

Yes, evil will increase in the days ahead, but so will righteousness.

And that is why I, along with many other leaders, am believing for one billion new souls in the end-time harvest (Rev. 7:9). The harvest will not "just happen," however. We must contend for it with the world's most powerful weapon—prayer. We have addressed God's response to the coming crisis throughout this book. But this—prayer—is, in fact, at the very heart of *our* response to the coming crisis. And as we pray, I believe the Lord will move on our behalf, just as He has always desired to do among His people.

Chapter 10

PUTTING TRUTH
INTO PRACTICE

T HE CHURCH WILL continue to be even more irrelevant when
it quotes letters from 2,000 years ago as their best defense."[1]
I could hardly believe what I was hearing. I expected a statement like that to come from an atheist, an agnostic, a humanist,
or someone still stewing from a bad experience with the church—
not from a *pastor*. Certainly not from a pastor who started a con-
servative evangelical church that quickly grew to more than ten
thousand people and who then became the voice for young con-
servative evangelicals everywhere. This was the same guy who had
been heralded as one of the most influential evangelical leaders
in the world. The guy whose books and videos were instant best
sellers. And the guy who was now sitting with Oprah on her television show claiming that the church's acceptance of same-sex
marriage is "inevitable" and that any church not endorsing it will
"continue to be even more irrelevant."[2]

I was not shocked by this leader's words regarding same-sex
marriage since he had given clues to his about-face on homosexuality in recent years. But his statement about the Bible was like a
punch to the gut because it was emblematic of the devastatingly
painful shift now occurring—not among unbelievers but *within*
the leadership of the body of Christ.

In previous chapters of this book I have referred to the great
falling away that will occur in the end times. Jesus warned
believers more about deception in the end times than anything

else. But sadly we do not have to look hard to find evidence that this fast-growing deception and falling away have already begun.

The debate over same-sex marriage takes most of the current headlines when it comes to mainstream culture's increasing rejection of biblical standards and disdain for believers who publicly stand up for them. But equally as disconcerting is the internal shift on other fundamental beliefs of our faith.

More pastors than ever before now hedge on saying Jesus is the only way to God and to salvation, while some go so far as to preach that there are many paths to heaven. Not long ago a California pastor held numerous Easter services in a mosque "as a needed expression of mutual respect between cultures" yet never once mentioned Jesus's death and resurrection. "I know that I don't believe in the physical resurrection of Jesus, but I do believe his spirit ascended and his teachings are very valid and transformative," the pastor said in an interview.[3] A recent study claims that only one in three young evangelicals now believes that Jesus is the only way to heaven.[4]

Other studies prove that more believers think the Bible is not necessarily the inspired Word of God. In general, 28 percent of Americans believe the Bible is "the actual Word of God" and not just an inspired text, according to a recent Gallup poll.[5] Shockingly that number is no different among believers. In 2001 41 percent of all professing Christian adults said the Bible is accurate;[6] today approximately 28 percent say that the Bible is "the actual word of God and should be taken literally."[7] In fact, almost half of all Americans think the Bible, the Quran, and the Book of Mormon are different expressions of the same truth.[8]

These are not encouraging statistics—and we have not even touched on what believers think the Bible has to say about topics such as sexuality, marriage, relationships, sin, and grace. Clearly a radical shift is taking place within the church. Mainstream culture's views on God and truth are now accepted by many believers more than what the Word of God says.

Evangelical believers are increasingly succumbing to secular beliefs, and as the crisis expands and Christ's return grows closer, we can expect them to continue to do so.

BIBLICAL TRUTHS BEING QUESTIONED

Before moving on to what we should do in light of these faith-shifts within the church, I believe it is important for us to identify some of the biblical truths that are currently on the "hot seat," so to speak. This is not meant to be a comprehensive list or a thorough explanation of what Scripture says about these essential truths. But it does give an indication of the extent to which even the most foundational biblical principles are now being questioned or even denied by those who profess to be Christians. Sadly more and more Christians are waffling in their stance on these issues.

Here are some of the biblical truths from which believers are drawing back due to the stigma related to them.

The Bible as the final authority on all matters of faith and practice

Once the authority of Scripture is questioned and rejected, people are left without biblical absolutes to determine what is true. God's Word is timeless; it is an eternal truth that applies to all humanity. Some people say that because the Bible is to be understood within its own time frame and context, we have the liberty to dismiss various moral commands of God as not being applicable to us. Thus they interpret and change the meaning of some passages by filtering them through the so-called "advanced understanding" of our time frame and context.

A prime example of this is how some people seek to make evolution fit with the biblical Creation account in Genesis by arguing that Adam was merely a symbolic figure rather than a literal man. Others follow this line of thought by arguing that large sections of the Old Testament are not really an account of God's perspective but are simply a story simply told through the lens of the ancient Israelites. They conclude, therefore, that neither God's agenda for Israel and the nations nor His moral requirements are literal.

Yet 2 Timothy 3:16 refutes their argument. It says, *"All* Scripture is given by inspiration of God, and is profitable for doctrine, for reproof, for correction, for instruction in righteousness" (NKJV, emphasis added). As Psalm 119:160 states, "The entirety of Your word is truth" (NKJV). And for those who doubt the validity of the Old Testament as God's account rather than just Israel's, Christ spoke directly on the matter when He said, "Do not think that I have come to abolish the Law or the Prophets. I have not come to abolish, but to fulfill. For truly I say to you, until heaven and earth pass away, not one dot or one mark will pass from the law until all be fulfilled" (Matt. 5:17–18).

When we begin dismissing parts of Scripture as merely symbolic—particularly when Scripture itself refrains from telling us to interpret it as such—then we tread on shaky ground and are mere steps away from falling into increased deception.

The divinity of Jesus Christ

Believing that Jesus is God is one of the most fundamental truths in the kingdom of God. We are to confess Jesus as Lord of all and follow Him as His disciples. Jesus said, "My Father and I are one" (John 10:30). It would take several pages to list the affirmations throughout Scripture that Jesus was indeed God in flesh upon the earth—fully God and fully man—that He now reigns in heaven, and that He will come again to rule on the earth with His bride.

The doctrine of Jesus as the only way to salvation

Despite what Oprah, Hollywood, and the rest of pop culture say, all roads and religions do not lead to God and salvation. Jesus clearly says, "I am the way, the truth, and the life. No one comes to the Father *except through Me*" (John 14:6, emphasis added). And Acts 4:12 reiterates Jesus's claim with Peter's words: "There is no salvation in any other, for there is no other name under heaven given among men by which we must be saved."

The reality of original sin and the need for Jesus's atonement

We must resist the "good without God" heresy, which claims that morality is linked to humanity needing only education and socialization rather than salvation and regeneration. Romans 3:23 says, "All have sinned and come short of the glory of God," while verse 10 of the same chapter says, "There is none righteous, no, not one." Because of Adam's original sin and our perpetuating nature of sin, we are born sinful. "But God demonstrates His own love toward us, in that while we were yet sinners, Christ died for us" (Rom. 5:8).

Jesus's substitutionary atonement for the sins of humankind

This theological phrase simply means that Jesus died in our place as a necessary sacrifice for our sins so that we could be reconciled to the Father. His death was for all humanity, for all time. Because He was the only sinless person to ever live, He was therefore the only perfect, unblemished "lamb" qualified to pay the price for our sins. Because of His sacrifice, "we have an Advocate with the Father, Jesus Christ the Righteous One. He is the atoning sacrifice for our sins, and not ours only, but also for the sins of the whole world" (1 John 2:1–2).

The grace of God freely given to empower us to live godly lives

As stated before, I believe the distortion of grace may be one of the biggest battles of our era within the church. Titus 2:11–12 makes it obvious what God's grace is truly about: "For the grace of God that brings salvation has appeared to all men, teaching us that, denying ungodliness and worldly desires, we should live soberly, righteously, and in godliness in this present world."

God's grace frees us from the law and freely provides us with full and final forgiveness for our sins—thank You, Lord! It empowers us to rest with confidence that we are fully accepted by God and to resist sin and walk in love with a spirit of obedience to Jesus and to do the works of the kingdom in deep partnership with Him and more. Many today proclaim the glorious truth of our free forgiveness and our freedom from the law but never call people to walk in a spirit of obedience to Jesus's leadership. Though I am grateful for anyone who emphasizes the glory of God's extravagant forgiveness and our freedom from the law, it is essential that we proclaim these truths in a way that does not give people "confidence" to walk in compromise and to not take seriously the call to resist sin and walk in obedience to Jesus.

The sanctity of marriage and sex

Immorality is defined as all sexual activity with someone outside the covenant of marriage between one man and one woman. Sexual immorality in the church occurs far more often between heterosexuals than between homosexuals. Yes, the Bible defines homosexual sex as sinful (Lev. 18:22; 20:13; Rom. 1:24–27; 1 Cor. 6:9–10), but Scripture actually says far more about heterosexual immorality (Matt. 5:8; 19:4–5; Eph. 5:5, 31; Heb. 12:16; 13:4; Rev. 22:15). As followers of Christ we must refuse a wrong application of tolerance, inclusion, and equality related to sexual immorality, and instead we must call God's people to the beauty and glory of walking in purity as defined by the Scriptures. All human beings are equal in their significance and value to God; however, not all lifestyle practices are pleasing to God (Rom. 1:18–32; Gal. 5:16–26; Eph. 4:17–5:7; Col. 3:1–17; Rev. 22:15).

The body of Christ is called to show love to all people and to give honor and dignity to all humans, regardless of their sexual orientation. We are not to participate in "homophobic prejudice and violence" against any who support the gay agenda but are instead to love all people—even those who fiercely oppose us or even vilify us. We are all fallen human beings who daily need grace in many areas of our lives. We can each find great hope in knowing that Jesus forgives all of us for immorality (heterosexual and homosexual) and much more, and that He enables us to enjoy a relationship with Him as we receive His mercies new every day. As Lamentations 3:22–23 says, "It is of the Lord's mercies that we are not consumed; His compassions do not fail. They are new every morning; great is Your faithfulness."

Eternal judgment for those who deny Christ

The Lord releases His judgments in this age and in the age to come to remove the things that hinder love from the earth. One day Jesus will create a new earth that will be filled with His glory and in which all His people will walk in His perfect love.

In the age to come Jesus will call every person to account for how they responded to His grace and leadership. As John 5:28–29 says, "For the hour is coming in which all who are in the graves will hear His voice and come out—those who have done good to the resurrection of life, and those who have done evil to the resurrection of judgment." Some today reject the idea of God's wrath, yet God's wrath is very real and "is revealed from heaven against all ungodliness and unrighteousness" (Rom. 1:18). Those unwilling to accept Jesus will be "cast into the lake of fire" and face eternal damnation (Rev. 20:15).

Literal interpretation of biblical end-times prophecy

As some often say, God said what He meant and meant what He said. Although some of the Bible's end-times prophecies certainly involve symbolic imagery, as a whole biblical prophecies concerning the end times are not to be dismissed as merely symbolic but are to be taken at face value, giving the body of Christ insight that is significant to equipping them to walk in victory as overcomers.

The importance of the local church

Scripture emphasizes the primary place of the church in God's eternal purposes. Jesus is building His church so that the gates of hell will not prevail against it (Matt. 16:18), and He is coming back for a glorious church that will make known His wisdom to principalities and powers (Eph. 3:10; 5:27). Many today put down and devalue the local church; however, the Holy Spirit is restoring and raising up strong local churches that will give a family expression of God's love to an unbelieving world that is searching not only to belong but also to be part of a healthy, functioning community.

God's purpose and sovereign calling for Israel

The church has not replaced ethnic Israel in God's purposes. This idea, called replacement theology, is gaining traction throughout the global church while anti-Semitism once again rises in cultures everywhere. Liberal theology in the church has ushered in the belief that the nation of Israel is no longer the "Israel" referred to throughout the Bible. For this and other reasons it is popular among younger Christians to resist God's biblical purposes for Israel. But Scripture is clear that the Lord has not rescinded His sovereign choice of the nation of Israel, both as a people and a nation:

> God has not rejected His people whom He foreknew....I say then, have they stumbled that they should fall [completely]? God forbid! But through their transgression salvation has come to the Gentiles, to make them jealous....For I do not want you to be ignorant of this mystery, brothers, lest you be wise in your own estimation, for a partial hardening has come upon Israel until the fullness of the Gentiles has come in. And so *all Israel will be saved.*
> —Romans 11:2, 11, 25–26, emphasis added

The Lord requires the whole church to stand with His end-time purposes for Israel. This includes declaring to all the nations with gladness that *God will gather and keep Israel* as a shepherd does his flock:

> For thus says the Lord: Sing with gladness for Jacob, and shout among the chief of the nations; publish, praise, and say, "O Lord, save Your people, the remnant of Israel!" See, I will...gather them from the remote parts of the earth...a great company will return here....Hear the word of the Lord, O nations, and declare it in the coastlands far off, and say, "He who scattered Israel will gather him and keep him, as a shepherd does his flock.'"
> —Jeremiah 31:7–10

Racial reconciliation and believers dwelling in unity and honor

As racial tensions increase in America and many nations, the church must stand in unity with all other believers and express genuine honor to all people—black, white, Native American, Asian, Hispanic, and those of Jewish and/or Middle Eastern descent. Jesus prayed that all His people be unified—by *seeing the value of one another* through God's eyes (John 17:21–23).

> May they also may be one in Us, that the world may believe that You sent Me.
>
> —JOHN 17:21

The Lord wants His children to love and honor all people and to demonstrate that they are a part of a kingdom community that embraces the King's ways. All believers are mandated to participate in their city as peacemakers and ambassadors for reconciliation, especially as racial tensions are increasing all over the earth.

The sanctify of human life

Malachi prophesied that the Lord would raise up many leaders who would care for children and thus turn their hearts to children (as we see in adoption, pro-life movements, anti-sex trafficking efforts, and so on).

> And he [Elijah] will turn the hearts of the fathers to the children.
>
> —MALACHI 4:6

I believe we will see the largest adoption movement and outreach to the fatherless in history before the Lord returns. The Holy Spirit is calling the body of Christ to take a stand to stop abortion, to express value for the fatherless, and to work to end human trafficking. There are 50 million abortions worldwide each year (over 100,000 per day).[9] In the United States nearly 60 million babies have been aborted since 1973. Estimates of the total number of abortions worldwide (from 1920–2000) are well over 500 million.[10]

Biblical prophecy describes slavery, which includes human trafficking, as a predominant sin in the end times (Rev. 18:13; see also Joel 3:3). Slavery combines violence and immorality in a significant way. There are currently 35 million slaves on the earth.[11] This practice is currently growing. More than 80 percent of human trafficking victims are female and children, forced into the rapidly growing sex trade that generates more than $32 billion per year.[12]

Loving the poor and working for justice

The prophet Micah famously thundered God's requirement for all who seek to love God wholeheartedly: "He has told you, O man, what is good—and what does the Lord require of you, but to do justice and to love kindness, and to walk humbly with your God?" (Mic. 6:8). Loving people by doing justly is the *visible* measurement of our *invisible* (but real) love for God. It is impossible for us to say that we love Jesus without loving people by expressing mercy and compassion to people in need (1 John 3:17–19; 4:20). Jesus calls His church to respond to the challenge of systemic injustice that afflicts the nations. Works of justice include feeding the poor and caring for the needy, orphans, widows, and homeless. It also includes alleviating the oppression of abortion, poverty, hunger, misogyny, and racism in the marketplace, law enforcement, education, and employment arenas, and many other issues. When we encounter God's heart for us and His heart for justice, works of justice become a priority to us in the use of our time, finances, and energy. A commitment to do justly is costly. It is inconvenient, but it is worth it.

Doing justly requires a view of finances that embraces what the Scripture teaches about generosity, simplicity, prosperity, and so on. We believe God for a supernatural supply of finances but voluntarily take less for our personal lifestyles so that we can give more to the poor and missions. As believers it is our privilege to make our personal resources available to serve the needy.

The gifts of the Holy Spirit operating in the church today

The increased activity of the Holy Spirit over the past thirty years, particularly in the body of Christ in Africa and South America, has caused many believers to open their hearts to not only a more Charismatic expression of worship but also a definition of the gifts of the Holy Spirit that is more in line with what happened in the Book of Acts. For more on this topic I highly recommend R. T. Kendall's book *Holy Fire* and Jack Deere's *Surprised by the Power of the Spirit.*

The increase of the number of believers with "Charismatic" theology and experience has grown from *one million* (1920) to *60 million* (1970) to *600 million* today.[13]

A careful consideration of Acts 2 will show that what was prophesied by Joel (Joel 2:28–32) was only partially fulfilled on the Day of Pentecost. Joel prophesied much more that has yet to be completely fulfilled. This includes the Spirit's being poured out on "all flesh" and God's showing great signs in the earth and wonders in heaven—signs such as blood, fire, and smoke; the sun becoming dark; and the moon turning into blood:

> And it shall come to pass in the last days, says God, that I will pour out of My Spirit on all flesh; your sons and your daughters shall prophesy, your young men shall see visions, your old men shall dream dreams. And on My menservants and on My maidservants I will pour out My Spirit in those days; and they shall prophesy. I will show wonders in heaven above and signs in the earth beneath: blood and fire and vapor of smoke. The sun shall be turned into darkness, and the moon into blood, before the coming of the great and awesome day of the LORD.
>
> —ACTS 2:17–20, NKJV

COUNTERING CULTURE WITH PRAYER

We have just identified several foundational truths and biblical values from which some believers are drawing back. Let's now turn our attention to ways we can refuse to draw back from God's truths and instead grow closer to the Lord.

One of the fundamental keys to such growth with God is talking with Him. I have never met a believer who was experiencing true spiritual growth who was not also praying more. Prayer is the place of our greatest intimacy, our deepest conversations, and our most profound insights about God. Everything that bears lasting fruit starts in the place of prayer and communion with Jesus (John 15:4–5).

As the global crisis grows in reach and intensity, believers will increasingly face situations for which they have no answers and that they have no natural ability to resolve. Though some of these situations will be attacks from the enemy, some will be designed by God to press the body of Christ further into a place of greater dependency on and trust in Him. This is why prayer is more than just another spiritual discipline to consider; as the end times near, prayer will be a life-and-death matter for *every* believer.

In Tim Keller's book on prayer he tells of a season in his life when everything seemed to be crumbling around him. New York City, where he serves as pastor of Redeemer Presbyterian Church, was reeling from the horrors of 9/11. His wife continued to face the effects of Crohn's disease. And to make matters worse, doctors told him he had thyroid cancer.

He and his wife knew they needed to pray, and they committed to pray together every night—something they had not been able to do for long before. Yet when his wife shared the following analogy, Tim had a newfound reason for praying that sparked something deep inside:

"Imagine," she said, "you were diagnosed with such a lethal condition that the doctor told you that you would die within hours unless you took a particular medicine—a pill every night before going to sleep. Imagine that you were told that you could never miss it or you would die. Would you forget? Would you not get around to it some nights? No—it would be so crucial that you wouldn't forget, you would never miss. Well, if we don't pray together to God, we're not going to make it because of all we are facing. I'm certainly not. We *have* to pray, we can't let it just slip our minds."[14]

I believe Christians are soon entering a time when we can't let prayer "just slip our minds," or else we will be helpless in the face of multiple life-and-death situations. Without prayer we will be not only unable to cope with these challenges but also incapable of doing anything about them. The church will face both an increasing number of trials and an increasing intensity of them. We must become a praying people, or we will not survive.

GROWING IN PRAYER

We can talk until we are blue in the face about our need to grow in prayer and how essential it will be in the coming days of increased life-and-death situations. But until we begin to *actually* pray, the idea of returning to the Lord with all our hearts will be just that— an idea. To grow in prayer takes—you guessed it—*praying!*

So how do you grow in prayer? This is one of the most common questions people ask me regarding prayer. I typically answer them not with biblical insights into why we pray or inspirational stories that prove what happens when we pray, though those things are extremely helpful. I have found that people are most often looking for some basic, practical, applicable guidance to help them develop a stronger prayer life. In a nutshell, they want a *plan of action.*

Loving God with all your heart is key to prayer. But there is more to developing a consistent prayer life than just loving God; there are indeed practical matters. Given that, here is a practical plan to help you along the way. Though growing in prayer is anything but a guaranteed three-step process, the following plan has helped me and countless others for many years. In 2014 I wrote a book called *Growing in Prayer.* In it I laid out many principles that I believe are necessary to continually grow in prayer and to actually enjoy the process. I will share just a few practical points that are developed more extensively in my previous book.

Set a schedule for regular prayer times.

A schedule establishes *when* you will pray. If you schedule time for prayer and make a prayer list, you will pray ten times more than you do now. Though I am not a scientist or professional researcher, I have proven the truth of this in my own life for the past thirty-five years, and I have also witnessed the results of others who have applied the plan in their lives.

We all have numerous demands on our time. If we do not set our schedules ourselves, others will set them for us, and the result will be that once again prayer gets bumped for something else, leaving us little—if any—time in the day to actually pray.

When we place something on our schedules, though, we are far more likely to do it. For whatever reason, it carries more weight and seems more important. Of course we may not keep our schedule 100 percent of the time, but we will keep it more often than not. I do not always stay in prayer for the entire time that I intended. But I set my heart to show up at the time I have scheduled to start it, and then I go from there.

Conversely, I do not limit my prayer life to my scheduled prayer times; I pray "on the run" during the day. This is actually part of what it means to "abide in Christ" (John 15:4–9). Abiding in Christ is one of the foundational principles of prayer. Jesus said, "If you abide in Me, and My words abide in you, you will ask what you desire, and it shall be done for you" (v. 7, NKJV). He was talking about prayer! However, some people read scriptures like this out of context and focus almost exclusively on the last part of this verse: "You will ask what you desire, and it shall be done for you." By neglecting to read the verses surrounding this one, they miss the point entirely.

When we abide in Christ, we first "bear much fruit" that glorifies the Father (v. 5, 8), and second, we realize continually that without Christ we can do absolutely nothing (v. 5), including praying! Again, we can bear lasting fruit only when we abide in Him.

Although abiding in Christ consists of more than just talking with Him, it is not only one of the core ways we abide but also one of the simplest. You can talk to Jesus anytime, anywhere, even when you are "on the go." Keeping that posture of continual prayer helps in gaining a proper perspective on prayer. It helps us see that there is value in the three-second "Help me, Lord!" prayers we make, just as there is value in our scheduled times of prayer, however long they are.

Keep in mind, however, that if our prayer lives consist of nothing but short bursts of prayer, then we will not grow to the full extent that is possible for us. We will sustain an "abiding dialogue" with Jesus throughout the day much more consistently if we also have regular times to talk with God set into our daily schedules.

Some people protest that it is robotic and legalistic to schedule time for prayer or to use a prayer list. Though it can be, it does not have to be. We move into legalism when we seek to *earn* God's love by praying or obeying rules. The good news of the gospel is that we do not have to earn it; God offers His love and grace freely. Consistency in prayer—talking with the Lord regularly and with focus—simply positions us to sit before Him more often so that we can experience more of His grace.

Setting regular times for prayer is not an attempt to earn God's love; it is a reflection of our desire to take control of our schedules so that we can make prayer a priority. I regularly schedule activities that I greatly value—ones that I want to make sure I do not inadvertently neglect through busyness in my life.

I urge you not to fall for the age-old lie that calls all discipline "legalism." This lie has robbed many believers of the blessing of a consistent prayer life. Experiencing the liberty of God's grace does not necessarily mean we are aimless or passive. The spirit of liberty speaks of what happens in the heart *while we are praying*. It describes a tender heart flowing in God and not weighed down with bitterness, lust, and dullness. As Paul says, "You, brothers, have been called to liberty. Only do not use liberty to give an opportunity to the flesh" (Gal. 5:13).

Scheduling time for the Lord is an expression of both our love for Him and our hunger for more and our value of pursuing Him more. It is not an attempt to earn love from the One who gives His love freely and abundantly.

One more note before we move on: during scheduled prayer times it is important to turn off your phone and "unplug" from e-mail, Facebook, Twitter, and other social media. The person who is overly stimulated with information and communication will not connect with God in the same way as when he turns off his devices during times of prayer.

Make a prayer list.

A prayer list helps you to focus on *what* to pray. I recommend that you prepare a prayer list (or several lists) so that you go into your scheduled times with purposeful direction. A list is a simple tool that can help keep us focused during our prayer times. Often when I begin to pray, my mind is blank. I need a little "jump start" to help me focus, so I still use prayer lists, which I have found invaluable.

I do not limit my prayers to the things on my lists but use them simply as a guide. I depart from them whenever I feel led to pray in a different direction. The goal is not to check off items on a list; the goal is to partner with God in prayer and follow His leading. I enjoy praying with the inspiration that comes from the leading of the Spirit, so even as I continue through my list, I always seek to follow His prompting.

Over the years I have developed three prayer lists—for my personal life, for people and places, and for justice issues.

- **For my personal life:** This list includes praying for my inner man, my ministry, and my circumstances (physical, financial, and relational). Some years ago I developed two different acronyms that help me pray for strengthening my inner man and for communing with the Holy Spirit. (To download these, go to mikebickle.org and search for "Prayers to Strengthen Your Inner Man.") I encourage you either to use mine or to create something similar that makes it easier for you to remember what to pray for regarding your own life.

- **For people and places:** I keep a list of individuals, ministries, cities, and nations that I pray for regularly. I pray for individual people (family and friends), ministries (including my local church), missionaries and mission endeavors, and so on. I pray for my own city, Kansas City, and for other cities that the Lord has laid on my heart, such as Cairo. I take extra time to "pray for the peace of Jerusalem" (Ps. 122:6; Isa. 62:6–7) and for the nation of Israel, as Scripture commands. And I pray for nations in great need (e.g., Haiti, Malawi) and particularly for the persecuted church in places such as North Korea, Syria, Egypt, and Afghanistan. Finally I also follow Paul's exhortation in 1 Timothy 2:1–2 to pray for those in authority positions.

- **For justice:** This is a broad topic that includes governmental and social issues such as the ending of abortion, human trafficking, unfair educational systems, and financial injustices. My list sometimes includes situations related to economic injustice, civil unrest (e.g., terrorism, riots), natural disasters (e.g., hurricanes, tsunamis, tornadoes, drought), disease (e.g., AIDS, tuberculosis), social crises (e.g., famine, genocide), and more.

Cultivate a right view of God.

This may not seem like a practical step toward growing in prayer. But cultivating a biblical perspective of God is not only practical for effective prayer; it is also essential. A right view of God causes you to *want* to pray. When we see God the way He truly is, our desire to know Him and talk with Him increases.

Too many believers have a wrong view of God. They live under the wrong assumption that God is an angry taskmaster who forces us to pray and endure conversation with Him to prove our devotion to Him. Or they view him as a stoic God who has no interest in our lives.

The truth is that God is a tender Father who deeply loves His children, and Jesus is a Bridegroom King filled with desire for His people. As we believe and understand the biblical truth of God as our tender Father and Jesus as the Bridegroom King, we are energized to seek God and experience new delight in our relationship with Him. Our prayer lives look radically different when we come to Him with the confidence that He does not just bear us but that He actually *enjoys* us. Think about it: Isn't it more enjoyable to talk to someone who really likes you? Of course! It is no different with God.

We grow in *our* passion for *God* by understanding the truth about *His* passion for *us*. This is the key to awakening true intimacy with God. It makes sense, then, that it is also foundational for growing in prayer. Encountering the father-heart of God awakens our own hearts for Him. This is exactly what Jesus prayed for just before He went to the cross. He prayed "that the world may know that You have sent Me, and have loved them as You have loved Me" (John 17:23).

Jesus wants us to know that the Father loves us just as He loves Jesus. How remarkable! If that concept has not already blown your mind, then think about this: we are valuable to our heavenly Father. In fact, He has taken us in as sons and daughters and given us "the Spirit of adoption, by whom we cry, 'Abba, Father'" (Rom. 8:15). In Hebrew *Abba* is a term of endearment for a father, much like *Papa* in our culture; it indicates respect but also affection and intimacy. The understanding of God as Abba and the knowledge of our identity as His children equip us to reject Satan's accusations—which are often disguised as our "own" thoughts—that we are hopeless failures. Nothing could be further from the truth!

The fact that Abba God enjoys us, even in our weakness, is a stabilizing anchor that gives us confidence in prayer. How we view God determines how we approach Him in prayer. If we view Him as aloof or angry, we will not want to pray much. But when we see Him as a tender Father and passionate Bridegroom who desires for us to come to Him, then we will pray much more. And the more we see ourselves as sons and daughters of God, the more we will approach His throne with confidence and without shame or hesitation.

As mentioned in the previous chapter, the Lord is actively seeking those who will partner with Him in prayer (Ezek. 22:30). But He is not looking for legalistic robots praying out of duty; He desires real, authentic, intimate relationship. Even better, He wants it because He not only loves us but also truly likes and enjoys us! This foundational truth is where we must begin in prayer, and it is the key to growing—and remaining—in God amid the surging spiritual crisis of our times.*

---

* For more on how to grow in prayer, see my book *Growing in Prayer* at mikebickle.org.

Chapter 11

STANDING VICTORIOUSLY
WITH JESUS IN THE END TIMES

ONLY ONE GENERATION will see the escalation of history's greatest and worst hour. Only one generation will see the Day of the Lord come to completion as the end times unfold. The question is: Is the generation that will see these things alive now?

In my opinion there are people today who might see the return of the Lord. I cannot be certain of that; it is my personal opinion, based on seeing what I interpret as the biblical signs of the times that will occur in the generation the Lord returns. But for now, only God knows when that generation will exist on the earth.

What we do know, however, is that God loves that generation deeply. He holds them close to His heart and is zealous to see them stand in victory in the end times. We know this because no generation is talked about, referenced, and addressed more in the Bible than the generation that will live during the end times.

Jesus spoke of the last-days generation and outlined a number of the signs of the times in which they would live. The apostles spoke of that generation and mentioned what would happen during that hour of history. The Old Testament prophets spoke of that generation and described various details related to the end times. There is more in the Bible describing that generation than most people who read the Word realize. Why? Because it is the most glorious and dangerous generation in history. Glorious in that it will usher in the biggest harvest of souls ever and see the church walk in the greatest levels of supernatural power, holiness, love, purity, and unity. And dangerous because that generation will also usher in the greatest darkness, destruction, despair, and death known in history; and because a significant number of people in that generation will fall away from the faith (Matt. 24:9–13; 2 Thess. 2:3; 1 Tim. 4:1–2; 2 Tim. 3:1–7; 4:3–5).

In Luke 21 Jesus does more than just speak *about* that generation as a Prophet, declaring what is to come; He speaks *to* that generation as a Pastor, warning them of the troubles they will face and urging them to stay close to Him as the great Shepherd. Indeed, Jesus was the great Prophet and the great Pastor, and in Luke 21 we see Him in both roles, announcing to the world the peril of the last days while also speaking tenderly to the heart of His people as one who "lays down His life for the sheep" (John 10:11).

Throughout this book we have examined God's answer for the coming crisis. We have seen that *the Psalm 2 crisis requires a Joel 2 response, resulting in an Acts 2 outpouring of the Holy Spirit.*

For those who are looking expectantly for the end-time outpouring of the Spirit and who seek to understand the unique dynamics that occur in the generation in which the Lord returns, I recommend that they prayerfully study Luke 21—it is one of the most extensive passages in which Jesus exhorts His end-time church.

Though His is a sobering message, it is also gives assurance that those who stay close to Him can stand in victory with Him through history's brightest and darkest hour. So let's take a look.

LIVING IN PERILOUS TIMES

For those reading Luke 21 for the first time, the passage can seem like nothing but gloom and doom. In other biblical accounts of what will happen in the end times, the writers include more positive elements than Luke 21. In fact, many of those passages make it clear that this will be the time of the great harvest, the outpouring of the Spirit in full measure released in all nations as the church walks in unity, purity, and power even beyond the Book of Acts. Yet here in Luke's account Jesus highlights mostly the negative. (We will soon see why.)

In the first two-thirds of Luke 21 Jesus paints a vivid picture of the Day of the Lord as He goes through the various signs of the times (i.e., wars, famines, earthquakes, and so on). But in verse 25 He makes a strong prophetic declaration intended to alert us. Amid describing the tumultuous cosmic signs and tsunamis that will come in this season, He also declares, "On the earth [there will be] distress of nations." This will be a time of distress that is unique in its intensity—the measure of unrest will be unprecedented and unparalleled. It will include financial crises, terrorism, racial clashes, violent weather, persecution, and many other things. But what makes this time unique is that the distress will continually increase until the Lord returns.

The nations of the world throughout history have always experienced some level of distress—whether from the chaos of a fallen natural world or from man's own hands (or most often, both). Throughout history even unusual distress has come in cycles, meaning there was always a reprieve. But we are now entering a season in which distress will continually increase. Things will never go back to how they were in the "good ol' days" of safety and security (whenever that was). The places in the world that refuse Jesus's leadership will continue to get darker and more chaotic. Sin will continue to escalate to higher levels. The demonic influence in the earth will increase.

Because the Lord is an excellent Pastor, He has told His people ahead of time what they should know and do. Throughout His Word—including here in Luke 21, where His instructions are explicit—He gives enough information to awaken our hearts spiritually and prepare us mentally so that we will not be surprised or overwhelmed. Jesus knows the human condition, mindset, and capacity more than anyone. He knows that we are prone to overreact when we initially experience distress. He knows we can process only small amounts at a time. And so He tells us in this passage, "Pay attention! Don't ignore what's happening. If you do, when the distress of this day comes—when it hits you all at once—then you will be overcome with fear. You don't want this to surprise you; there is no *need* for it to surprise you, for I am with you and can give you understanding. You can interpret the signs little by little as things unfold. My people will be able to understand more and experience more grace even as they observe things intensify more and more over several decades." But the important thing He is saying is this: "*Stay close to Me.*"

Indeed, in each season of increasing distress we must realign ourselves with the Lord so that the intensity of the distress does not overwhelm us. As we come closer to Him and rely on Him for strength and wisdom, we will grow in understanding of what He is doing and in our dependence on Him. This is not just the safe way to respond; it is the *only* way God's people will be able to succeed spiritually in the days ahead.

Fainting From Fear

The "distress of the nations" in Luke 21:25 will be dangerous. As the natural world becomes increasingly chaotic—with earthquakes, tornados, tsunamis, hurricanes, and the like—people will recognize this is not business as usual. Even the man-made chaos—wars, terrorism, riots, crime, political upheaval—will catch people off guard. But even more dangerous than the physical distress will be the *spiritual distress* Jesus mentions in verse 26 of "men fainting from fear and expectation of what is coming on the inhabited earth." The New King James Version translates this as "men's hearts failing them..."

Fear is a dangerous, powerful force. It grabs hold and does not let go. It immobilizes. It incapacitates. And in a spiritual sense, it paralyzes people, causing them either to not respond to Jesus's leadership at all or to respond in inappropriate ways. The fear Jesus refers to here is not a brief episode of being scared, after which a person quickly moves on. No, people will "faint" from this kind of fear in a figurative sense in that they will fall out of sorts and lose their spiritual (and even emotional) cognizance. In a literal sense, they will be overcome—taken over—by the spirit of fear.

A stronghold of fear in their life will render them unresponsive to Jesus, which is the worst thing that could happen to them during this time. It will be, in fact, a death sentence for many.

When Jesus speaks of "men's hearts failing," He is generally not talking about a pandemic of heart attacks among men, though I am sure that will also happen from the sheer terror of the surrounding events. No, Jesus is addressing a more prominent question: As the distress rises to unimaginable levels, will God's people turn their hearts to Him? Will they commit to staying closer to Him than ever before and trusting Him in the darkness of the times? Or will they succumb to the rampant fear that will be everywhere they turn?

Notice in verse 26 that fear will overwhelm people during this time not only because of the actual distress they can see but also because of the mere thoughts and expectations of "those things which are coming on the earth" (NKJV). This is a perfect picture of anxiety running rampant, and as any psychologist knows, fear and anxiety work hand in hand to cause overwhelming emotional turmoil.

Because of the potential impact of fear Jesus tells His people to pay close attention to what is transpiring in their hearts. The danger of what could happen on the inside of us spiritually is actually greater than what could happen on the outside of us physically. This is a very serious statement, given the upheaval in the nations and the persecution that many believers will experience during this time. Yet whatever pressures we may endure externally will not be as dangerous as being driven by fear that will cause some to make decisions that will cause them to draw from the Lord.

Some of the internal danger will emerge as a result of the sheer shock of what will be transpiring externally. Those surprised by the increasing distress will be more vulnerable to being overwhelmed by fear, as the events of this time and the emotional turmoil it causes will "come on [them] unexpectedly" (v. 34, NKJV). The intensity of the distress and the development of negative things will come without warning for most and will surprise multitudes. Even some of the most astute political analysts, financial forecasters, and cultural watchdogs will be shocked by the manner and intensity of what will take place.

This is exactly why the great Shepherd gave His people reliable insider information two thousand years in advance. He does not want us shocked or even mildly surprised to see the crisis continuing to grow. He wants us to know that when we see all these distressful things begin to happen, we can recognize them as that which was prophesied in His Word regarding the generation in which He returns. The logic is clear. Since He has the supernatural ability to prophesy these events accurately two thousand years in advance, it stands to reason He also has the supernatural power to help His people in that hour.

We must not neglect or dismiss these signs but instead must pay close attention. We do not need to know every detail or nuance of what will happen, but we can know the main trends occurring in that hour. We will be braced for the negative events and able to interpret them in a redemptive way, knowing that Jesus is leading history to a time when God's glory and love will cover the earth.

Only one group of people in the earth need not be surprised in those days, and that is the praying, Bible-believing church. God's people are to be aware so "that Day does not come upon them unexpectedly" (v. 34). "That Day" includes the actual day of His appearing as well as the events and trends associated with and leading up to that day. God's people are the only ones on the earth who know where it is all headed and how it will fulfill God's redemptive purposes.

Jesus gave this biblical information two millennia ago so that no one can dismiss it as if it came from modern-day social forecasters in the aftermath of a global crisis. He said this long before there was a global economy in crisis, a potential third world war, or a new pandemic on the horizon. His information can be trusted because it was provided long *before* this growing global crisis, not in its aftershocks. The only people on the earth who have understanding of what will happen are the praying church because they believe the Bible and have a connection with the Man who has the power and the plans.

Only one Man, the Architect of history who created the nations, calls us to connect with Him and live without fear in this hour. He is the sovereign King of all kings and possesses all power. He is filled with beauty, and His plans are rooted in love—a perfect love that drives out all fear. He gives us great hope.

At that time some will faint with fear (v. 26) while others will be filled with faith, *looking up* to King Jesus for the full release of their redemption or salvation instead of only *looking out* at the growing distress (v. 28). From this posture of faith and trust will come a sincere, deep, and tested love for our glorious Savior. In this context He will bring forth the greatest number of people at the deepest level of love in the context of the distress of nations and the outpouring of the Spirit combined together. His plan is remarkable, and it will succeed.

THE THREE TRAPS

In the ancient world people were not able to just run down to the grocery store and buy five pounds of hamburger meat to cook for dinner. Neither were they able to simply shoot an animal for their dinner because they didn't have guns. They had to capture animals—their food—in a trap. They had to ensnare them with a device that required patience and cunning. So when Jesus compares the Day of the Lord to a trap or a snare in Luke 21:35, those listening at the time understood the analogy.

> For as a snare it will come on all those who dwell on the face
> of the whole earth.
> —LUKE 21:35

Though Jesus's audience that day may have been familiar with His word picture, I wonder if they grasped Jesus's deeper meaning. There is a twofold nature to a snare or trap. First, a trap is hidden. If an animal walks near it, he does not realize it is there. An animal will not step into a trap it can see. Second, a trap captures and holds its prey. Once an animal steps into a trap, it cannot get free. No matter how much it struggles, it will not be able to break free from the bondage.

Jesus uses this intense analogy to highlight the extreme danger of the end times. Just as a baited snare was hidden to lure its prey into the trap and was designed to hold that prey, the enemy of our souls, Satan, will lay countless traps during the difficult days of extreme darkness on the earth.

Let me ask you a question: Whom do you think Jesus is addressing in Luke 21? Whom is He really talking to? He is giving specific directions for those who follow Him—His church. So this passage is not about or directed primarily to the unsaved; it is primarily a warning and valuable guidance for believers like you and me.

That means Jesus is warning the church of the traps laid out both now and in the end times. Too many believers are not actively alert to the enemy's traps. They think that just because they have received salvation and the forgiveness of sins, they will somehow clearly see all of Satan's hidden snares. Wrong! We have been warned because we too can fall prey to these hidden traps; therefore we must stay alert. We must remain vigilant as the distress of the nations increases.

Jesus is concerned primarily with the state of our hearts. He does not want our hearts to be "burdened" by anything. For this reason He highlights three emotional traps in verse 34:

> Take heed to yourselves, lest your hearts be burdened by *excessiveness* and *drunkenness* and *anxieties of life*, and that Day come on you unexpectedly.
> —LUKE 21:34, EMPHASIS ADDED

Though there are certainly other traps Jesus could have mentioned, I believe He highlighted these three as the main ones because they are and will continue to be the biggest ones into which believers are most susceptible to fall. Each has the power to ensnare the heart of a believer and "burden" it in a bondage that has eternal consequences.

1. Excessiveness

Most Bible translations replace the word *excessiveness* with the word *dissipation*, which is a synonym for lustful physical pleasure. Jesus used a word that conveys overindulgence that dissipates or diminishes one's strength. Its primary expression is immorality, but it is not limited to immorality. Carousing is about seeking relief through pleasures that are outside the will of God.

As the end times near, the sexual darkness via technology and the online world will increase beyond anything we can imagine. Immorality will be at its highest levels both in the virtual world and the physical one—in schools, businesses, government offices, and, unfortunately, even in churches. We have already mentioned the staggering rates of pornography addiction in every generation (particularly the younger ones) and in both men and women. Studies prove that the numbers are not so different in the church than outside it. I have seen young men and women come through our own ministry struggling with porn. Just because they commit to joining a prayer ministry does not mean they are instantly set free from this trap. Yet the truth is that right now is the *easiest* hour to get free from pornography because things will only get worse from here. The pornification of our culture will intensify far more than we assume, and the temptations will grow stronger as sexual immorality becomes even more prevalent in our culture than it is now.

2. Drunkenness

Many people seek to escape their pain and the pressures around them by finding comfort through the abuse of alcohol, drugs, and other mind-altering substances instead of seeking relief by connecting with Jesus. *Drunkenness* in this context points to more than only intoxication with alcohol. There are various other ways to escape, such as with drugs—both legal and illegal. Whatever the outlet, this trap will be far more intense as the pressures from the various crises in the coming days increase.

3. The anxieties of life

This may be the most common snare of all because it is often the subtlest.

The *anxieties of life* refers to concerns about our families, our jobs, and our circumstances. They typically fall into one of four categories: provision, protection, position, or promotion. When someone blocks us from achieving one of these goals to gain honor or secure a position that we rightly deserve, bitterness sets in because we feel as if we are not getting what we are entitled to. What begins as anxiety gradually turns into self-pity and then into full-fledged bitterness.

Thus the anxieties of life also include the negative bitter emotions associated with not receiving the honor, privilege, or recognition that we feel we deserve. By not receiving the position or promotions we hoped for, we end up in fear that we will not "have enough" in terms of provision and protection, and more.

This trap has become so effective at ensnaring people today partly because of the entitlement culture that prevails in our time. Entitlements are not just government payouts; people everywhere are raising the bar on what they "deserve" and "need" to survive. When they don't get it, they believe they are being mistreated: "They should know I'm worth more than that. I deserve more honor and respect than this. People aren't giving me what I'm entitled to."

This sentiment is exploding today with the aid of social media that, though originally intended to build community, has instead nurtured narcissism, criticism, and bitterness. A sense of entitlement can cause major tension between "what is" (the reality) and "what should be" (the ideal). Sadly the more that people are disappointed in the disparity between the two extremes, the more they tend to just give up and quit—falsely believing that there is always greener grass somewhere else in a place where people will *finally* recognize who they are and give them the honor they deserve. "If you don't want to honor me like I deserve, then fine—I quit!" They quit their job, marriage, church family, ministry team, or other relationships. Worse still, they quit God or the church because they feel exasperated and spiritually burned out.

Jesus told those who follow Him that they would have to deny themselves, lose themselves in Him, and find their identity in their relationship with Him. Satan has already trapped many believers with this "anxieties of life" snare; I shudder to think of how many more will be bound in the bitterness that comes with disappointment as the distress of the growing crisis comes to fullness.

We avoid each of these three traps by being aware of them, watching out for them, and most importantly remaining close to Jesus and alert to what the Bible informs us about His end-time plans. The Lord does not want any of us to be ensnared by the enemy's traps, and this is why He has specifically warned us of them. As the pressures of the Day of the Lord rise, it will be common for people to succumb to fear or to self-medicate their discomfort with immorality, drunkenness, or self-pity that results in bitterness rather than to stand strong against the pressures by finding their identity and source in the Lord. If we are unprepared for the day's pressures or not alert to the enemy's traps, then we will be surprised or shocked. And those who are caught off guard will be far more vulnerable to seeking temporary comfort in immorality, drunkenness, or the cares of life. Tragically those caught in these traps and weighed down by them will be unresponsive to Jesus's leadership in the most glorious and dangerous hour of human history, and they will miss out on the greatest revival to ever occur among the nations.

God's people do not need to succumb to this. We have the information. The Lord will lead His people with clarity in this hour. While others numb themselves with self-medication and fall into traps, God's people can stay sharp and alert. We do not have to try to seek relief in lust or be overwhelmed with fear. We can stay close to Jesus and overcome even in the face of chaos and crisis.

FINALLY... A GOOD WORD

Amid all the negativity of Luke 21—the distressing events, disastrous responses, and sobering warnings—Jesus offers several exhortations. Like light at the end of a tunnel, these encouraging directives give us hope that despite the darkness of the coming crisis, we can stand with the Lord in victory.

Though Jesus points out many things in Luke 21, He gives two main exhortations, as found in verses 34 and 36: first, we are to take heed, and second, we are to watch and pray.

> *Take heed* to yourselves, lest your hearts be burdened by excessiveness and drunkenness and anxieties of life, and that Day comes on you unexpectedly. For as a snare it will come on all those who dwell on the face of the whole earth. *Therefore watch always and pray* that you may be counted worthy to escape all these things that will happen and to stand before the Son of Man.
>
> —LUKE 21:34–36, EMPHASIS ADDED

Take heed

In the New King James Version the Lord encourages us to "take heed" twice in Luke 21 (vv. 8, 34). To heed something is to pay close attention to it.

"Take heed to yourselves" (v. 34, NKJV). Other Bible versions translate this as "Be on your guard" or "Watch yourselves." The focus here is internal, to take inventory of what is happening inside us. This means paying attention to what is transpiring in our hearts.

Once again Jesus is most concerned with our heart condition. We are to pay close attention to our hearts so that they will not be weighed down. We are accountable for our own internal condition, yet thankfully the Lord, as always, provides sufficient grace for the task. Though it may sound strange to those who routinely put others' conditions before their own, we *must also* prioritize the strengthening of our own hearts. Why is this such a big deal? Because the outward, increasing distress in the nations will not be the most significant danger or challenge to our lives. The greater threat is internal because it can do more harm to our spiritual lives.

Jesus exhorts us to take heed or see to it that our hearts are growing in strength spiritually. Yes, the external situation will be dangerous and troublesome, but the internal battle for our hearts will be even more dangerous.

The greatest danger will be having a heart that is weighed down because when this happens, many will not access the power of grace and thus will not be able to respond to Jesus's leadership. We must be intentional about making the spiritual condition of our hearts our top priority so they do not become weighed down, unresponsive, and spiritually dull. Many will be preoccupied with wrong things; we must remain focused on what Jesus said are the right things.

As God's people connect to Jesus the King, they will have access to the information, power, and love needed to walk in victory. They will also have the strength they need to escape the snares of fear and lust. In verse 36 Jesus tells us to stay alert and pray "that [we] may *have strength* to escape all these things that are about to take place, and to stand before the Son of Man" (NASB, emphasis added).

A heart that is weakened or weighed down with sin and fear is unresponsive to the truth of Jesus. The Lord tenderly warns us of this spiritual assault. It is clear in Scripture that what we do with our bodies (immorality, drunkenness, and so on) greatly affects the spiritual condition of our hearts. By falling into compromise, we can become spiritually dull and lose godly perspective, courage, and motivation to seek God.

Though the Modern English Version translates the phrase in verse 36 "that you may be counted worthy," other modern Bible translations say "have strength." Jesus was exhorting His people to pray to be strengthened. In the Lord's grace—first by asking Him for this in prayer—we will be able to stand in victory and "escape" compromise, sin, and fear.

This is the call to be strengthened in the Lord so as to overcome fear and temptation. There is only one kind of person on the earth—we are all weak and broken in terms of our own human strength. No one is born a spiritual giant. There are no "super saints" who just waltz through life unaffected by the pull of this world. In our flesh we are all weak and broken people. James says that even one of the Bible's greatest prophets, Elijah, was a man weak like us (James 5:17).

Given this truth, victory is attainable for all—yes, even for people like us. Victory is not out of reach or for only the spiritual giants of history. Weak people like us *can* overcome—if we talk to Jesus, if we do what He says, if we stay close to Him. His grace is sufficient. For where sin abounds, grace abounds more (Rom. 5:20). Where darkness increases, light increases more.

Watch and pray

Jesus's second main exhortation in Luke 21 for His people in the end times is to watch and pray (v. 36). When I first read this forty years ago, I thought the directive was really impractical. Here Jesus has talked about how the nations will be distressed, the world will be in utter chaos, darkness will grow, the church will be persecuted, there will be wars and famines and earthquakes and pestilence…and then all He tells us to do is to watch and pray?! Is that really all He has to say?

I remember thinking, "Surely there's something better He could come up with. He is the smartest Man who ever walked the earth; He is the great Shepherd who is addressing His beloved end-times generation—the generation spoken of more than any other in the Bible. Surely there are more effective instructions that He could leave us with. What about a couple of verses about storing up water and food, blankets, batteries, or something?"

No, that was it.

Watch. And pray.

Over the years I have changed my response to this—significantly. Let me explain why.

Jesus's urging for us to watch is an exhortation that focuses on the mind—He wants us to grow in understanding by watching the biblical signs of the times unfold in society.

We "watch" what Jesus, the apostles, and the prophets in the Bible said would be happening so that we grow in our understanding of the end-times narrative, and we "watch" what is happening in the natural world and society to see how it lines up with biblical prophecy so we are not caught off guard. As we watch, we process the information bit by bit with the Holy Spirit guiding us. And through our processing we can realign ourselves with the Lord's plan and leadership.

Several things happen when God's people watch the biblical signs of the times. Urgency increases in our hearts as we see prophecy progressively unfold before our eyes and we grow in understanding little by little over the years. I have insight on things today that I was clueless about ten, twenty, or thirty years ago. As our team at the International House of Prayer of Kansas City (IHOPKC) has studied the signs of the times, we have challenged and encouraged each other in the Word. This is a glorious benefit of "watching" together in a community of believers (remember, Jesus was talking to the church, not just to individual believers).

People always talk about what they "watch." For example, when someone watches a good movie or a football game, they talk about that movie or game to those who they know share a common interest in it. They bond with people when talking about things that express their common values and interests.

Likewise, when something important happens in society, we watch and thus talk about them.

As we talk about what the Bible says and how those truths line up with current events or trends, our connectedness and unity with others grows. Simply put, we end up talking more—both with each other and with God in prayer—which draws the community closer together around a unified purpose and vision. We begin bonding more with people around us over Jesus's leadership, His magnificence, His wisdom, His end-times plans as set forth in Scripture, and His grace that sustains us.

Watching the end-time trends and events that Scripture prophesied gives people urgency about talking to God and praying to release His power and protection. Watching also gives people urgency to talk to like-minded people; thus they connect more in unity of vision. By watching, we increase in confidence as we see the Lord's leadership and plans unfold before us in society in a way that the Scriptures accurately prophesied.

But Jesus's exhortation to watch and pray is not just so that a community of believers can gain knowledge and feel more confident in His leadership. No, God wants to change lives and expand His kingdom on the earth through partnership with His people. And this is where prayer comes in.

As watching focuses on the mind, so prayer focuses on the heart. It strengthens our hearts, helping us to connect with Jesus. Prayer helps us grow in intimacy with the Lord, and through prayer we release His resources, power, and protection into the earthly realm.

When God's people do this together—watch and pray—they position themselves to receive the Lord's specific and practical counsel for their neighborhoods and cities in times of crisis. The church will shine forth God's light when it finds its strength in intimacy with the Lord and receives insight on what the Holy Spirit wants them to do in their local area as distress increases.

PART OF THE ANSWER AND NOT THE PROBLEM

The Lord calls us to position ourselves by watching so that we can receive greater insight (by watching) to understand what He is doing in the world and by praying so that we can receive greater strength to love well as pressures continue to increase. Those who grow in understanding and strength will not fall but rather will stand in victory and will overcome the enemy's snares in that day. Jesus's call to watch and pray is a call to empower believers to love others well. Multitudes will need to be helped by those who are walking in power and courage and who have insight into what God is doing. People with understanding will be a part of the solution instead of contributing to the confusion (Dan. 11:33; 12:3, 10).

I want to be part of the answer, not part of the problem; I want to be part of the solution, not part of the confusion—and I suspect you do too. The good news is that God is raising up ministries all over the world that are beginning to watch and pray with new zeal and urgency. They are growing in their understanding of the biblical end-times storyline. They are watching the signs of the times increase with both negative and positive events and trends, and they prioritize connecting to God through prayer.

I believe this activity will increase significantly as the crisis grows; we will hear of more communities of believers first hearing from the Lord about what to do regarding practical issues such as food, provision, and protection and then responding to their local area's unique situation. Rather than retreating to hide in a cave somewhere, these believers will walk confidently as lights and release hope where otherwise there would not be any.

Jesus, the great Prophet and Pastor, knew what He was talking about when He said for us to *take heed* and to *watch and pray*. He was not dumbing down anything for us in a simplistic way. These will be the most essential things we can do. And they will change not only our lives but also the lives of those around us.

Indeed, this is the greatest hour in history to be alive—for those of us who love the leadership of Jesus. Yes, there will be great darkness in the coming days. It will be the most distressing and dangerous time in history. The enemy will rage; man will walk in deeper levels of sin beyond any time in history. But the Lord will oversee it all. As things get worse, He has promised that His people will get stronger as we stay close to Him—this, ultimately, is the message of Luke 21. Meanwhile we eagerly watch and pray for the time when God's people will rejoice to "see the Son of Man coming in a cloud with power and great glory... [and can] look up and lift up [their] heads, for [their] redemption is drawing near" (Luke 21:27–28).

DAVID'S MESSAGE OF HOPE

This book centers on the prophetic, increasingly relevant message of Psalm 2. It is fitting, then, that we end by focusing again on David's concluding remark. In a psalm filled with the raging conspiracies of the nations (v. 2), the terrifying release of the Father's wrath (v. 5), and promises of the annihilation of Jesus's enemies (v. 9), David leaves us with a hopeful truth—it is good news for every believer.

The last line of Psalm 2:12 is a promise of hope: "Blessed are all who seek refuge in Him."

Do you get a sense of what David was saying? While calamity surrounds us, we can be filled with joy because of Him who shelters us. Though we find the turmoil of Psalm 2 everywhere we look, we can enjoy the God who enjoys us. When the world's crisis reaches levels we never thought possible, we can trust the One who holds the universe in the palm of His hand. And even when we are persecuted beyond what we think we can take, we can rejoice because the altogether worthy One is our true refuge.

God called David a "man after My own heart" (Acts 13:22), meaning the king intimately knew God's heart. He enjoyed authentic relationship with Him and talked with Him as friends talk. He understood the Father's love for him, and he delighted in the King's passionate desire for him. Out of this understanding and revelation of God's love David wrote Psalm 2. That may seem oxymoronic, given the bleak outlook for the millions or billions of people who reject Jesus. But for those who return to Jesus, who trust Him, who partner with Him in prayer, and who run to Him for refuge, we understand. We know the truth behind what is happening now in our day. We know the plans of our Savior.

David prophesied of a coming crisis like no other, and all the signs point to the fact that we are beginning to see that time come to pass. The crisis is growing. Leaders are conspiring. Nations are raging. The world is shifting.

Will you commit to taking refuge in Jesus, no matter what comes? Will you remain steadfast in the light even as the storms of crisis grow darker?

I pray you will join me as we stand with Jesus, our only hope. We can join in with the great cry of God's people across the earth as the Spirit and the bride cry, "Come, Lord Jesus!" (Rev. 22:20, NKJV).

NOTES

INTRODUCTION

1. Emily Brown, "Murder on Social Media: Killer Wanted the World to Watch," *USA Today*, August 26, 2015, accessed May 26, 2015, http://www.usatoday.com/story/news/nation/2015/08/26/two-dead-virginia-shooting-live-tv-social-media/32401101/.

2. Melanie Eversley, "9 Dead in Shooting at Black Church in Charleston, S.C.," *USA Today*, June 19, 2015, accessed May 26, 2016, http://www.usatoday.com/story/news/nation/2015/06/17/charleston-south-carolina-shooting/28902017/.

3. Heather Clark, "'Are You a Christian?' Report Confirms Oregon Gunman Shot Those Who Professed Christ in Head," ChristianNews.net, October 1, 2015, accessed May 26, 2016, http://christiannews.net/2015/10/01/are-you-a-christian-report-confirms-oregon-gunman-shot-those-who-professed-christ-in-head/.

4. Wesley Bruer, "DOJ Pivots From ISIS to U.S. Anti-Government Groups With New Position," CNN.com, updated October 15, 2015, accessed May 27, 2016, http://edition.cnn.com/2015/10/14/politics/justice-department-domestic-terror-council/.

5. David K. DeWolf and Seth L. Cooper, "Teaching About Evolution in the Public Schools: A Short Summary of the Law," Discovery Institute, June 20, 2006, accessed May 27, 2016, http://www.discovery.org/a/2543.

6. Steven Ertelt, "57,762,169 Abortions in America Since Roe vs. Wade in 1973," LifeNews.com, January 21, 2015, accessed May 27, 2016, http://www.lifenews.com/2015/01/21/57762169-abortions-in-america-since-roe-vs-wade-in-1973/.

7. Warren Richey, "Supreme Court Splits on Ten Commandments," *The Christian Science Monitor*, June 28, 2005, accessed May 27, 2016, http://www.csmonitor.com/2005/0628/p01s03-usju.html.

8. Jack Jenkins, "Atheists Score Major Win in Federal Court," ThinkProgress.org, November 3, 2014, accessed May 27, 2016, http://thinkprogress.org/justice/2014/11/03/3587801/district-court-declares-secular-humanism-a-religion/.

9. Michael Vasquez, "Broward Schools' Runcie Says Bible Controversy 'Should've Been Handled Differently,'" *Miami Herald*, May 6, 2014, accessed June 15, 2016, http://www.miamiherald.com/news/local/education/article1964003.html.

10. Deepak Chopra, "Will God 2.0 Be Indispensable in Ten Years?," *Huffington Post*, updated February 7, 2015, accessed May 27, 2016, http://www.huffingtonpost.com/deepak-chopra/will-god-20-be-indispensa_b_6289724.html.

11. "America's Changing Religious Landscape: Christians Decline Sharply as Share of Population; Unaffiliated and Other Faiths Continue to Grow," Pew Research Center, May 12, 2015, accessed May 27, 2016, http://www.pewforum.org/2015/05/12/americas-changing-religious-landscape/.

12. "Most American Christians Do Not Believe that Satan or the Holy Spirit Exist," Barna Group, April 13, 2009, accessed September 30, 2016, https://www.barna.com/research/most-american-christians-do-not-believe-that-satan-or-the-holy-spirit-exist/#.V-qFE_ArIdU.

13. "Barna Survey Examines Changes in Worldview Among Christians Over the Past 13 Years," Barna Group, March 9, 2009, accessed May 27, 2016, https://www.barna.org/barna-update/transformation/252-barna-survey-examines-changes-in-worldview-among-christians-over-the-past-13-years#.

14. Ibid.

15. Dan Weil, "James Rickards to Newsmax TV: 'Ugly' Financial Crisis to Jolt US Within 5 Years," Newsmax.com, May 20, 2014, accessed May 27, 2016, http://www.newsmax.com/Finance/StreetTalk/James-Rickards-Dennis-Kneale-Financial-Crisis-Economy/2014/05/20/id/572264/.

16. Catey Hill, "45% of Americans Pay No Federal Income Tax," MarketWatch, April 18, 2016, accessed May 27, 2016, http://www.marketwatch.com/story/45-of-americans-pay-no-federal-income-tax-2016-02-24.

17. "States Most Likely to Go Bankrupt," *The Daily Beast*, January 26, 2011, accessed May 27, 2016, http://www.thedailybeast.com/articles/2011/01/26/states-most-likely-to-go-bankrupt.html; "32 States Have Borrowed From the Federal Government to Make Unemployment Payments; California Has Borrowed $7 Billion," EconomicPolicyJournal.com, May 21, 2010, accessed May 21, 2016, http://www.economicpolicyjournal.com/2010/05/32-states-have-borrowed-from-treasury.html.

18. Merrill Matthews, "We've Crossed the Tipping Point; Most Americans Now Receive Government Benefits," *Forbes*, July 2, 2014, accessed May 27, 2016, http://www.forbes.com/sites/merrillmatthews

/2014/07/02/weve-crossed-the-tipping-point-most-americans-now
-receive-government-benefits/.

19. Mark Murray, "A Long Division: Political Polarization Is Worse
Than Ever, and Here to Stay," NBCNews.com, October 17, 2014,
accessed May 27, 2016, http://www.nbcnews.com/politics/first-read
/long-division-political-polarization-worse-ever-here-stay-n228441.

20. Kenneth T. Walsh, "Americans Have Lost Confidence…in
Everything," USNews.com, June 17, 2015, accessed May 27, 2016, http://
www.usnews.com/news/blogs/ken-walshs-washington/2015/06/17
/americans-have-lost-confidence-in-everything.

21. Ibid.

22. M. Auguste Molinier, *The Thoughts of Blaise Pascal*, trans. by
C. Kegan Paul (London: George Bell and Sons, 1889), 12. Viewed at
Google Books.

23. Patrick Wintour, "David Cameron Warns of Looming Second
Global Crash," *Guardian*, November 17, 2016, accessed May 27, 2016,
http://www.theguardian.com/world/2014/nov/16/david-cameron-third
-eurozone-recession-g20-warning.

24. Helena Horton, "There Are More Slaves Today Than EVER
Before in the History of the World," Mirror.co.uk, October 14, 2014,
accessed May 27, 2016, http://www.mirror.co.uk/news/ampp3d/more
-slaves-today-ever-before-4435373.

25. Chris Morris, "Things Are Looking Up in America's Porn
Industry," NBCNews.com, January 20, 2015, accessed May 27, 2016,
http://www.nbcnews.com/business/business-news/things-are-looking
-americas-porn-industry-n289431; "TopTenREVIEWS Reports Worldwide Pornography Market at Least $97 Billion; Every Second 28,258
Internet Users View Pornography," prweb.com, March 13, 2007,
accessed May 27, 2016, http://www.prweb.com/releases/pornography
/toptenreviews/prweb511051.htm.

26. Mary Elizabeth Williams, "Stoya's James Deen Bombshell: The
Porn Star's Shocking Revelation Could Change How We Talk About
Consent," Salon.com, November 30, 2015, accessed May 27, 2016,
http://www.salon.com/2015/11/30/stoyas_james_deen_bombshell_the
_porn_stars_shocking_revelation_could_change_how_we_talk_about
_consent/.

27. "Porn Use and Addiction," in Pornography Survey Statistics,
ProvenMen.org, accessed August 2, 2016, http://www.provenmen.org
/pornography-survey-statistics-2014/.

28. Matthew Lee, "Australian Woman Battles Porn Addiction That
Started at Age 8," Metro.us, updated December 11, 2015, accessed

May 27, 2016, http://www.metro.us/viral/australian-woman
-addicted-to-porn-since-8-years-old/zsJolk---IUb1X2rwbpGzk/.

29. Patrick Howse, "'Pornography Addiction Worry' for Tenth of
12 to 13-year-olds," BBC.com, March 31, 2015, accessed May 27, 2016,
http://www.bbc.com/news/education-32115162.

30. Todd Starnes, "Could Obama's Nuke Deal Unleash Iran's Apocalyptic Muslims?" FoxNews.com, January 18, 2016, accessed May 27,
2016, http://www.foxnews.com/opinion/2016/01/18/could-obamas
-nuke-deal-unleash-irans-apocalyptic-muslims.html.

31. "Quick Facts: What You Need to Know About the Syria Crisis,"
MercyCorps.org, updated June 16, 2016, accessed May 27, 2016, https://
www.mercycorps.org/articles/iraq-jordan-lebanon-syria-turkey/quick
-facts-what-you-need-know-about-syria-crisis.

32. David Graham, "Violence Has Forced 60 Million People From
Their Homes," TheAtlantic.com, updated June 18, 2015, accessed May
27, 2016, http://www.theatlantic.com/international/archive/2015/06
/refugees-global-peace-index/396122/.

33. Faith Karimi, Catherine E. Shoichet, and Ralph Ellis, "Dallas
Sniper Attack: 5 Officers Killed, Suspect Identified," CNN.com,
updated July 9, 2016, accessed July 15, 2016, http://www.cnn.com
/2016/07/08/us/philando-castile-alton-sterling-protests/.

34. "Black Power Political Organization Claims Dallas Shooting on
Facebook, Vows More Attacks," RT.com, July 8, 2016, accessed July 15,
2016, https://www.rt.com/usa/350178-dallas-black-power-claim/.

35. Norman Grubb, Rees Howells, Intercessor (London: Lutterworth
Press, 1952).

36. Ibid., 233.

37. Ibid., 234–235.

38. Ibid., 235.

39. Ibid., 237.

40. Ibid., 239.

41. Ibid.

42. Ibid.

43. Andrew Roberts, "Dunkirk: A Miracle of War," Telegraph, July
25, 2009, accessed June 2, 2016, http://www.telegraph.co.uk/comment
/5902668/Dunkirk-a-miracle-of-war.html.

44. Grubb, Rees Howells, Intercessor.

CHAPTER 1
THE BIBLE TELLS US SO

1. Justin Lafferty, "#LoveWins: How the Same-Sex Marriage Decision Spread Through Social," *Social Times* (blog), Adweek.com, June 30, 2015, accessed June 2, 2016, http://www.adweek.com/socialtimes /lovewins-how-the-same-sex-marriage-decision-spread-through-social /622661.

2. "When the World Goes Mad—TransNorway," YouTube video, uploaded October 26, 2015, accessed June 2, 2016, https://www .youtube.com/watch?v=nXwEM30L3NI.

3. Ibid.

4. Cordelia Hebblethwaite, "Sweden's 'Gender-Neutral' Pre-School," BBC.com, July 8, 2011, accessed June 3, 2016, http://www.bbc.com/news /world-europe-14038419.

5. Joseph Patrick McCormick, "Norwegian Government Proposes Extending Trans Protections to Children," PinkNews.co.uk, June 25, 2015, accessed June 3, 2016, http://www.pinknews.co.uk/2015/06/25 /norwegian-government-proposes-extending-trans-protections-to -children/.

6. Associated Press, "Kim Davis Calls Herself a 'Soldier for Christ' in Recently Acquired Emails," MSNBC.com, October 22, 2015, accessed June 3, 2016, http://www.msnbc.com/msnbc/kim-davis-calls -herself-soldier-christ-recently-acquired-emails.

7. "Oregon Bakery Owners Refuse to Pay Damages in Gay Wedding Cake Case," FoxNews.com, October 1, 2015, accessed June 3, 2016, http://www.foxnews.com/us/2015/10/01/oregon-bakery-owners-refuse -to-pay-damages-in-gay-wedding-cake-case/; Michael Gryboski, "Christian Couple Forced to Close Bakery Due to Gay Activism May Face Over $150K in Damages," ChristianPost.com, October 2, 2014, accessed June 3, 2016, http://www.christianpost.com/news/christian -couple-forced-to-close-bakery-due-to-gay-activism-may-face-over -150k-in-damages-127331/.

8. Todd Starnes, "The Christian Purge Has Begun: Chaplains Banned From Preaching That Homosexuality Is a Sin," FoxNews .com, August 11, 2015, accessed June 3, 2016, http://www.foxnews.com /opinion/2015/08/11/chaplains-banned-from-preaching-that -homosexuality-is-sin.html?intcmp=hpbt3.

9. Andrew Welsh-Huggins, "Board: Ohio Judges Can't Choose Marriage Type They Perform," Yahoo.com, August 10, 2015, accessed June 3, 2016, http://news.yahoo.com/board-ohio-judges-cant-choose -marriage-type-perform-192249584.html; Ken McIntyre, "Christian

Judge's Objection Prompts Ohio Supreme Court's Board to Tell All Judges to Perform Gay Marriages," DailySignal.com, August 11, 2015, accessed June 3, 2016, http://dailysignal.com/2015/08/11/ohio-supreme -courts-board-orders-all-judges-to-perform-gay-marriages-after -christian-judge-objects/.

10. Amanda Terkel, "Apple Breaks Ties With Anti-Gay Alabama Lobbyist," HuffingtonPost.com, updated February 19, 2015, accessed June 3, 2016, http://www.huffingtonpost.com/2015/02/17/_n_6699054 .html.

11. "Swedish Anti-Abortion Midwife Sues County," *The Local*, July 11, 2014, accessed June 3, 2016, http://www.thelocal.se/20140711/anti -abortion-nurse-takes-firing-case-to-court.

12. Ellie Buchdahl, "Christian Doctor Sacked for Emailing a Prayer to Colleagues to Cheer Them Up Loses Appeal Against Dismissal," *Daily Mail*, September 25, 2013, accessed June 3, 2016, http://www .dailymail.co.uk/news/article-2431814/Christian-doctor-sacked -emailing-prayer-colleagues-cheer-loses-appeal-dismissal.html.

13. John Hall, "Christian Guest House Owners Lose Court Fight Over Turning Away Gay Couple," *Independent*, November 27, 2013, accessed June 3, 2016, http://www.independent.co.uk/news/uk /home-news/christian-guest-house-owners-lose-court-fight-over -turning-away-gay-couple-8966573.html; Paul Vale, "Peter and Hazel-mary Bull, Christian B&B Owners Who Refused Gay Couple, Forced to Sell Hotel," *Huffington Post*, September 19, 2013, accessed June 3, 2016, http://www.huffingtonpost.co.uk/2013/09/19/christian-bed --breakfast-bull_n_3954992.html.

14. Peter J. Smith, "Germany Jails Eight Christian Fathers for Removing Children From Sex-Ed Class," LifeSiteNews.com, December 11, 2009, accessed June 3, 2016, https://www.lifesitenews.com/news /germany-jails-eight-christian-fathers-for-removing-children-from-sex -ed-cla.

15. James J. Ponzetti Jr., ed., *Evidence-Based Approaches to Sexuality Education: A Global Perspective* (New York: Routledge, 2016).

16. "Anti-Abortion Doctor Fired," *Warsaw Voice*, August 1, 2014, accessed June 3, 2016, http://www.warsawvoice.pl/WVpage /pages/article.php/27522/article; Natalia Dueholm, "Lynched, Fined, and Dismissed: An Interview With Poland's Dr. Bogdan Chazan," LifeSiteNews.com, July 18, 2014, accessed June 3, 2016, https://www .lifesitenews.com/news/lynched-fined-and-dismissed-an-interview -with-polands-dr.-bogdan-chazan.

17. Gudrun Kugler, keynote address at OSCE High Level Conference on Tolerance and Non-Discrimination, Tirana, Albania, May 21, 2013,

on behalf of Observatory on Intolerance and Discrimination Against Christians in Europe, OSCE.org, accessed June 3, 2016, http://www .osce.org/cio/101779?download=true.

18. Jessilyn Justice, "7,000 Churches Fasting, Praying Over Terrifying New Persecution Law," *Charisma News*, July 8, 2016, accessed August 3, 2016, http://www.charismanews.com/world/58295-7-000 -churches-fasting-praying-over-terrifying-new-persecution-law.

19. Chase Madar, "The Bitter Tears of the American Christian Supermajority," America.Aljazeera.com, March 30, 2014, accessed June 3, 2016, http://america.aljazeera.com/opinions/2014/3/christians -persecutioncomplex.html.

20. Benjamin Dixon, "Please Stop With the Christian Persecution Complex. You're Embarrassing the Faith," Patheos.com, July 9, 2015, accessed June 3, 2016, http://www.patheos.com/blogs/godisnota republican/2015/07/please-stop-with-the-christian-persecution -complex-youre-embarrassing-the-faith/.

21. "Barna Survey Examines Changes in Worldview Among Christians Over the Past 13 Years," Barna Group, March 9, 2009, accessed June 3, 2016, https://www.barna.org/barna-update/transformation/252 -barna-survey-examines-changes-in-worldview-among-christians-over -the-past-13-years#.

CHAPTER 2
THE DIVINE DRAMA OF PSALM 2

1. C. H. Spurgeon, *The Treasure of David: An Expository and Devotional Commentary on the Psalms*, vol. 1 (Grand Rapids, MI: Baker Book House, 1983), 11.

2. Born to Reform, "32 Things You Might Not Know About Charles Spurgeon," Evangelical Channel, Patheos.com, January 30, 2013, accessed June 3, 2016, http://www.patheos.com/blogs/borntoreform /2013/01/32-things-you-might-not-know-about-charles-spurgeon/.

3. "2540. *kairos*," BibleHub.com, accessed August 4, 2016, http:// biblehub.com/greek/2540.htm.

4. Harbour Fraser Hodder, "The Future of Marriage," *Harvard Magazine,* November–December 2004, accessed June 3, 2016, http:// harvardmagazine.com/2004/11/the-future-of-marriage.html.

5. Brigid Schulte, "A Longtime Proponent of Marriage Wants to Reassess the Institution's Future," *Washington Post,* January 3, 2015, accessed June 3, 2016, https://www.washingtonpost.com/local /a-longtime-proponent-of-marriage-wants-to-reassess-the-institutions -future/2015/01/03/c0960e4a-8ada-11e4-8ff4-fb93129c9c8b_story.html.

6. Ken Taylor, "Should Marriage Be Abolished?," PhilosophyTalk
.org, accessed June 3, 2016, http://philosophytalk.org/community/blog
/ken-taylor/2015/04/should-marriage-be-abolished; Edward Zelinsky,
"Strengthening Marriage by Abolishing Civil Marriage,"
HuffingtonPost.com, updated October 26, 2012, accessed June 3, 2016,
http://www.huffingtonpost.com/edward-zelinsky/abolish-marriage
_b_1831271.html; "Should We Abolish Marriage?" Debate.org, accessed
June 3, 2016, http://www.debate.org/opinions/should-we-abolish
-marriage.

7. As cited in Wikipedia.org, s.v. "Religion in Nazi Germany," note
13, accessed August 4, 2016, https://en.wikipedia.org/wiki/Religion_in
_Nazi_Germany.

8. "The German Churches and the Nazi State," United States Holocaust Memorial Museum, accessed June 3, 2016, http://www.ushmm
.org/wlc/en/article.php?ModuleId=10005206.

CHAPTER 3
ACT I: THE GLOBAL OPPOSITION

1. "There Are 7 Mountains of Influence in Culture…,"
7CulturalMountains.org, accessed June 6, 2016, http://
www.7culturalmountains.org/.

2. Chris Morris, "Things Are Looking Up in America's Porn
Industry," NBCNews.com, January 20, 2015, accessed June 6, 2016,
http://www.nbcnews.com/business/business-news/things-are-looking
-americas-porn-industry-n289431.

3. Emily Empel, "The Future of Sex? 5 Trends That May Completely
Transform Our Sex Lives," Alternet.org, April 18, 2012, accessed June
6, 2016, http://www.alternet.org/story/155049/the_future_of_sex_5
_trends_that_may_completely_transform_our_sex_lives.

4. Mark Judge, "Jennifer Lawrence Attacks Christians: 'People
Holding Their Crucifixes, Which May as Well Be Pitchforks,'"
CNSNews.com, November 13, 2015, accessed June 6, 2016, http://www
.cnsnews.com/blog/mark-judge/jennifer-lawrence-attacks-christians
-their-crucixies-which-may-well-be-pitchforks.

5. Carol Hartsell, "This May Be Bill Maher's Most Intense Rant
Against Religions—All of Them—Yet," HuffingtonPost.com, updated
March 17, 2014, accessed June 6, 2016, http://www.huffingtonpost
.com/2014/03/15/bill-maher-god-psychotic-mas-murderer_n_4970831
.html; Bill Maher, "Jesus Forgives Sins So the Person You Molested
Doesn't Have to," BillMaher.tumblr.com, accessed June 6, 2016, http://

billmaher.tumblr.com/post/121791578846/jesus-forgives-sins-so-the
-person-you.

6. "8 Black Celebrities Who Don't Believe in Jesus," Atlanta Black Star, August 29, 2013, accessed June 6, 2016, http://atlantablackstar .com/2013/08/29/8-black-celebrities-dont-believe-god/2/.

7. Leah Marieann Klett, "Miley Cyrus Mocks Christians Who Believe in Old Testament 'Fairy Tales,' Says Those Who Oppose Homosexuality 'Shouldn't Get to Make Laws,'" GospelHerald.com, June 10, 2015, accessed June 9, 2016, http://www.gospelherald.com/articles /55983/20150610/miley-cyrus-mocks-christians-who-believe-in-old -testament-fairy-tales-says-those-who-oppose-homosexuality-shouldnt -get-to-make-laws.htm.

8. Yasmine Hafiz, "Candace Cameron Bure Explains Being 'Submissive' to Husband," HuffingtonPost.com, updated January 25, 2014, accessed June 6, 2016, http://www.huffingtonpost.com/2014/01/06 /candance-cameron-bure-submissive_n_4550818.html; "'I Let My Man Be a Leader': Full House Star Candace Cameron Bure Explains How 'Submissiveness' Is the Key to Her Marriage," *Daily Mail*, January 7, 2014, accessed June 6, 2016, http://www.dailymail.co.uk/femail /article-2535401/I-let-man-leader-Full-House-star-Candace-Cameron -Bure-explains-submissiveness-key-marriage.html; Patrick Gomez, "Candice Cameron Bure Opens up About Her Faith and 'Submissive' Marriage," People.com, April 26, 2014, accessed June 6, 2016, http:// www.people.com/article/candace-camerom-bure-faith-submissive -marriage; Patrick Gomez, "Candace Cameron Bure: I Know People Don't Agree With My Beliefs," People.com, April 23, 2014, accessed June 6, 2016, http://www.people.com/article/candace-cameron-bure -evangelical-christian-beliefs-dancing-with-stars.

9. "Tim Tebow Still Can't Find the End Zone as Girlfriend Olivia Culpo Breaks It Off Over Lack of Sex," NYDailyNews.com, November 26, 2015, accessed June 6, 2016, http://www.nydailynews.com /entertainment/gossip/confidential/tim-tebow-find-zone-article -1.2447008.

CHAPTER 4
ACT II: THE FATHER'S RESPONSE

1. Matthew Henry, *Matthew Henry Commentary on the Whole Bible*, "Psalms 2," BibleStudyTools.com, accessed June 6, 2016, http:// www.biblestudytools.com/commentaries/matthew-henry-complete /psalms/2.html.

2. *Merriam-Webster Online*, s.v. "derision," accessed August 12, 2016, http://www.merriam-webster.com/dictionary/derision.

3. J. I. Packer, *Knowing God* (Downers Grove, IL: InterVarsity Press, 1993), 151.

4. C. S. Lewis, "Christian Apologetics," in *God in the Dock: Essays on Theology and Ethics*, ed. Walter Hooper (Grand Rapids, MI: Eerdmans, 1994), 89–103.

5. Os Guinness, *The Call* (Nashville: Thomas Nelson, 1998), 188.

6. Tom Doyle, *Killing Christians* (Nashville: W Publishing Group, 2015), xi.

CHAPTER 5
ACT III: JESUS'S RESPONSE

1. *Merriam-Webster Online*, s.v. "decree," accessed August 12, 2016, http://www.merriam-webster.com/dictionary/decree.

2. Unless otherwise noted, summaries are gathered from my book *Growing in Prayer* (Lake Mary, FL: Charisma House, 2014), 247–252.

3. George Thomas, "24/7 Christian Prayer Movement Sweeps Muslim Indonesia," CharismaNews.com, August 2, 2013, accessed June 7, 2016, http://www.charismanews.com/world/40484-24-7-christian -prayer-movement-sweeps-muslim-indonesia.

4. Tom Hess, "Rise of the Praying Church," CharismaMag.com, May 1, 2011, accessed June 7, 2016, http://www.charismamag.com/site -archives/1441-0511-magazine-articles/features/13395-rise.

5. Ibid.

6. Oswald Chambers, "Greater Works," *My Utmost for His Highest* (Westwood, NJ: Barbour and Company, Inc., 1935, 1963), October 17.

CHAPTER 6
ACT IV: DAVID'S EXHORTATION

1. Mark Carey, *In the Shadow of Melting Glaciers* (Oxford, UK: Oxford University Press, 2010), 149–150; "January 10, 1962: Avalanche Kills Thousands in Peru," History.com, accessed June 7, 2016, http:// www.history.com/this-day-in-history/avalanche-kills-thousands-in -peru.

2. Carey, *In the Shadow of Melting Glaciers*, 149–150.

3. Ibid.

4. Charles Sawyer, "Political Landslide," NewScientist.com, November 14, 2012, accessed June 7, 2016, https://www.newscientist .com/letter/mg21628910-800-political-landslide/; Carey, *In the Shadow of Melting Glaciers*, 149.

5. Carey, *In the Shadow of Melting Glaciers*, 149.

6. Annie Theriault, "Yungay 1970–2009: Remembering the Tragedy of The Earthquake," PeruvianTimes.com, May 31, 2009, accessed June 7, 2016, http://www.peruviantimes.com/31/yungay-1970-2009 -remembering-the-tragedy-of-the-earthquake/3073/.

7. John Bevere, *The Fear of the Lord* (Lake Mary, FL: Charisma House, 2006), 3.

8. Tom McTague and Martin Robinson, "Republican Jeremy Corbyn Will Kiss the Queen's Hand and Pledge His Loyalty Despite Campaigning to Replace Her With a President and Evict Her From Buckingham Palace," *Daily Mail*, September 14, 2015, accessed June 8, 2016, http://www.dailymail.co.uk/news/article-3234276/Republican -Jeremy-Corbyn-pledge-loyalty-Queen-Right-Honourable-member -Privy-Council.html.

CHAPTER 7
THE CHURCH'S STAND:
RESPONDING TO THE PSALM 2 CRISIS

1. Tobin Grant, "The Great Decline: 60 Years of Religion in One Graph," ReligionNews.com, January 27, 2014, accessed August 15, 2016, http://tobingrant.religionnews.com/2014/01/27/great-decline-religion -united-states-one-graph/.

2. Kyle R. Beshears, *Empty Churches: The Decline of Cultural Christianity in the West*, accessed August 15, 2016, http://www.kylebeshears .com/emptychurches/empty_churches.pdf.

3. *Today in the Word* (Chicago: Moody Bible Institute, October 1991), 21.

4. "Jonathan Edwards: America's Greatest Theologian," *Christian History*, accessed June 8, 2016, http://www.christianitytoday.com/ch /131christians/theologians/edwards.html.

5. Jonathan Edwards, "Sinners in the Hands of an Angry God," sermon, Enfield, Connecticut, July 8, 1741, accessed June 8, 2016, http:// www1.cbn.com/churchandministry/sinners-in-the-hands-of-an-angry -god.

6. Ibid.

7. Harry S. Stout, Nathan O. Hatch, and Kyle P. Farley, *The Works of Jonathan Edwards, Vol. 22: Sermons and Discourses, 1739–1742* (New Haven, CT: Yale University Press, 2003), 34.

8. Lawrence Wright, "The Counter-Terrorist," *New Yorker*, January 14, 2002, accessed August 16, 2016, http://www.newyorker.com /magazine/2002/01/14/the-counter-terrorist.

9. Ibid.
10. Ibid.
11. Ibid.
12. Ibid.

CHAPTER 8
ENGAGING IN A JOEL 2 RESPONSE

1. Michael Hernandez, "More than 70,000 'Brave Rain to Encounter God' at Azusa Now Rally," *Citizens Journal*, April 13, 2016, accessed August 16, 2016, http://citizensjournal.us/more-than-70000-brave-rain -to-encounter-god-at-azusa-now-rally/.

2. Robert Morley, "The Inspiring History Britain Should Never Forget," *Trumpet,* March 2008, accessed June 9, 2016, https://www .thetrumpet.com/article/4747.24.102.0/britain/the-inspiring-history -britain-should-never-forget?preview; Elmer L. Towns, *Fasting for Spiritual Breakthrough* (Minneapolis, Minnesota: Bethany House Publishers, 1996).

3. Andrew Murray, *With Christ in the School of Prayer* (Peabody, MA: Hendrickson Publishers, 2007), 80–81.

CHAPTER 10
PUTTING TRUTH INTO PRACTICE

1. Carol Kuruvilla, "Former Megachurch Pastor Rob Bell: A Church That Doesn't Support Gay Marriage Is 'Irrelevant,'" HuffingtongPost .com, updated February 21, 2015, accessed June 10, 2016, http://www .huffingtonpost.com/2015/02/20/rob-bell-oprah-gay-marriage_n _6723840.html.

2. Ibid.

3. Eryn Sun, "Calif. Pastor Who Believes in 'One God, Many Paths' to Hold Easter Services at Mosque," ChristianPost.com, March 22, 2012, accessed June 10, 2016, http://www.christianpost.com/news /calif-pastor-who-believes-in-one-god-many-paths-to-hold-easter -services-at-mosque-71866/.

4. Stoyan Zaimov, "Only 1 in 3 Young Born-Again Evangelicals Believe Jesus Is Only Way to Heaven, Apologist Says," ChristianPost .com, October 12, 2013, accessed June 10, 2016, http://www .christianpost.com/news/only-1-in-3-young-born-again-evangelicals -believe-jesus-is-only-way-to-heaven-apologist-says-106500/.

5. Lydia Saad, "Three in Four in U.S. Still See the Bible as Word of God," June 4, 2014, accessed August 17, 2016, http://www.gallup.com /poll/170834/three-four-bible-word-god.aspx; Morgan Lee, "Less Than a

Third of Americans Say Bible Is Actual Word of God, Should Be Taken Literally," ChristianPost.com, June 5, 2014, accessed June 10, 2016, http://www.christianpost.com/news/less-than-a-third-of-americans -say-bible-is-actual-word-of-god-should-be-taken-literally-120964/.

6. "Religious Beliefs Vary Widely by Denomination," Barna Group, June 25, 2001, accessed June 10, 2016, https://barna.org/component /content/article/5-barna-update/45-barna-update-sp-657/53-religious -beliefs-vary-widely-by-denomination.

7. "New Research Explores How Different Generations View and Use the Bible," Barna Group, October 19, 2009, accessed June 10, 2016, https://barna.org/barna-update/faith-spirituality/317-new-research -explores-how-different-generations-view-and-use-the-bible.

8. "What Do Americans Really Think About the Bible?," Barna Group, April 10, 2013, accessed June 10, 2016, https://barna.org/barna -update/culture/605-what-do-americans-really-think-about-the-bible.

9. "Abortions This Year," Worldometers, accessed July 18, 2016, http://www.worldometers.info/abortions/.

10. Steve Jalsevac, "Shock: 1 Billion Abortions in World Since 1920," LifeSiteNews.com, December 24, 2014, accessed July 21, 2016, https:// www.lifesitenews.com/news/global-life-campaign-new-international -abortion-stats-org-reveals-1-billion.

11. Euan McKirdy, "World Has 35.8 Million Slaves, Report Finds," CNN.com, updated January 4, 2015, accessed July 18, 2016, http://www .cnn.com/2014/11/17/world/walk-free-global-slavery-index-2014/.

12. "Human Trafficking: The Facts," United Nations Office on Drugs and Crime, updated May 11, 2009, accessed July 18, 2016, https://www .unodc.org/documents/blueheart/Fact_sheet_english.pdf.

13. "Christian Movements and Denominations," Pew Research Center, December 19, 2011, accessed July 21, 2016, http://www .pewforum.org/2011/12/19/global-christianity-movements-and -denominations/.

14. Timothy Keller, *Prayer: Experiencing Awe and Intimacy With God* (New York: Dutton, 2014), 9–10.

International House *of* Prayer

INTERNSHIPS

ENCOUNTER GOD. DO HIS WORKS. CHANGE THE WORLD.
ihopkc.org/internships

Each of our five internships are committed to praying for the release of the fullness of God's power and purpose, as interns actively win the lost, heal the sick, feed the poor, and minister in the power of the Holy Spirit. Our vision is to work in relationship with the larger Body of Christ to serve the Great Commission, as we seek to walk out the two great commandments to love God and people. Our desire is to see each intern build strong relationships and lifelong friendships.

INTRO TO IHOPKC

Two three-month tracks designed to impart the vision and values of the International House of Prayer, along with the practical skills necessary to succeed long-term as an intercessory missionary. For singles, couples, and families. Classes for children available.

FIRE IN THE NIGHT

Come and behold the beauty of Jesus in the night hours. Grow in love for God and take your stand in intercession as a watchman of the night. Fire in the Night is for young adults, ages 18–30.

ONE THING INTERNSHIP

A six-month residential program for single young adults, ages 18 to 25.

SIMEON COMPANY

Two three-month tracks for over-50s, married or single.

HOPE CITY INTERNSHIP

A three-month internship program equipping intercessory missionaries to minister in the inner city, serve in the soup kitchen, lead in our inner-city prayer room, and minister to gang members, drug addicts, and the homeless.

International House of Prayer Missions Base, 3535 E. Red Bridge Road, Kansas City, MO 64137
(816) 763-0200 | info@ihopkc.org | ihopkc.org

MIKE BICKLE
TEACHING LIBRARY
—— *Free Teaching & Resource Library* ——

This International House of Prayer resource library, encompassing more than 25 years of Mike's teaching ministry, provides access to hundreds of resources in various formats, including streaming video, downloadable video, and audio, accompanied by study notes and transcriptions, absolutely free of charge.

You will find some of Mike's most requested titles, including *The Life of David*, *The First Commandment*, *Jesus, Our Magnificent Obsession*, *The Book of Romans*, *The Book of Revelation*, and much more.

We encourage you to freely copy any of these teachings to share with others or use in any way: "our copyright is the right to copy." Older messages are continually being prepared and uploaded from Mike's archives, and all new teachings will be added immediately.

Visit mikebickle.org

International House of Prayer Missions Base, 3535 E. Red Bridge Road, Kansas City, MO 64137
(816) 763-0200 | info@ihopkc.org | ihopkc.org

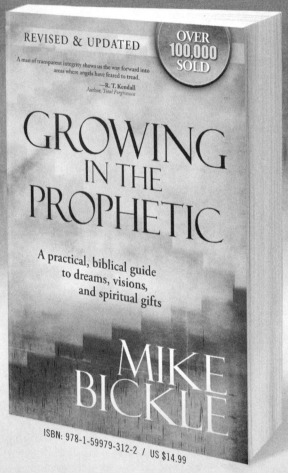

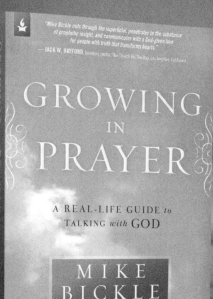

SUBSCRIBE TODAY

Exclusive Content

E-mailed to You

Stay Informed

Update Others

CHARISMA MEDIA

FREE NEWSLETTERS
TO EMPOWER YOUR LIFE

 PROPHETIC INSIGHT
Receive prophetic messages from respected leaders in the body of Christ.

 STANDING WITH ISRAEL
Do you have a heart for Israel? Stay informed of Israel-related news with articles and information from around the world.

 CHARISMA MAGAZINE
Stay up-to-date with top-trending articles, Christian teachings, entertainment reviews, videos, and more from your favorite magazine and website.

 CHARISMA NEWS DAILY
Get the latest breaking news with a Christian perspective from the editors of *Charisma*.

SIGN UP AT: nl.charismamag.com